Creating
Your Life
Collage

STRATEGIES FOR
SOLVING THE WORK/LIFE DILEMMA

Kathy McDonald and Beth Sirull

Three Rivers Press
New York

Published by Three Rivers Press, 201 East 50th Street, New York, New York 10022. Member of the Crown Publishing Group.

Random House, Inc. New York, Toronto, London, Sydney, Auckland
www.randomhouse.com

THREE RIVERS PRESS is a registered trademark of Random House, Inc.

Printed in the United States of America

Design by Meryl Sussman Levavi/Digitext, Inc.

Library of Congress Cataloging-in-Publication Data

McDonald, Kathy.
    Creating your life collage : strategies for solving the work/life dilemma /
Kathy McDonald and Beth Sirull.—1st paperback ed.
        1. Women—Psychology.   2. Women—Employment—Psychological
aspects.   3. Women—Job stress.   4. Women—Conduct of life.   5. Self
realization.   I. Sirull, Beth.   II. Title.
HQ1206.M3664   2000
158.1'082—dc21   99–42375

ISBN 0-609-80410-3

10 9 8 7 6 5 4 3 2 1

First Edition

To Anne Marie,
who provided encouragement and
divine intervention every step of the way.
You renewed my sense of wonder,
and restored my faith in the generosity of others.
—Kathy

To my parents—Bob and Elsie Sirull.
Although I am a writer, I am without words
to express my gratitude for all that you are
and all that you have given me. May God bless.
—Beth

Acknowledgments

No book is written without the immense generosity of knowledge and spirit from so many. This book would not have been conceived without the Kellogg Alumni Association Women's Committee members who prodded my cochair, Joanna Baker, and me to do an event around the topic of work/life balance. From that event the glimmer appeared that became this book.

Thank you to Linda Roghaar, our agent and friend, who fearlessly supported the making of this book. To Dina Siciliano, a caring and kind editor, who shepherded this project through complex publishing waters, my abundant gratitude. Special thanks to the rest of the Crown Publishing Group, whose enthusiastic support continues to overwhelm me.

Many thanks to all of the women whose stories comprise this book, who dared to believe there was a way to make the collage work. You blazed your own trails when you found none and generously shared your experiences so that others may benefit.

To my partner, Beth Sirull, my appreciation knows no bounds. Without you, this dream would not have come true. It's been a wild ride—what a pleasure it's been to have someone with whom to share it! Thank you for all of your tireless enthusiasm, professional expertise, and sheer stamina to make it through the crunch periods.

Thank you hardly seems sufficient to offer my sister, Beth Tuttle, for her thorough and tireless reading of the manuscript. Beth, your many suggestions meaningfully improved this book. Hearty thanks to Randi Killian—through your belief that writers should support other writers, you unselfishly donated your time to lead our book-naming brainstorm session. Thanks goes to all of those who participated in the session. My abundant gratitude goes to my personal board of directors, Mara Hauser and Sally Hodge, who continuously gave their encouragement, wisdom, and professional expertise. To my writing instructor, Carol LaChapelle, heartfelt thanks for helping me find my path back to the writer within.

To my parents, John and Terry Hastings—you always taught me I could accomplish anything I set my mind to and you supported and encouraged me every step of the way. Thank you hardly seems enough for all you have done for me. A tender thank-you to my beautiful Sammie Scrumptious and sweet little Liam—you are my constant reminder why this book is so important for so many. A special thank-you to Dora, in whose able and caring hands I placed my children for uninterrupted time while completing this project.

And finally, my deepest gratitude goes to my husband, John, who dreamed of a life bigger and bolder than even I could have imagined and who crafted a way to make it happen. You were my inspiration and role model that there was life beyond all-consuming work. Through your true partnership you gave me the space to pursue this dream.

Kathy McDonald, September 1999

First and foremost, I would like to thank the nearly 1,000 women who gave of their time to be interviewed or to respond to the questionnaire we posted to the Internet. Your stories are a constant source of inspiration to me.

I would like to thank Harvey Bergholz and Sue Flaster, who led us to Linda Roghaar, agent extraordinaire. Without Linda there would be no book and I would be minus a warm, endearing, and supportive friend. Special thanks to Miriam Krasno, for reviewing numerous drafts of the book proposal as well as the manuscript and for being a constant source of ideas, information, and encouragement throughout this project. To the members of my personal board of directors—Joanna Baker, Claudia Braun, Miriam Krasno, and Cheryl Rodgers—I appreciate your many ideas and consistent

The women who contributed their stories to this book knew it was time to make a change when . . .

". . . I started dreaming about work issues in my sleep. . . ."

". . . I was spending too much free time preparing for work instead of enjoying my time off work. . . ."

"I booked and paid for an airline ticket to take a week's vacation. I was so involved in work that I forgot to go. That was when I realized that I had to start putting myself first instead of my clients."

"I turned forty and decided that it was time to stop being a workaholic. There had to be more to life than work, work, work. . . ."

". . . I couldn't sleep well . . . I was nervous. I was anxious. I did not experience a good feeling at the end of each day that I had accomplished anything worthwhile. The morale in the office was low and I was afraid it was rubbing off on me. I thought if I stayed at that job, that I would become a different person, a person I did not want to be. . . ."

"My mother died six months after she retired. I saw myself putting in too many hours, and realized that I was doing the same thing my mother did. Her whole life was her job. She didn't attend my college graduation because she didn't feel she could miss work. . . ."

". . . It seemed that everything was falling apart at once, my emotions, my work, my family, everything. . . ."

"I found myself working seventy to eighty hours a week in a challenging position for a major retailer. . . . When I wasn't at work, I was thinking about work and/or bringing it home. Weekends didn't exist much, and a vacation was hard to come by. I truly knew it was time for a change when all I knew about was my job. . . . My world had narrowed significantly. I found myself defining my life by my job and its successes and failures. . . . I had little to show for all I was doing. No time for travel, no time to visit my family, no time for volunteering in the community. . . ."

*Find out how these women and many others like them moved **from** overwhelmed, overworked, exhausted, bleary- and dreary-eyed, out-of-shape, one-dimensional lives **to** satisfied, fulfilled, multifaceted, collaged lives.*

support. I am grateful to Amy Yoffie and her company, Research Connections, Inc., for enabling us to conduct research via the Internet. For their encouragement, assistance, and unique contributions to this book, I would like to thank Julie Benton Fleischer, Ellen Gabriel, Marian Gibson, Dawn Gray, Susan Klein, Hope Langer, former U.S. Secretary of Labor Lynn Martin, Andrea Meltzer, former Congresswoman Susan Molinari, Joanna Moran, Sue Shellenbarger, Julian Sirull, David Shuster, Joyce Smith, Carol White, and Mike Wien.

To the crew at Random House—Tina Constable, Joan DeMayo, Alison Gross, Christian Red, Kim Robles, Carter Shaw, and Dina Siciliano—thanks for leading us through the wonderful, exciting maze of writing and publishing a book.

A special thank-you to Julie Benton Fleischer and Joanna Baker, for introducing me to Kathy McDonald. It goes without saying—but I'll say it anyway—that this project was a true collaboration. I could not have done it alone. I would not be here, writing the acknowledgments section of my first book, if not for Kathy. Thanks, Kath, for undertaking this with me, for all your hard work, passion, and commitment, and for putting up with my assorted foibles along the way.

Abundant thanks to my parents, Bob and Elsie Sirull, for all the years of guidance, love, support, and encouragement. Thanks also to my in-laws, Susan Klein and Arnold Shuster, who, in addition to constantly egging me on in this project, raised a remarkable son, thereby making an immeasurable contribution to my life. To my husband, Jon Shuster, my soul mate, life partner, friend, confidant, and lover, go more than thanks. You envelop my heart, nurture my soul, bolster my psyche, and challenge my brain. I love you more than I can convey. Last, but not least, my thanks to Sadie DeVine, aka The Divine Miss Sadie, wherever you are. I wouldn't be here without you.

Beth Sirull, September 1999

Contents

Exercise Contents

Part I

The Storm Before the Calm:

Life Before the Collage

Introduction:

The Journey to Creating

a Conscious Life Collage

I snapped out of my commuter daydream only to discover that I had been dreaming I had pneumonia, was in the hospital, and had a big smile on my face because I was resting peacefully and didn't have to go to work. . . .

MEET THE AUTHORS—BETH AND KATHY

Beth and Kathy are two women just like you.

Beth's Story

"In 1993 my life looked something like this: Monday through Friday, up at 6 A.M., out by 6:45 to be at work by 8 A.M. At work until anywhere from 6 P.M. to 8 P.M., home somewhere between 7 P.M. and 9 P.M. Opened mail, paid bills, or returned important calls, ate

dinner, and went to bed. Started over at 6 A.M. the next day. Friday night, I dropped on the family-room couch, read the People *magazine that my husband generously bought me to help me unwind, and fell asleep. Saturday and Sunday generally consisted of life's errands, maybe dinner or a movie, work-related reading or writing, and sleep—lots of it—to be ready to get on the merry-go-round again on Monday morning.*

"I cared deeply about women's issues, particularly issues regarding domestic violence and women's economic equity. I belonged to several relevant organizations, but felt unable to assume any leadership roles due to my work and business-travel schedule, which generally precluded my meeting any ongoing commitments. At the same time, avoiding these commitments left me feeling unable to make a difference on these important issues.

"Not only had my involvement in community affairs lessened, but the attention I paid to my hobbies and other interests had all but evaporated. As a teenager, I had been a successful seamstress and had dabbled in several other three-dimensional arts such as stained glass and clay. I was a regular lap-swimmer. I had no interest in swimming competitively but did find that swimming helped me keep fit—both mentally and physically. In college I had assumed an active role in religious life. Somehow, as I ambitiously undertook my career, these varied interests had been shed at the altar of ladder-climbing.

"In the fall of 1993, not only was I dissatisfied with my paltry contribution to my community and philanthropic work, I was neglecting hobbies and interests. I was increasingly unhappy at work. It took enormous energy to drag myself out of bed in the morning; I came home more and more exhausted each night.

"As I grew increasingly unhappy, my husband and I considered whether I should quit my job. It seemed senseless and impossible. After all, what would I do? Plus, my husband had just finished graduate school; his job was brand-new—nowhere near secure. We had almost no savings, and we were drowning in our combined student loans. However, I say all of this in hindsight. At

the time, I had a gnawing sense of unhappiness. I could never have articulated my growing despair in just a few paragraphs. And then it happened—my epiphany experience.

"One Tuesday morning in early September 1993, I set off on my normal commute to work at about seven A.M., just as I did every day. I knew the route so well that I had taken to lapsing into daydreams as I left my driveway to "wake up" an hour later as I pulled into the office parking lot. At first, this morning was no different. But then, about one mile from the office, I snapped out of my daydream. Unlike other days when I could not have told you what I had been envisioning during that hour commute, on this day it was crystal clear:

> *"I snapped out of my commuter daydream only to discover that I had been dreaming I had pneumonia, was in the hospital, and had a big smile on my face because I was resting peacefully and didn't have to go to work. . . .*

"Having no idea what I was going to do or how we were going to make ends meet, I quit my job that very day.

"Today, I am the designer of an ever-evolving life collage: Professionally, I manage a successful marketing- and training-consulting practice and teach a college marketing course. More important, I participate regularly in aerobics, am an avid cook, sometime hiker, and, with this book, fulfilling a lifelong dream to be a published author. As a member of the board of directors of a domestic-violence agency and as a participant in my synagogue community, I make a difference in the world around me."

Kathy's Story

"A few years back, I arrived home late, again—really late—exhausted, and tried to engage in a few minutes of quality time with my husband, John, before going to sleep. Our discussion centered on our workday, and I shared all the fire drills I was currently handling since the product I worked on was under severe competitive threat.

"As John and I were both getting a little exasperated with my schedule, I tried to reassure him (and me, I'm sure) that things would improve after December 8, the latest deadline I had to meet. John held up his hands and said patiently, 'Stop. Just stop. . . . Do you know how many times you have said that to me? I am in full support of what you want to do with your life, and I want you to be happy. I'm just not seeing a happy wife before me. Your life has become work, sleep, commute, and eat—in that order. Are you happy with that balance? If you are, I'll go on giving you my full support, but I just find it hard to believe that you are happy living your life this way. You don't see your friends much anymore. You don't see your family. You don't have time for hobbies. Is this what you want out of life?'

"Wham! It was the first in a series of epiphany experiences that helped me begin to recognize that my life was horribly off-track. Sure, on the surface everything was great: I had a great career that many graduate students envied. I worked in marketing for a Fortune 50 consumer-packaged-goods company on one of their most important products. I was making a good living and had a great marriage. But John was right. He also had a successful career and yet still had time for friends, family, golf, and other leisure activities. I kept rationalizing, 'Well, that's your industry. Everyone I know is in the same boat I'm in.' I couldn't figure out how to balance my life because no one around me demonstrated an alternative path. I was surrounded by workaholics who were more than willing to take my place on the career track. It was an endurance test.

"Somewhere between the time I started my career and this juncture, the notion of paying my dues early in my career for easier times ahead was thrown out (perhaps with the downsizing craze of the nineties). Every time management changed (and it was changing often in those days), I had to prove myself all over again. And I soon learned that the people ahead of me on the career track were no more balanced than I or my peers.

"And forget having kids. I always thought I would want them some day when 'things settled down.' I was so exhausted just managing my own life, I couldn't fathom how I would care for another human being. Women around me were either plowing right back into work after the baby was born, going part-time, or chucking the career altogether to nurture their children. All three options scared me. So I kept putting it off.

"It took another year, a move to another company, two more promotions, and another big salary jump for the next big epiphany experience (see Chapter 2) to happen before I was ready to consider that there had to be an alternative way to live.

"By redefining success and balance, my life now encompasses considerably more than work and family. I am a committee chair for NAWBO (the National Association of Women Business Owners); I'm writing this book; and I am in the envisioning stage of creating a new business. I've taken up gardening, painting, and other creative activities. I regularly attend plays, concerts, and other cultural events. I've made many new friends and work to foster the growth of those friendships, and I spend more quality time with my family. I regularly engage in physical-fitness activities, and I take time to reflect for my own mental well-being. Finally, and most important, I can envision that family I've always wanted—my husband and I are thoroughly enjoying nurturing our two children."

IN THE BEGINNING . . .

When Beth and Kathy met in the fall of 1996, each was well along the collage-creating path. Each had re-created her work to open up her life to other elements of the collage. Beth and Kathy shared their stories and the stories they had heard from so many other women. Together, they came to the same conclusion: There is "a story" to be told here, one that will inspire, comfort, and educate women just like them—and you.

And so Beth and Kathy began their journey together. Beth's and Kathy's journeys—along with the parallel, but unique, journeys of nearly one thousand women just like you—are the substance of this book. The women who contributed their stories have moved *from* overwhelmed, overworked, exhausted, burned out, sleep-deprived, bleary- and dreary-eyed, out-of-shape, one-dimensional lives *to* satisfied, fulfilled, multifaceted, collaged lives. Nearly one hundred women ranging in age from twenty-five to fifty-five from a variety of economic and professional backgrounds were interviewed for this book. In addition, more than eight hundred women responded to an Internet-based survey; many of these women wrote at length about their experiences redesigning their work/life.

The reader might be tempted to assume that "those women can afford to take chances. I can't make the changes they did because I don't have their resources." The women interviewed for this book were consciously chosen to represent "typical" professional women. Therefore, with few exceptions, very wealthy and/or famous women were not interviewed because their circumstances are often unique. The intent is for every woman to see herself in these pages.

While a number of the women who contributed to this book are mothers, many do not have children. Work/life issues are not for mothers only. Many single and childless married women simply want a life made up of other elements. Childless women want an enriched life as deeply as working mothers.

Career-development professionals shared their perspective on the stress that often accompanies all-consuming work, as well as the stress that comes with making the transition to (and maintaining) a multifaceted lifestyle. Finally, human-resource and executive-search professionals contributed their views of the evolving new options for work, offering their success tips for evaluating the right option for you.

In interviews and through the Internet, women discussed the nuts and bolts of how they changed their work/life but, more important, shared the emotional process they went through to create their solution to the work/life dilemma. Women shared how they moved from "stuck"—where they saw no options—to exploring and choosing an option. Women generously shared the ups, the downs, the fears, the coping mechanisms, the satisfaction, the frustration, and the impact on relationships. Once work was no longer all-consuming, women shared how they brought new interests into their life and how they managed the fluidity of their life to keep it continually fresh and satisfying. Finally, the women shared the payoff—and the cost—of adopting a multidimensional lifestyle. These women's stories are told throughout this book; while the women are quoted anonymously, their stories are true. As Beth and Kathy culled through these stories, a new paradigm for women's lives emerged: **The conscious life collage.**

THE CONSCIOUS LIFE COLLAGE—A NEW PARADIGM FOR MANAGING YOUR WHOLE LIFE

Remember making collages as a kid, combining images and colors to create a unique piece of art? A *conscious life collage* applies this artistic concept to life, creating a lifestyle thoughtfully composed of many roles, including career and family, but goes beyond to include hobbies, interests, spirituality, and community; unified to form a fruitful, fulfilling, and joyful life. Some women talk of "balancing" work and life (and most people read "life" as "family"). Balancing implies a two-dimensional, unsustainable precision where the slightest shift can put life out of kilter. In practice, balance is rarely achievable; women are left with a pervasive sense of dissonance. Other women speak of "juggling," which connotes a sense of the frantic, with balls precariously teetering. *Collaging* **offers a new approach to work and life—one that works for managing your** *whole* **life.**

Most working women's lives are consumed by their work and everything that goes with it—commuting, traveling, office politics, entertaining clients, and, of course, unrelenting demands and dead-lines. Working women with children often find themselves squeez-ing their kids into an overcrowded calendar. For many women, something is missing. There is too little time for family, never mind hobbies, friendships, community service, and spirituality, among other activities. If just some of the time that work consumes can be reclaimed, a conscious life collage becomes possible.

Using the strategies in this book, you can redesign your work to reclaim this time. Then, you can rediscover old interests and explore new ones, consciously choosing how to spend your "new" time. Your conscious life collage is your own unique artwork. As your needs change, you can modify your collage, removing or reducing one element and introducing another. As one activity becomes more important, you may brighten its color. At the same time, another element may fade. The result is a life collage that is consciously assembled, representing the life you want, which evolves over time to meet your changing desires.

"HOW CAN THIS BOOK HELP ME?"

This book is based on three beliefs:

1. **Many women feel that "something is missing" in their lives.** They want to lead multifaceted lives, weaving profes-sional, family, community, and personal roles into one fulfill-ing life.
2. **There are many more options for redefining work than most women think.** Many women have leveraged their cre-ativity and ingenuity to manage and grow their careers with-out sacrificing everything else in their lives. The possibility exists for every woman to create a full life that works for her.
3. **Women benefit from hearing other women's success sto-ries.** Too many women feel that they are all alone when faced

with redesigning work. Despite what you may think, success stories abound. These stories must be shared and celebrated. Learning about what has worked for other women helps every woman craft a life that meets her needs. As women consider their journey to more dynamic lives, they will be reassured and inspired by the practical, emotional, and financial experiences of their peers.

This book is designed to help you create a multifaceted life that works for you—your own unique life collage. Specifically, this book will:

- **Help you get unstuck.** In Chapter 2, you will learn how to recognize the signs that it is time for a change. Do not languish in discomfort out of fear and uncertainty. No one is going to hand you this life—you have to claim it, create it, and maintain it.
- **Help you face what stops you.** Chapter 3 will help you identify the internal roadblocks that keep you from moving on. By sharing what has worked for other women, this book will help you recognize and face your roadblocks with confidence.
- **Help you consider options.** This book examines the full spectrum of alternatives and will help you figure out which option will work best for you. Chapter 4 will help you begin to consider what is possible. In Chapters 5–8, you will explore ten different options for redesigning work to reclaim your life. You will benefit from the experiences, tips, triumphs, and pitfalls of women who have "been there and done that."
- **Help you rediscover your talents.** In Chapters 9–11, you will look at your life after you have redesigned your work. You will identify those interests that have long been buried beneath your one-track career. Once you have redesigned your work, there will be room for the rest of your life collage. Learn to manage your collage to grow and evolve as you do.

- **Show you how you can help make a conscious life collage a reality for others.** Once you have built your conscious life collage, you can help others do the same. Chapter 12 will give you ideas of what you, as an individual, as well as what employers, the government, and media can do to support people in creating work that works in their lives. Not only are individuals happier and more productive when they lead a multifaceted life, but communities also benefit when people take on multiple roles.
- **Provide inspiration and guidance.** Throughout, this book will supply you with the inspiration and tools to make your chosen option a reality. You *can* redesign your work and reclaim your life.

COMMON THREADS

A number of common themes emerged from the many interviews and Internet survey responses. Keep these ideas in mind as you read this book.

Creating your life collage is a journey, not a destination. Redesigning work and creating a life collage is a dynamic, ongoing process. One woman calls her collage "an extraordinary continuum." Creating your life collage will go more smoothly if you view the process as a journey, rather than a destination or series of destinations. Destinations are often fraught with disappointment. You work hard to get there only to find that "there" is not such a great place to be. If you tend to be a very destination-focused person, as many of the women who contributed to this book are, you may find yourself agreeing with one woman who commented, "Each destination I reached, I celebrated for all of thirty-five seconds. And then I was on to the next one." If you shift your paradigm from destination to journey, you will experience less disappointment, and greater joy, achieving milestones along the way. And, in your worst moments, you will know that on a journey, everything— including the bad patches—passes.

As you proceed along the journey, it is unlikely that you will reexamine your work/life, adopt an option, and then have a solution for the rest of your career. Rather, it is more likely that you will re-create work for your collage today. It will work for a while, perhaps a long while, providing a resting place along your journey. Then, at some point, you may find that it no longer works the way it once did and you will want to re-create it again. The first time you redesign your work will be the hardest. After that, making adjustments should become easier and more natural.

Trade-offs are inherent in the journey. Life is comprised of a series of trade-offs. You make trade-offs every day, many times a day. If you currently spend many hours working, you are trading off other things you could be doing. As Molly, a human-resources professional, says, "Personal choices involve trade-offs that we're often not willing to make. We think they're forever. They're not." You cannot avoid making trade-offs. However, by clearly defining what is important to you and making conscious choices, you can make the optimal trade-offs for you.

You are in good company—past and present. As Beth and Kathy began their journeys, each thought that she was alone, the only one "who just could not take it anymore." Each thought that her friends and colleagues in similar positions were doing fine. Yet, there is a widespread movement of women working to redesign work.

Today's women who are struggling to incorporate more than work, or work and family, into their lives have numerous peers engaged in the same struggle. These women also have a little-known but inspiring legacy of simultaneously working, raising families, pursuing interests, and contributing to their communities. The "traditional" American nuclear family of the 1950s, with a working dad, stay-at-home mom, and two kids, was, in fact, more of a historical aberration than a true heritage. Women have led multifaceted lives, combining work, family, and community, almost since the dawn of humanity. Even in cave times, men hunted while women, with children by their side, gathered plants and berries to contribute to the household.

When the American West was being formed, women worked alongside men to build communities. Margaret Frink, Mary Jane Megquier, and Luzena Stanley Wilson are not exactly household names, but each operated a business, had a family, and contributed to the development of the West. Other women, such as Madame C. J. Walker, America's first African-American female millionaire, and Victoria Woodhull, the first woman to trade on the New York Stock Exchange, are perhaps slightly more well known. Each had a child even as she made history. As role models, these historical figures, along with thousands of others whose stories have not been told, remind today's women that they are not alone. Legions of women have traveled this road before.

Remember this heritage as you move forward. As Miriam Krasno, a career-development and life-planning consultant, counsels, "Don't do this alone. Find a buddy who is going through a similar journey. Understand that sometimes the people who love you most can't help you. This can be a major life change for some women. You will need support to get you through the difficult days." No one goes through this process without some difficult emotional times. By sharing women's stories, this book will help you through these tough moments. However, redesigning work and creating your own life collage will be much easier, and more fun, if you seek additional support. This book will help you to find the support you need and to make the best use of it.

Ask for what you want. If you do not ask, you have no shot of getting what you want. At least if you ask, you have a shot. You may be surprised to find you get what you desire! Ginny, a commercial–

real estate executive, found her stodgy firm met her needs for a professional part-time position. Her advice: "My encouragement to others would be to 'ask.' You spend too much time having dialogues with yourself and not with the person who needs to be hearing what you want to say. . . . My boss wasn't going to come in and say, 'You're working too hard, don't do this project.'" Too many times women assume they will be turned down. Meanwhile, with work/life policies on the books at many firms, managers are wondering why the policies are not utilized and everyone is still complaining. These managers say that it is the employee's responsibility to propose the schedule she wants while addressing the impact on management and the rest of the department.

"I would have done it sooner." Finally, all of the women who contributed to this book were asked what they would do differently if they had it to do all over again. By far, the most common answer was, "I would have done it sooner." Ginny spoke for many when she continued, "I'd do everything sooner. I look back and say, 'Wow, you [were] either a wimp or a coward.' I guess it is a maturing process that we all go through. You think back to these things that seemed so overwhelmingly important and so critical, and you know what? They just don't matter." Out of almost one thousand stories, very few women regretted reexamining their professional lives to forge satisfying careers that also allow room for family, community, hobbies, and other activities.

You *can* create a life that is more satisfying and fulfilling. You do not have to come home exhausted at the end of every day, depleted. Just as your life did not get offtrack overnight, restoring it will not happen overnight either, but it will happen if you are *really* ready to begin. You are taking a big step forward by reading this book. Do not wait until you are done reading to take the next step. Participate. Take small steps along the way as you read the chapters that follow. If you do, by the end, you will have gone a long way toward creating your conscious life collage. It is time for your journey to begin.

t w o

Something Is "Out of Whack"

"THAT GNAWING FEELING": EARLY WARNING SIGNS

Is it time for you to make a change—or are you just having a bad week? There are a number of "early warning signs," indicators that perhaps you should be making changes in your work/life. Unfortunately, most women who contributed to this book identified these warning signs in retrospect, after they had become so burned out, stressed out, frustrated, exhausted, and/or physically ill that they were forced into action.

If you are reading this book, you already suspect that something needs to change in your life. To help you tune in to your own alarm bells, below are some of the early warning signs that women experienced. If you find yourself nodding in agreement, start your journey *now*. Do not wait until you are physically sick or emotionally kaput.

You find yourself starting most conversations with "Sorry I didn't call you back sooner, but I've been *so* busy. . . ." This had become Emily's mantra. Even though she cherished her friends and family, she always felt too busy to spend time talking or visiting with them. As she raced from one deadline to the next, her dissatisfaction with being out of touch with loved ones mounted. A friend helped Emily to see how much her relationships were slipping, prompting her to initiate change. Another woman chimed in: "I didn't know what was going on in my friends' and family's lives, and I didn't have time to live a life, much less know what was going on in it."

You feel in a constant state of exhaustion and/or are frequently sick. Mindy was sick almost constantly during the last two years before she made changes in her life. "I would go from a cold to allergies to flulike exhaustion and back. It took me a month of lying in bed, after I quit, to get better." Delaney would get migraine headaches. "They would put me out," she says. "I didn't have time for that. I went to the doctor and said, 'Fix it.' He said, 'I think stress is causing this,' but I didn't get the message. I wasn't ready to change anything." Another woman confided, "I began getting anxiety attacks. I got dizzy spells. I had to run to the bathroom at least once a day to dry-heave or vomit bile."

You could win a *People* magazine trivia contest. Kathy loved to read but was so mentally exhausted at the end of a workday that following a story in a book was an insurmountable task. She took to taking baths and reading a *People* magazine to unwind from the day. One evening, when watching TV with her husband, John, she informed him that one of the actors they were watching in a program was married to an actress from another program they usually watched. John looked at his formerly intelligent, interesting wife incredulously and said, "You've got to lay off the *People* magazine. You're scaring me!"

You keep telling yourself it will get better next week, next month, or after the next deadline. Molly said, "Work was at the top of my list. I kept telling myself that next month will be better. It never was."

As Nicole put it, "I kept saying, 'As soon as . . . [I make this presentation, I hire that person, I meet that deadline] . . . then I'll get this under control.' It never happened."

You no longer find satisfaction from your work. Sylvia said, "I was doing my job on autopilot. There was no more challenge. I like a challenge. It offered me nothing new." Another woman confided, "I felt my work was meaningless and all-consuming. One day I looked in the mirror, saw the sadness in my eyes, and said, 'No more.' . . ." Some women expressed this warning sign as having nothing to look forward to in the next twenty-four hours.

You dread going to work—the Sunday-night funk/Monday-morning blues are a weekly occurrence. Some women experienced a funk every Monday morning. Over time, this funk expanded, creeping into Sunday evening, as they mentally prepared themselves for the week. These women found their weekends becoming shorter— squeezed between de-stress time needed on Friday evening and the beginning-of-the-week blues starting on Sunday. As Becky put it, "I struggled to get up in the morning and get to work. I was tired all the time; I napped on weekends." Another woman said, "I no longer looked forward to going to work. Getting out of bed and motivating myself to even be slightly interested in the day ahead was a major struggle."

When the pleasure you derive from your accomplishments becomes increasingly fleeting. To boost herself up, Mindy sought out recognition by winning awards, or getting public acknowledgment for her accomplishments in the company newsletter. "The pleasure I derived from each accomplishment kept getting more fleeting." April, now a freelance marketing-communications consultant, said, "When my company promoted me to vice president my first thought was, 'What things are going to be painful now?'"

You have no desire to have your boss's job. Mindy was an account executive at an advertising agency. Her boss once said to her, "You're talented. I'll support you in anything you decide to do. But I have to ask, What are you doing here? You come alive when you're working with the creative team. The client side just doesn't light you up." She knew he was right. She had no desire to have his job. She wanted to be with the writers. She went on to forge a successful freelance writing career.

You find yourself buying a lot of little things "because you deserve it." Some women run out during lunch to buy a pick-me-up gift for themselves to boost their spirits. Others treat themselves to a manicure or a massage. It is okay to treat yourself once in a while, but it becomes problematic when you find yourself buying little treats with greater frequency. As Mindy explains, "The last six months I was at the agency, I would regularly get manicures, go out to lunch, peruse bookstores, just to make myself feel better. Once I left, I didn't need that anymore."

That rising star of yours is beginning to fade. A market-research professional, Dana was working in a "very frustrating environment. . . . I was told that my mission was to change the way the department worked. Every time I'd go to make a change, they'd say, 'That's not the way we do this.' I went from employee of the year to nonfunctional inside of one year." Another woman lamented, "I realized I was not enjoying my work and was no longer challenged. My performance was slipping." If you are nodding in agreement with this early warning sign, make a move before your performance slips. Do not wait until others notice your sliding commitment.

You cannot remember the last time you laughed, did charity work, or had a hobby. When Kathy and John were getting married, their religious advisor had them fill out a form describing their interests and hobbies. "I was ready to cry right there," Kathy says, "because

I no longer had any." Becky lamented, "I cut back on charitable efforts because I needed the weekends free to go to the office." For another woman, it was her kids that brought her back to reality. "My kids started asking when I would be in a good mood again because they could not remember me happy."

You find yourself snapping at coworkers or acting crabby to family and friends. Becky reflects, "I found myself routinely disappointing friends and family because I had to work. In the rare times I had with my husband and friends, all I wanted to do was complain about work. For them, it was a really disheartening and confusing time. They didn't know what to tell me to cheer me up." As another woman put it, "I kept hearing myself say how sick I always felt from the stress of the day, and how tired I felt by the time I got home. Then I realized I was sick and tired of being sick and tired."

You have the feeling of being stuck. "There is nothing worse than the feeling of being stuck," says Cindy, now the owner of a multimillion dollar gift business. "My advice to others is to understand that if you are feeling stuck, you're already in the worst place. *Any* change you make will be a change for the better." When Sylvia felt stuck, she found she was talking to herself. "'What am I going to do? What can I do? I've got to do something! I've got to get out of here.' I was so obsessed. It was a constant tape recording going around in my head. When I quit, the tape shut off, and there was quiet!"

Friends and family repeatedly express concern for you. When Judi accepted a promotion to vice president of finance at her company, her mother's response was one of dismay: "I can't believe you did that!" Her mother knew that Judi's life was out of balance and that Judi was seeking to get back in line with what was important to her. Her mother knew that this promotion would mean more work and longer hours. Judi credits her mother with helping her keep her personal commitment. Jill credits her husband and sons with helping her to see the need for change. "[They] really wanted me to quit my job because all I did was complain about it."

Lack of time with the children in your life. For other women, it is children who provide the eye-opener. As one woman put it, "I was working eighty hours a week. One day, my niece asked me, 'Why?' I couldn't answer her!" Another woman experienced every working woman's nightmare. She recounted, "My nine-month-old daughter began calling the baby-sitter Mama. When my daughter became ill, she didn't want to have anything to do with me. She wanted her 'mama.' That was quite an eye-opener." Yet another woman recounts an absurd incident in her office: "My boss didn't speak to a coworker for a month because she took two hours off to see her new grandchild be born." Still other women shared that their kids resorted to making appointments to see them.

"THAT'S IT! I CAN'T TAKE IT ANYMORE": EPIPHANY EXPERIENCES

More of Kathy's Story

"I was sitting in a conference room in a meeting with my peers and several of the directors. At the front of the room, a consultant was presenting his perspective on how messed up our organization was and how he had the cure that was going to make everything all right. He was the latest in a long line of consultants we'd burned through. I had heard this story before, and, quite frankly, I was sick of hearing it. So I started grilling him. . . . 'And what are your assumptions based on? . . . And what examples do you have that what you propose works in our industry? . . .'After several minutes of this, I checked my watch and realized I needed to leave for yet another meeting. This company loved meetings. As I stepped

outside the conference room door, my mentor followed me out and asked, 'So why did you just chew that guy out?' The words that popped out of my mouth, before I could think or retrieve them, were, 'Because I hate my job!'

"Now, I'm the first one to admit that I had been blocking for a long time. If you had asked me even ten minutes before if I hated my job I would have told you, 'No, my division's just going through a rough time right now. It will get easier after. . . .' But when those words popped out of my mouth there was no turning back. I had to face the fact that I needed a change and I needed it fast. It wasn't the job. It wasn't the company. It was me. I wasn't enjoying this anymore."

For most women, the warning signs begin to happen more frequently and with greater intensity, until they reach a breakthrough volume—known in collage parlance as "epiphany" level. For many women, the need for change becomes crystal clear in a particularly powerful instant or event, a defining moment when, all of a sudden, it hits you—"Aha. I have to make a change." There is "a point of no return," after which women begin to move toward change in both attitude and behavior. Some women make a change immediately. For others, the epiphany experience launches their committed effort to determine "What's next?" The actual move may not happen for some time.

As one woman said, "My kids were sick. I was unhappy. My home life was disrupted. Work was stressful. There was a collision. I couldn't breathe. I cried all day. . . . My husband and I looked at what we could afford. . . . It became clear that we couldn't afford for me *not* to quit. . . ."

No two women have the same experience deciding to make a change. And yet, listening to one woman share her epiphany evokes a completely different "aha" in others. As you read the following epiphany experiences, "listen" for what they highlight in your own life. Perhaps something similar has already happened to you. Or perhaps a life event is leading you in that direction. Miriam Krasno, a Chicago-based career-development and life-planning consultant, says, "For many women, an epiphany experience is often precipitated by some life event—family illness, having or adopting a child, or the desire for marriage and/or children that doesn't happen." Maybe you see yourself heading for one of these moments.

Illness and exhaustion grow into a malady requiring medical attention. You may recall Beth's bout with "imaginary pneumonia" described in Chapter 1. While Beth was fortunate—her pneumonia was only a fleeting image in her head—many other women report that it took coming face-to-face with significant mental and physical health issues to get them to recognize the need for change. Career coach Krasno highlights that for some women, "a health crisis manifests itself in alcohol and drug abuse, eating disorders, or as a devastating shopping addiction."

Sylvia, a thirty-one-year-old single mom and a local news producer for a television station, wanted to be a journalist since she was twelve. Even before she finished college, she was on-air for her local station. "I liked it the first year, the second year had exciting times, but after that . . . I was working long hours and there was no more challenge. . . . News happens all the time. People would constantly be calling me at home. I was never not working. I would leave my stressful job and create stress at home. I'd say, 'Jack (my three-year-old son), let's cram all our fun into two hours.' That was all the time I had. *I knew it was time to go when I realized that I was popping so much Tylenol that I got kidney stones.* I couldn't do news anymore. It was killing me. . . . I quit without any safety net." Sylvia took two months off and then began a journey that landed her a position with a special-interest radio program that broadcasts nationally—a position she loves and one that allows her time for Jack as well as her other interests.

Another woman had both mental and physical symptoms: "I knew it was time to make a change when I physically and mentally fell apart. Physically, my allergies went haywire, I needed a hysterectomy, and my nerves were so bad that I felt as if I was shaking and twitching all day! Mentally, I found it hard to concentrate, exhibit patience, and, more important, have compassion for those who were having problems. I continued working like this for about six months, progressively getting worse. When I finally had a confrontation with my new boss, I knew it was time to leave. Amazingly, the moment I handed in my resignation, I felt better. . . ."

For some women, it takes the diagnosis of a life-threatening illness to signal their wake-up call. As one woman confided, "I knew it was time for a change when I was diagnosed with a bleeding ulcer. The doctor told me I had to make changes in my life or I could die." Yet another woman shared, "The day the doctor told me that I had an aneurysm in my brain, I decided that it was time to cut my hours and start to enjoy life more. . . ."

Monday-morning dread metamorphoses into full-blown job dissatisfaction. As Kathy did, many women have come face-to-face with just how much they dislike (okay, hate) their jobs. And they realize, "It doesn't have to be this way. I can make a decent living doing something I like." Or, as one woman put it, "I just couldn't do it anymore. I felt like I was playing charades."

Margaret worked for a video-production agency in the advertising field. "I was very ambitious and saw this as a way to fast-track into a lucrative, glamorous advertising/media career. One day, I realized that I was sitting in a small room listening to two grown men argue about how best to photograph a hamburger. I am a vegetarian. The full impact of the absurdity of this hit me all at once. 'This is not what I was put on earth to do,' I thought. I switched to the nonprofit sector, making less money but salvaging my soul. I have never looked back. . . ."

Judi laughs now when she recounts her story. At the time, she was assistant controller for the cheese division of a manufacturing company. "I was at an off-site meeting where they were discussing the commodity price of cheese curds. Chart after chart after chart of cheese curd trends flashed before my eyes. I knew I should care about this stuff. This meant millions of dollars to my division and all I could think of was, 'Who gives a shit?' I started interviewing after that meeting."

Megan provides another example. A consultant for a nationally recognized firm, Megan found the work "intellectually, pretty interesting, but, emotionally, I didn't buy into it. I wasn't invested. One day I was at the client's office when one of the marketing managers I had been working with walked in. He had been watching focus groups of women talking about vacuum cleaners. He was so excited! His eyes were shining! I said, 'That's it.' That was the defining moment for me. I said, 'If he can be that excited about vacuum cleaners and I'm not that excited about this job that's supposedly an intellectually stimulating, sought-after glamour job, I'm in the wrong place. I've got to do something else.'" Megan went on to become a successful freelance computer trainer.

Stephanie worked in advertising when, one Christmas week, she was stuck in a meeting with her client until four A.M. "I looked around at this meeting. There were twenty-seven other M.B.A.'s in the room. I asked myself, 'Does this room really need a twenty-eighth M.B.A.?' I love to sing. I had recently been offered a professional singing job, one that many people didn't think I could get. It could [have launched] me as a professional singer. I was fired before I even began because on the first night of rehearsals I was stuck in this meeting with my client. There I was, in the wee hours of the morning, driving home, having lost my singing job because of a client meeting. I had to pull my car over on the expressway because I was crying so hard. I had given up something I loved for something I wasn't all that fond of. That was it for me. Something had to change." Stephanie began counseling shortly thereafter. She eventually found her way into the nonprofit sector, where she is thriving, working in the arts.

"What friends? What family?": Your relationships become strained.
Some women find they have compromised their relationships with family and friends before they finally realize they have let things go too far. Laura, a public-relations professional, put it succinctly when she said, "After seven years, I was burned out. I was disillusioned. I was working sixty hours a week. The client always came first. One year I was out of town on Valentine's Day, my husband's birthday, and our anniversary. It was simply costing too much." Laura's journey took her first to a job share and then to a part-time job in her field.

Delaney, an attorney and mother of two, relates a similar experience. "I was working full-time in the law department at the bank. It was right after Christmas. I had managed to get through Christmas. Only after the holiday did I realize that I didn't enjoy it. I didn't 'do' it—I got through it. The two big presents I bought for my kids were gifts I didn't approve of! I thought, 'What have I done? This isn't how I want to do it. Something is wrong. I don't have time to think. If I just had one more day. . . .'" Delaney went on to negotiate a part-time arrangement with her employer.

Friendships can bring about similar realizations. Molly, a human-resources professional, was working for a midsize company. Like so many other women, Molly was working "mega hours." "My job was at the top of my list. I tried, but I had no energy left for anything else. I kept telling myself that next month would be better. Finally, the mother of one of my childhood girlfriends died. I thought about whether I could fit going to the funeral into my schedule. I almost chose work over going to support one of my oldest friends. I thought, 'This is insane.' It became a matter of when I would leave, not if."

For many women, it is their children who provide the final impetus for change. One woman recounts an incident right after the birth of her child. "I was a court reporter in Florida. I knew I was in trouble when a firm I was working for called me at the hospital the morning after I had a baby via C-section and asked me if I could transcribe and turn in a deposition I had taken a couple of months earlier. . . ." Another woman explains, "It finally hit home the day my daughter came to my office on a Saturday night to show me how she looked for the prom!"

Your fantasy life turns destructive. Like Beth, Melinda imagined self-harm. "I knew it was time to make a change when I realized I had no life outside of work and I hated my job. I would drive to work each day and think, 'If I drive into that tree over there, I won't have to go to the office today.' When the tree started seeming more and more like the way to go, I quit. . . ."

"No matter how much I do, they always want more." Betsy explains, "I was tired of it 'never being enough' even though I was on call twenty-four hours a day, seven days a week in a management position. It was nothing to put in seventy hours a week. To top it off, the CEO was passive-aggressive in managerial style, totally demoralizing. It reached a point where I was starting to doubt my own abilities. . . . One day I just said, 'Enough,' wrote my resignation, walked away from the computer for two hours, dealt with problems, came back to my office and hit 'Print.' That was it. . . ."

Monica recounts, "I remember the day I knew I needed to make a change very clearly. It was almost eight o'clock at night on a Thursday, and I was still at my desk at work. I had the perfect window view of the city and the most beautiful sunset, right behind the Wrigley Building clock tower. That sunset, coupled with the huge clock, reminded me of how late it was, which stirred something in me. It was almost as if someone was telling me that I was wasting too much time in the office and not [spending] enough time living, enjoying the things I love to do and the things that make me happiest. Right then I decided that I needed to give up the office job for good and go back to school to pursue my real dream. . . ."

Regardless of the type of epiphany you have, once that flash hits you—"something absolutely has to change"—there is no turning back. It may take some time before you can implement the change, but at least now you will actively engage in figuring out what the next step should be and how to make it happen.

Stop for a moment and congratulate yourself. You may feel as though you have not made much progress so far. But truly you have taken a significant first step. Realizing that you must make a move is a giant leap forward toward your new, more enjoyable life.

"HOW DO I KNOW WHEN I'M READY FOR CHANGE?": THOSE FIRST SUBCONSCIOUS STEPS— RECOGNIZING YOUR READINESS FOR ACTION

Many women complain for years about their unhappiness with the pressures of work but fail to take steps toward doing something about it. Sometimes, a simple readiness to head in a new direction holds women back. Krasno explains that there are numerous signals people display when they are finally ready to shift direction in their lives. "In working with my clients," she says, "I find that most take small, unconscious steps, such as cleaning out closets and throwing away little-used items in their house and office. There is an intentional, cleaning out of the clutter in one's life to make room for the new. Other women make and keep a commitment to get fit. It is these small steps that prepare them for taking bigger steps."

Krasno has found that as her clients prepare for change, they often fear that they have to make major shifts all at once. She counsels, "It is okay to have fear about making a change. Just remember that it's your life. It's your process. You decide the pace—how much to take on at each step. If you prefer to make changes over time, then let your coach know you wish to take things slowly. If you want to make a change in under a month, prepare to do a lot of hard, intensive work quickly."

In order to prepare for exploring new possibilities, Krasno advises clients to get control of their finances. "Evaluate your level of debt. Work out a plan, or get professional assistance for eliminating your debt. Many people have been using spending money as therapy for the pain they experience with work. First you need to get your current debt under control, and, second, you need to change your spending habits." Krasno offers this tip: "Keep a log of everything you spend your money on over the next three months. You will start to see where some of your money is wasted and budget yourself accordingly."

Finally, if you find yourself in a moment of discomfort at the thought of making changes, Krasno advises, "Do an envisioning exercise. Close your eyes and envision living a life you love, where your life, including work, is flowing effortlessly. You don't have to know what you want to do next to begin 'living' with the idea that your next move can bring more peace to your life."

three

"So What's Stopping Me?":
Recognizing Your Roadblocks
to Moving On

Whether an early warning sign or an earth-shattering epiphany makes you recognize a change is in order, you are likely to experience some internal roadblocks to moving on. Most of the women who contributed to this book confronted one or more of the roadblocks described in this chapter. These roadblocks are often culturally ingrained—almost hardwired—in women. But, just as other women have gotten over these hurdles, so can you. By sharing what has worked for other women, this chapter is designed to help you recognize and face your roadblocks with confidence.

"I CAN'T GIVE UP_____!": EXPLORING YOUR RELATIONSHIP TO MONEY, POWER, AND TITLE

If you still truly believe that Success = Money + Power + Title, this book is not for you. If, on the other hand, you suspect that this equation is somehow flawed, keep reading.

The pervasive American culture celebrates the workaholic as the ultimate success story. As the story goes, the more you earn, the greater the title you hold, the more power you wield; the one who wields the most power wins. Success is defined solely on this monetary, hierarchical structure. It is easy to understand. It is measurable. The problem is, it is wrong.

Think about your own life. Whom do you consider to be successful? At first, you might think of people you know who have reached a high level of monetary success. Perhaps you are thinking of the family at the end of your block who has added on to their home, turning it into a McMansion. Their kids have the latest and best of everything. Both spouses have brand-new, pedigreed cars. But how much fun are they to be around? If you were in need of neighborly assistance, would they be the first you would call? Would you consider them great friends or parents?

Now, think of people you admire. They are rarely the same people. The people you admire most are probably those who contribute to their communities, raise solid families, and inspire others. These same people have probably also attained a level of professional success, but there is much more to their lives than that. As one woman put it, "My definition of success has changed tremendously. It used to be based on how much money a person made. Now it means more to me if a person has made a difference in the lives of others."

This monetary, hierarchical measurement system is pervasive; it is very difficult to begin measuring yourself by a new, less clearcut yardstick. Nancy, a former banking officer in transition, put it this way: "You tend to stay stuck, surrounded by others who are stuck in competitiveness, blinded by their materialism, their consumerism. That's what helps keep score." Megan, a computer trainer, has learned to handle her moments of monetary competitiveness. "Occasionally, when I get into a comparative situation with friends and peers, I just remind myself that I really do like what I'm doing."

One general strategy to help wean you away from this narrow definition of success is to broaden your network. It is important to include friends and colleagues who define themselves by more than their work. Another strategy is to take a critical look at your definition of success and balance. Stephanie, a former advertising supervisor who found career fulfillment in the non-profit arts community, shares how the meaning of success and balance changed for her. "Why live by someone else's definition? . . . You have to ask yourself, 'Am I being true to my soul?' At the end of the day ask yourself, 'Whom did I help?'" Molly observes that "before, success equaled money, power, and title. Now, success equals power—power over my own life, not power in an organization."

Most women have found that their definitions of success and balance changed significantly as they redirected their work/life. Where balance was not even a consideration early in their careers, its importance grew significantly as work took over their lives. To make building a life collage a reality, their definition of success necessarily changed. And while these same women claimed they wanted more "balance" in their life, few had really defined what that meant for them, making it elusive.

For many women who have shifted direction, the definition of success now includes a commitment to their life collage—be it spending time with family, community involvement, exercising, pursuing spirituality, or taking up a new hobby. The impetus for this revised definition was the point at which success and balance collided—the point where you may now find yourself.

◼ EXERCISE 1
Redefining Success and Balance

Take out your journal or a piece of paper. First, write down your current definition of success. To help you, think of people you know or have read about who you think epitomize success. What makes them successful in your eyes? Be as specific as possible. What signals you that they are successful? Is it the things they have or the way they are as people? Is it the amount of control they have over their time, their earnings, their work, or their commitments? Next, picture yourself as a success. Write down what it would take for you to consider yourself a success. How would you know when you are officially "successful"? Once you achieved this success, then what?

Now write down your current definition of balance. Be as specific as possible. What does balance look like to you? Do you know anyone who is balanced? What makes him or her so, in your eyes? Over what period of time do you measure balance—a day, week, month, or year? Perhaps, even a lifetime?

Now reflect constructively on your definitions. Are they in conflict? For instance, do you want to be a Fortune 50 general manager and be home nightly by 5:30 P.M. for dinner with the kids? How well do you measure up to these definitions? How likely are you ever to measure up? Perhaps you are getting a glimmer that you have been setting yourself up to fail. You have the power to define your own success; redefining these concepts may open a whole new freedom in your life.

Don't be afraid to create your own way. Listen to Catherine's advice: "Don't be afraid to be an individualist. You may appear to be different, but in the long run people will wish they were like you."

Now consider redoing each definition so that success and your life collage are in sync. What definition of success would allow you to realize your optimal collage? Think of nonmonetary interpretations of success. What makes up the components of your life collage? How much time or effort do you want to spend in each activity or role?

It might be helpful to draw two pie charts on your page. In the first chart, divide the pie to reflect how you currently spend your time. In the second chart, depict how you would ideally divide your time among your various roles and responsibilities. For instance, perhaps you currently spend the majority of your time working, sleeping, commuting, and parenting, with little left over for a significant other or yourself. Your ideal might include all of the above, plus a hobby, donating some time in your community, more time for spirituality and creative expression.

Now stop and pay attention to what thought came into your head as you were writing down all of the things that you want to do. Most likely, it was some negative thought discouraging you. "There is no time for all of that!" the voice says. "We don't have the money to allow me to scale back." Those are just fears creeping in that probably fall into one of the major roadblocks discussed in this chapter. Before you get too overwhelmed by listening to that inner voice discouraging you, read on to determine more about what is stopping you from realizing your ideal.

Human beings tend to express their attachment to money, power, and title in several ways. Having reconsidered your definition of success and balance, see if any of these messages resonate:

- "I can't afford to make less money!"
- "I haven't been financially dependent on someone else since I was a kid."
- "Who I am is what I do."
- "This is all I've ever wanted. What do I do now that I'm there and it isn't enough?"
- "My title gave me power. How will I be treated without it?"

"I Can't Afford to Make Less Money!"

One of the biggest obstacles many women cite in moving on to a more satisfying and workable career is their attachment to money. For many women, this is as much an emotional concern as a financial one. Many women derive their self-worth from the size of their annual salary. Some women automatically eliminate a potential career option if they think it will require a cut in pay. Yet, a pay cut may not have as big an impact as you think, if it coincides with a reduction in expenses. You may be surprised to see how little of your income is left after taxes and expenses due to your all-consuming work.

Many women redesign work without reducing their earnings. Some even get raises in the process. But if you are willing to at least consider (by completing the exercise on page 36) the possibility of making less money, you will have more options available to you. This exercise is meant to put the choice back in your hands—taking you out of a vicious cycle, where you work in a job you do not like to earn money to pay for the treats you need to sustain yourself in the job that you do not like.

Emily knew a change in her work/life was needed. A mother of one daughter, with another child on the way, she had talked about her turmoil this way: "I want to scale back while my kids are young, but I just don't see how Chris and I can afford to live without any part of my income." Emily learned that she could afford to earn less money because her work-related costs associated with an alternative work arrangement would be significantly lower, while her net buying power—what would be left of her salary after taxes and work-related expenses—would remain roughly the same.

Follow the worksheet and the instructions in Exercise 2 to determine what you really earn. While your tax return says you earn one thing, you will find your net buying value to be significantly less. If you are in a desperate situation, where you need to leave your current employer to save your sanity, you may be able to earn the equivalent net buying value (or cover your basic living expenses) in a new way. For instance, many women freelance part-time while looking for a permanent, more satisfying position. Also, as you evaluate possible new work options, use this worksheet to help you analyze your true financial situation.

If you look at this exercise and say, "Uggh! I don't want to go through all of this work!", stop yourself. Determining your net buying value is critical to creating freedom to pursue options that you may have previously considered impossible. Many women are surprised to discover that what they really earn and what they have to earn is less than they thought, giving them the freedom to consider options they once thought were unaffordable. You may even find you can afford to take a sabbatical to give you the time off you need to figure out your next move.

EXERCISE 2
Personal Financial Analysis:
Understanding What You *Really* Earn

Gross Income (you can find this on your W-2 form)	$
Deduct: total taxes (including state, federal, social security)	$
Deduct: tax-bracket adjustment (if necessary)	$
Net Income	$
DEDUCT WORK-RELATED EXPENSES:	
Meals	
Eating breakfast out (____ days/week x $____ average cost x ____ weeks)	$
Eating lunch out (____ days/week x $____ average cost x ____ weeks)	$
Eating dinner out (____ days/week x $____ average cost x ____ weeks)	$
Grocery-delivery costs	$
Work-wardrobe expense Spring suits/uniforms	$

Fall suits/uniforms	$
Dry cleaning	$
Tailoring	$
Other_____	$
Commute expense Mileage @ $0.325/mile	$
Parking	$
Car phone	$
Books on tape	$
Public-transportation expense (train and/or bus fare)	$
Other_____	$
Child- and/or elder-care expense Nanny/day care/au pair	$
School wardrobe/supplies/meals	$
Interim sick care	$
Baby-sitter	$
Meal and commuting expense for a family member providing care	$
Shuttle service	$
Other_____	$
Household-service provider expense Landscape services	$
Cleaning service	$
Dog walking	$
Window washing	$
Carpet cleaning	$

Snow removal	$
Home repair	$
Other_____	$
Personal care/improvement services/treats	
Massage therapy	$
Manicure/pedicure	$
Facial	$
Shopping therapy	$
Physicians' expense	$
Lessons/training (e.g., golf)	$
Other_____	$
Other_____	$
Total work-related deductions	$
Subtract total deductions from net income to determine what you REALLY earn.	$

INSTRUCTIONS

Review the above expense items, putting amounts in where appropriate. You probably do not incur all of these work-related expenses. If you incur expenses that are not listed, insert them. Make sure to include all of the expenses you incur due to your working outside of the house—or due to your work consuming so much of your time. Do not include expenses that you would incur even if you did not work. The idea is to determine how much of your salary is really left over for you or your family to use. Keep in mind, no one is suggesting that you have to give up your cleaning service or your massages. This exercise is meant to put your expenses into context. Then, you can decide how hard you want to work to pay for the services you want to use.

Income and Taxes

Gross income and all taxes deducted from your salary are straightforward and can be found on the W-2 form that you filed last year. If you are married and filing jointly, you may incur a hidden cost if your income pushes your household income into a higher tax bracket. Check the tax tables in last year's tax booklet or ask your accountant. If your income does push the household into a higher bracket, compute the tax savings by comparing the gross taxes owed on your husband's income at the higher tax bracket versus the lower bracket. The net difference between the two is the tax-bracket savings.

Meals

Estimate how many times you eat breakfast and lunch out per week. Estimate the average cost of eating each meal out. Determine the number of weeks you eat out. For instance, if you get a two-week vacation each year, the standard holidays and personal days, then you would use forty-eight weeks for your calculation. Say you eat breakfast in your car on the way to work or at your office on average three times a week and the average cost is $1.50. Then eating breakfast out due to work costs you $1.50 x 3 times per week x 48 weeks = $216/year. Now if you go to a gourmet-coffee shop and order the latte instead of a cup of coffee, the cost quickly jumps to $3.50 x 3 x 48 = $504. Use the same calculation for determining your lunch meals.

Your dinner calculation should include the number of times a week you order in or eat dinner out as a result of working late or not getting home in time to prepare a meal. If you order a meal for delivery at your place of employment but get reimbursed from your company, that meal does not count. If, on the other hand, your family orders a meal because you are not home to cook dinner, this does count. Remember to estimate only the extra cost incurred in eating out—your take-out or restaurant bill minus what you would have spent on groceries.

Many families are now making use of grocery-delivery services as a timesaving convenience. Typically, there are monthly fees for participating in such a service. Sometimes a delivery charge is also incurred. Determine which fees are involved with your service and estimate your total expenditure on an annual basis.

Work-wardrobe Expense

In some professions, uniforms are required, in which case, determining the cost of a work wardrobe is straightforward. In many other professions, the costs are less clear. However, if you are in a position that requires you to wear a suit or some sort of professional attire, scan your closet to identify new items you purchased this year. Do not forget to consider accessories such as blouses, shoes, scarves, pantyhose, dress socks, boots, purse, briefcase, and costume jewelry. If you use a personal financial–software program such as Quicken, you may be able to run a report to determine work wardrobe–related expenses. Otherwise, you will have to estimate the cost. Do not worry about coming up with the exact figure. A general estimate will do for the purposes of this exercise.

Now comes the task of determining the ghastly costs of maintaining that wardrobe. If you have to wear professional attire that must be dry-cleaned, estimate your average bill and multiply by the number of times a year you go to the dry cleaners. Some women need to have new work-wardrobe purchases tailored. Few stores include free tailoring. If you incur tailoring expenses each year with new wardrobe purchases, include the cost in your worksheet.

Transportation Expense

For simplicity's sake, determine the wear and tear on your car by using the rate used by businesses for tax-deductible expenses (the 1998 rate is $0.325/mile) times the number of miles you drive to and from work each day. Multiply this per-day figure by the average number of days you work each year (approximately forty-eight weeks a year, if you get a two-week vacation and the standard holidays along with a few sick days, which comes to roughly 240 days). This will cover your gas, maintenance, tolls, and insurance expense related to getting to and from work.

If you work in a city that requires you to pay for parking, you will need to include your annual parking expense. For those people who make use of a long commute by catching up with friends by cellular phone, estimate the monthly car-phone expense that would go away if your commute went away. Similarly, if you purchase or rent books on tape to while away your commuting hours, include the expense associated with this entertainment.

Alternatively, some women incur a commuting expense such as train or bus fare instead of car expense. Estimate your yearly expense associated with public transportation.

Child- and/or Elder-care Expense

Your child-care expense may not go away entirely with a move to another position, but perhaps it may decrease. Or you may be able to take greater advantage of after-school programs if you telecommute and are able to drive the kids from school to after-school activities. Either way, determine your entire child-care expense. This should include meals, insurance, and social-security tax expense of in-home child care. If you use a day-care center, do not forget to determine late pickup charges that you incur periodically, or interim sick–child care. If you use an au pair, do not forget the agency fee and any application fees incurred each year as well as health insurance. Even if your mother is watching the kids for free, determine the meal expense and any commuting expense associated with this arrangement.

One woman described how she regularly used a shuttle service in her community to get her daughters from school to after-school activities. If this is an expense you incur, include it.

Household-service Provider

Many women utilize household-service providers in order to free weekend and after-work hours for quality family or personal time. These services include household cleaning, lawn care, pet walking, carpet cleaning, window washing, and snow removal. For some women it may even include painting and other home repairs that they would be willing to do themselves if given more time. Determine the monthly and annual costs associated with maintaining your home by using service providers as a result of your work consuming so much of your time.

Personal Care/Improvement Services/Treats

Frequently women use personal-care services as a "reward" for all of their hard work or as a tool to de-stress from their work/life. Women also use shopping expeditions as rewards or entertainment to get away from the stress of work. In either scenario, these are work-related expenses because you would not incur them otherwise.

Other women find the incidence of illnesses requiring medical attention increases with their stress level. In this section, you need to include the costs of visits you made over the course of last year to: your general practitioner, a psychiatrist, psychologist, or counselor, and particularly any alternative-medicine providers who are not typically covered by insurance. These include chiropractors, acupuncturists, herbalists, and Reiki treatment providers.

Finally, if you have to entertain clients in your position and that entertainment requires that you learn a new skill, include the cost of training. For instance, women in sales positions frequently take golf lessons in order to entertain clients competently on a golf course.

Filling out this worksheet is not meant to depress you by showing how little you really earn after all of your hard work. Nor is it meant to suggest that women should give up working and go home if that is not what they choose to do. Numerous research studies have documented the intangible benefits of working on women's self-esteem. Working women also provide great role models for young girls. This exercise simply illustrates that you have more financial freedom than you think to consider a myriad of options for redefining work.

"I Haven't Been Financially Dependent on Someone Else Since I Was a Kid"

Depending on the career changes you are contemplating, you may need to consider depending on a relative, spouse, or friend for financial support while you get started. Or, you may have to use savings that you had not yet planned to tap. Many times, this creates a significant level of anxiety. Kathy knew her desire to be financially independent stemmed from events she witnessed as a child. "I watched some of my mother's friends face terrible situations. These women were raised to be good Christian women. They were told by their church, 'Be a good wife, be a good mother, and you'll be taken care of.' Their husbands left them at fifty for a trophy wife. Out of the workforce for over twenty years, these women no longer had marketable skills to support themselves. I never wanted to let that happen to me." Kathy overcame this hurdle, first by accepting that she was looking for financial support only as she got her new business off the ground. Second, she reminded herself that she and her husband have a partnership that is committed to both partners' growth and development. With her husband's full emotional and financial support, Kathy launched her business.

Nancy's willingness to rely on her husband for the short term had an unusual benefit. "I didn't realize ahead of time how much my letting go of work for the time being [while I figured out my next step] was a signal to him that I trusted him. He subconsciously knew [part of] my working out of the home was because I didn't trust him. I was hedging my bets in case, God forbid, I ever wanted out of this marriage."

Bridget, a former commercial–real estate executive in transition, had to dip into her savings to allow for a sabbatical so that she could determine "what's next." She reflects, "I wasn't anticipating needing this money for something like this. It was supposed to be for a rainy day. But I guess what was at stake was my happiness for the rest of my career. I mean, I was miserable! So I reconciled dipping into savings by acknowledging that this crossroads I'm at measures up to a decent-size rainstorm."

"Who I Am Is What I Do"

Susan Molinari, who left her seat in Congress in 1997 to spend more time with her family, said, "How much of me was a congresswoman? Almost all of me. It was who I was. I was twenty-six when I announced my intention to run for my first elective office, [a seat on] the New York City Council. I've been doing this fast track since then—Republican keynote speaker, head of the Dole campaign in Congress, a stint at CBS. And then one day it was all gone. I remember that shortly after I left CBS, I went to a store in the mall to get my contact lenses. I'm sitting there with my daughter, filling out the forms. I write down my name and our address. And then I got to occupation. I had a total meltdown! My palms were sweaty. I was really uncomfortable. It was the first time I had to confront not being able to fill in 'occupation.' What should I put down? I had to walk out of the store and go back later!" Molinari is currently on the journey to figuring out what is next for her.

Likewise, after Beth quit her job, she began doing some freelance work to help pay the bills while she figured out what she wanted to do next. Only a few weeks into her freelance life, she and her husband went to a friend's housewarming party. Beth knew that most of the other guests would be recent business-school graduates and the conversation would center on their new jobs. She was dreading this party. If not for the fact that the hosts were very close friends, she would have skipped it.

Beth was concerned that "people would invariably ask, 'What do you do?' I wasn't sure how I would answer, but I felt pretty certain I was going to feel about the size of an ant. After all, everyone else would be reporting on his or her experiences as a marketer, or consultant, or investment banker. For so many years, I had had a 'label' by which to identify myself and that others easily understood. All of a sudden, I had no title to explain who I was." Beth was nothing short of shocked when a flock of partygoers circled around her wanting to know how she had done it. How, they asked, had she mustered the guts to quit her job? Where was she getting the interim freelance work? "People found what I was doing more interesting than many of the other guests' jobs."

Evelyn, a lawyer, said, "Before I left the law, my whole identity was bound up with being a lawyer, being smart and quick, caustic if needed, unrelenting." At the same time, this attorney found out that by letting go of this identity, even though she didn't know what might replace it, she was allowing a new identity to emerge. "As I scaled back in work, I discovered a softer, more humane side of myself. I rediscovered the part of me that was drawn to ideas and self-expression, creativity. It was as if peeling away the layer of myself that was 'lawyer' enabled me to find the part of me that loved words and colors, loved to observe and record the world." Evelyn went on to forge a career in creative writing.

Most women, given the time to think about it, "know" that there is more to who they are than what they do. When they move toward changing or giving up that career identity, that "knowing" is truly tested. It is easy to define themselves and allow others to see them through their professional title. It is like a nickname, a shortcut to understanding who they are. Total strangers are often impressed by the power that is implied by a title. Trying to define themselves as "freelance marketer, wife, mother, community activist, hobbyist, spiritualist, etc.," is messier than describing themselves as "vice president of marketing" or "lawyer" or "congresswoman." And yet, these other roles are vital to their conscious life collage.

As Bridget explains, "It was like a tape recorder going in my head: 'What am I going to do? What if I can't figure it out?' All of a sudden I heard this screaming 'I!' in my head and realized that I was looking at my next move as a definition of who I am. I got it, that *I am who I am. What I do next is simply what I do next. What I do isn't the definition of who I am.*"

"This Is All I've Ever Wanted. What Do I Do Now That I'm There and It Isn't Enough?"

"I always thought that 'making money plus a good job equals fulfillment,' " said Mindy. "Further along in my career, I realized that was not enough." Many women like Mindy have worked very hard and spent much of their lives reaching lofty professional goals. They climb the ladder with high expectations. But when they reach the top, disillusionment sets in. They find the destination was not worth the climb. It is difficult to admit that all they have fought to achieve—what they thought they wanted—either is not for them anymore or at least is not enough.

As one businesswoman wrote, ". . . I was a success at the job I was in, I had made it to the top. . . . I drove myself hard to get there, and then was hit by the realization that I was not happy there. . . . I liked my job, don't get me wrong. . . . But, there was something missing, which was the passion, the joy, of really loving my work. . . . Suddenly I was out of balance, wanting more. . . . I realize now that being happy in my work and enjoying what I do is the success of my work. . . . *Instead of working harder to become something, I now work smarter to enjoy something. . . .*"

It is very difficult to let go of something that you have worked for years to achieve, even if, deep down, you know it does not make you happy. If you find yourself in this situation, it is important to remember—as one woman so aptly put it—"No decision, save the one to have a child, is irrevocable." No one can take away your achievements. Moving on does not lessen the value of what you have already accomplished. As one woman put it succinctly, "I knew that I could always go back to doing what I was doing before at a different company or go back to the same company in a different position."

Molinari reflected that had she not pursued her career in elective office, she would have always wondered what might have been, even though, once there, she chose not to stay. "Having left Congress and left CBS, I am a bit confused, a little up in the air. But it is nothing compared to the regrets [of not pursuing my goal] or wondering, 'What if?' Regrets are killers. I am proud of what I accomplished in Congress. I do not regret it [my time there]. For me, it was time to move on. . . . I'm on the journey, trying to figure out 'what's next.' "

If you have reached the pinnacle of your career goals and find it lacking, take a chance on a new, more satisfying path. Remember that, if all else fails, you can go back—maybe not to the exact position, but you can go back into the world you left. You will not go hungry or become homeless. But at the same time, do not allow yourself to go running back at the first rough patch. Re-creating work is *work*. Use your past successes to corral your confidence. You do not have to stay in a position that does not work for you anymore just because you have been working toward that goal for some time.

"My Title Gave Me Power: How Will I Be Treated Without It?"

Sarah moved from head of public relations for a major nonprofit organization to running her own firm. In her former role, Sarah was the one CNN called for comment when there was a major world disaster. She was the talking head on the morning news, commenting on the impact of the latest hurricane, war, or flood. Sarah was on call twenty-four hours a day. At some point, she said, "Enough," and started her own firm. But the adjustment was not without difficulty. "I went from being one of the most powerful communicators to virtual oblivion. I felt invisible." To help her accept this loss of power, she joined and assumed a leadership position with the National Association of Women Business Owners (NAWBO) where she used her former skills to benefit the organization. NAWBO has helped her maintain her identity and given her the ability to receive recognition from others while being on her own.

For some women, their title carried a level of power in their organization. That power became intoxicating. With the thought of moving on, these women had to face the loss of some or all of that power. The thought of losing the authority to order around minions is scary. Emma, a former sales manager who moved into an advisory position, confides, "It was hard to go from directing the action to advising someone else [on how] to direct the action. Particularly when I knew their skill set was all wrong and they would likely run the division into the ground." Emma handled this change in her power status by focusing her efforts on outside endeavors. She chuckles as she explains that she is currently building a manufacturing company with her husband in her "spare time."

THE FEAR OF FAILURE: "WHAT IF THE NEXT STEP I TAKE DOESN'T WORK OUT?"

Experiencing uncertainty when embarking on a major career change is normal! Mary left her insurance position to become self-employed shortly after her husband left her and her ten-month-old child. She shares that "the worst part of making this change in my life is the possibility of failure. . . . So far everything has been great . . . but there is always that possibility. . . ." Megan, who left a prestigious management-consulting firm, was having difficulty determining what was next for her. Her fear was centered on "Oh, my God, it's been five months, and I still don't know what I want to do. How am I ever going to figure this out? Oh, God, I'm going to have to go back and work someplace where I don't like it."

Most women have experienced a fear of failure at one time or another. It is only human. But the question to ask yourself is: "How do I act in the face of my fear?" Mindy had so many ideas in her head that it scared her to choose one to the exclusion of the others. What if the one she chose did not work out? She changed her thinking. "I realized I'm just picking one for now. It doesn't mean the others necessarily go away. I like the idea of a 'stash' of ideas for what can come next in my life. The different things I want to do don't have to compete because I'm not trying to do everything at once."

Many people let fear hold them back, keeping them from making changes and pursuing what is right for them. As Dana put it, "My fear of failure has made it hard to do new things. I've missed out on so many opportunities in life . . . fun, money, people—because of fear. I am determined not to continue that behavior." Others move forward despite their fear. As Stephanie, who left advertising for a nonprofit company, observed, "This was the first time in my life I had to say, 'Oh, my God, how can I do this?' I was working in a field I knew very little about. But I just kept myself focused on 'What single step can I take today? What single step can I take tomorrow?' and it just went from there."

Quitting is not synonymous with failure. Some women, particularly those who want to make a shift but do not know to what, think quitting their current job signifies a personal failure. Rather than seeing that something is wrong with their current position, these women think, "There must be something wrong with me." These women assume that because one job no longer suits them, their entire career is in question. Roberta was miserable working as a lawyer in a prestigious firm. "I started to ask myself, 'Did I make a huge mistake?' I was crushed. I felt like a loser." Roberta has since discovered she loves the law, but does not like private practice. She has moved to the public sector and is thriving. Quitting simply means that you are leaving a job. You do not have to attach any more meaning to it than that.

Some thoughts on overcoming the fear of failure. Molly frequently reminds herself that she is on a journey. "I realized there are no absolute rights and wrongs. When I stop trying to make things fit into right or wrong, I am more comfortable. 'Okay, this doesn't work'—no judgment . . . I need to keep journeying . . . I gave myself permission in this process to find *a* right place (not *THE* right place) . . . I have permission to keep making changes for the rest of my life." Molly has the right idea—re-creating work is a journey, not a destination. The next step you pursue may *not* be the best one. But it is important to take it to help you further clarify the right direction for you. It is hard not knowing exactly what your next move should be. Up to now, you may have been on a career path that was very clear-cut (e.g., financial analyst to senior analyst to finance manager to director of finance to vice president of finance to chief financial officer). And yet, if you are willing to ask the question "What's next?", the answer will emerge when you are ready to hear it.

Molinari remembers advice her father gave her. "He taught me to take risks and be prepared to fail. 'Failure is no loss of dignity,' he'd say. 'Not trying is.' "[1] She adds, "People need to detach from the weighty pressure of failure. All it means is you tried something and it didn't work out. Big deal. Get on with it. Our male peers were taught this on the playing field when they were little. You will make mistakes sometimes. Shake it off and get your head back in the game. Women need to let go."

Keeping a journal helps some women work through their fear. Getting a fear out on the page and exploring where it is coming from can go a long way toward defusing it. If you are plagued by fear, this is a good time to remind yourself of prior accomplishments. No one can take away your existing successes. The things you did to achieve past success will help achieve future success. Perhaps it is time to make a written list of the accomplishments of which you are most proud. As you create this list, remind yourself of times when you were afraid you would fail but did what you set out to do anyway.

---

[1]Susan Molinari with Elinor Burkett, *Representative Mom: Balancing Budgets, Bill, and Baby in the U.S. Congress* (New York: Doubleday, 1998), 269.

THE FEAR OF CHANGE: "I KNOW I'M MISERABLE, BUT HOW DO I KNOW TRYING SOMETHING ELSE WILL BE ANY BETTER?"

Mindy remembers her father's cautionary words: "Don't do what I did—thirty-five years with the same company. Don't let them drain your life force." Mindy used her father's advice to move beyond feeling stuck into taking action toward creating her collage. But many women experience trepidation about making a change—any change. As unhappy as they are, at least what they have is a known entity. When Judi was single and completing business school—a natural time to make a career change—she still resisted. She tormented herself: "I'm thirty-six, toward the top of my [financial] profession. I'm too old to be starting over." Even though she was unhappy—so unhappy she required a sabbatical—Judi still could not consider taking a chance on something new. At the end of her sabbatical she ended up back in finance, albeit at another firm that had a healthier culture. When asked why she returned, Judi responded, "It was easy. I knew it [how to do the work]." Another woman echoed Judi's concern but moved past her fear: ". . . My time was running out. I almost thought it was too late to change, but I did it anyway."

Some women who are thinking of making a major career switch are concerned that they lack the necessary training and will be forced to start over. If this concern is stopping you, remember Catherine's counsel: "Reflect on really successful people. Read their biographies. Very few succeeded in what they studied or trained for. Many times they just 'fell into it.' Training can be a myth." Don't let lack of training stop you from pursuing your life collage.

If fear of change is stopping you, remember that you are letting the fear of the unknown keep you stuck in the known—a known that is making you miserable. It is quite possible, as evidenced by so many of the women in this book, the change you fear most might lead you to the life you desire. Sometimes the grass *is* truly greener on the other side. By not taking a chance, you are risking your life. Ask yourself if you would rather risk your life or risk change. Every moment that passes, with you stuck in frustration and disappointment, is a moment that could have been spent in a life filled with possibility, hope, and joy.

THE FEAR OF "WHAT WILL EVERYONE SAY?"

Part of what kept Mindy stuck in a position she no longer enjoyed were the comments made by her friends and family. They kept telling her, "You have such a great job! . . . You're so lucky! . . . You're doing great!" When Mindy finally moved on to pursue writing, they all thought she was nuts. But she stuck to her passion and forged a successful freelance writing career. She finally did something that made her happy rather than worrying about meeting the expectations others had set for her.

It is human nature to care what other people think. As much as you think you do not care, you may find that you care very much. Sheila, a single mom, was a senior vice president at a financial-services company. Sheila's typical workweek was sixty hours; she was on the road about half the time. Sheila was looking for an alternative, one that would provide normal hours, less travel, and more time with her kids. And yet, when faced with the perfect offer, she wavered. "I had this ego thing. . . . Before, I'd be at a cocktail party and people would ask me what I do and I'd say, 'I'm a big shot with a Wall Street firm.' I thought, 'What am I going to tell people now? No one's ever heard of [this organization].' I finally got to a point where I said, 'I don't care what other people think. . . . What does it really matter?'" Sheila took the new job and is much happier.

The next time you are wondering what other people will think, ask yourself, "What people?" Upon critical reflection, you may find the impression you are concerned with is the one you make on total strangers or colleagues who are mere acquaintances. Often, when you are comfortable with your new direction, others will be comfortable as well. As Mona put it, "Your attitude goes a long way toward defining how others will interpret your move. They will take their cues from you."

Whose opinion really matters? Focus only on the people in your life whose opinion you respect. Many times you will find you already have the esteem of your friends and family. If you are in doubt, solicit their input on changes under consideration. Do not assume you know what those people will think. Ask! You may be surprised to find a deep well of support rather than criticism.

However, Miriam Krasno tells a cautionary tale. "Most people around you will be supportive of the career shift you pursue. Occasionally, however, I find some family members will be outright hostile about your change. It is tempting to get mad at them. Keep in mind, your career shift makes them reflect on their own lives, the changes that they haven't made. Many times, they are concerned with the stability of the family and the impact your shift will have on them. For peers, friends, and colleagues, they're not sure if your move will make you think less of them for not making one. They often justify staying in their own miserable situation by putting down your move. Don't let them sabotage you."

"You Never Could Cut It Anyway": Special Concerns for Women Leaving a Dysfunctional Corporate Culture. Some company cultures have a maverick mentality that employees cannot help but adopt. Peer pressure is intense in these environments, making it especially difficult for women to detach from the fear of what other people will think. "For some time, I had been thinking about leaving the technology company I worked for," says Kathy. "But I saw formerly well-respected people who had left the company being treated as if they couldn't take the pressure. It made it hard to leave because I didn't want to be thought of that way."

Nancy found, "There was a huge conflict between my values and the values my company espoused. I finally reached the point where I was ready to make decisions for myself and not worry about what others thought. It had nothing to do with anyone else. I was truly miserable, so I quit for me, rather than not quit to prove something to someone else. Why let someone else determine the rules to live by? . . . I realized, in the grand scheme of things, *I'm not that important to them*. I don't have to prove anything to them."

"Tempered Radicalism and the Politics of Ambivalence and Change"[2] by Debra Meyerson and Maureen Scully identifies how a company's culture can impact its employees by causing them to adopt a certain persona and values to "fit in." Some women find that to fit in to these organizations, they must take on traits they find undesirable. "I had become someone I didn't want to be," says Stephanie. "I had developed a very hard shell."

Women caught in these inhospitable work environments often forget that there are as many company cultures as there are companies. You can extricate yourself from a dysfunctional one and move to a company whose culture is in sync with your values. As Lucy, a wellness consultant to Fortune 500 companies is finding, "work culture is quickly becoming THE primary draw for prospective employees. Companies can have policies on the books, but if no one feels comfortable using them, then this isn't a culture where you will be happy."

Becky, a vice president at an advertising agency, now looks back on the advice she received out of college and laughs. "The prevailing thought was identify the company you want to work for, figure out what they are looking for in an employee, and go be that person in your interview. This is all wrong. It automatically sets people up for unhappiness because they are going into companies,

[2]Debra E. Meyerson and Maureen A. Scully, "Tempered Radicalism and the Politics of Ambivalence and Change," *Organization Science* 5:5 (September–October 1995).

pretending to be something they're not. Rather, go find a company that meshes with your values, appreciates the talents you have, and helps you develop them."

So before you continue to be stuck, thinking you cannot handle the pressure of competing in the big leagues, or you find yourself becoming someone you do not like, take a fresh look at the culture in which you work. Evaluate whether it reflects the values you hold.

"I'm Letting Down All Women": Reducing the Weight of Feminist Groundbreaking. For women who have been trailblazers, going into careers where few women have tread or into male-dominated industries, quitting frequently feels as though they are letting down all women, not just themselves. There is tremendous pressure when a woman is one of the very few women or the only one in a position. Her performance is scrutinized with a hotter, brighter spotlight, as if the mistakes she makes are representative of how every woman will perform in the same position. There is the fear of validating preexisting prejudices, making it that much more difficult for the women who follow.

Sandy, chief financial officer of a nonprofit organization fighting hunger, confided, "When I was in business school, I thought I was a woman who would push all women ahead, be somebody out there for women. I thought, 'I'll always work.' My friends started having kids, dropping out of the workforce. I looked, and thought, 'What are you doing? You're letting all women down.' Then I had my first child. It calmed me. It put everything in perspective. You learn where your priorities are. You make changes."

Molinari talks about her concern with letting down all women. "I've learned to brazen it out like a good marine, but gritting your teeth for years on end is hard on the enamel, both emotional and physical."[3] She continues, "I finally concluded that much of the

[3]Molinari with Burkett, 290.

feminist reaction [with my leaving Congress] was not really about the implications of my decision. . . . It was about the notion that I was giving up power. The subtext of their criticism was 'How dare a woman give up power when so few of us have any!' . . . [D]id that mean that I, as a woman, should be shackled to it [the Congress] indefinitely? . . . Women as some abstract collective might have lost some power, or at least some influence, when I left the House. I, on the other hand, took back my power in the process."[4]

While it is important to advocate for positive change, you do not have to—and indeed should not—stay in an unhealthy organization in a fruitless attempt to break new ground for women. Think how difficult it is to change your own views on many subjects. Now imagine how difficult it is to change an entire organization that does not see a reason to change. Your advocacy will be put to better use in an organization that is ready, willing, and able to change.

Remember that advocacy *is* important, particularly in leaving the world a better place for the next generation of women. It is wonderful that you want to make a difference. For the sake of all women, do break down barriers where you can. But this is not a dress rehearsal for your life. Your life is happening right now. You do not want to miss it or take all the joy out of it by fighting the impossible fight. You can make a difference advocating for change, and still lead a satisfying career.

[4]Molinari with Burkett, 254.

"I HAVE GOT TO GET OUT OF HERE, BUT I HAVE NO PLACE TO GO!": THE FEAR OF QUITTING ONE JOB WITHOUT HAVING ANOTHER

Ideally, people find their next job before leaving their current one. But, sometimes, that ideal is not realistic. If you are aching to quit your current job but afraid of how prospective employers will view such "rash behavior," this section is for you. How many times have you heard the cardinal rules of job searching?

- "Do not quit one job without having another."
- "It's much easier to find a job when you have one."
- "People like to hire people who already have a job."
- "Unemployed? A bright red flag."

These are all variations on the same theme. But do these rules still apply? Are you at a disadvantage looking for your next job if you are not working? If you are quitting your job with no idea what you will do next, the first thing to remember is you are not alone. Many women have quit one job and were "clueless" about what they would do next. If you can afford to leave your existing job before you have another, this fear alone should not keep you in a job you hate. There are strategies you can use to make your transition as smooth as possible:

- Take stock of your situation to make the most advantageous exit you can. You may be able to negotiate a favorable package.
- Even if you have no clue what you are going to do next, develop a positive "spin" to your situation to avoid looking directionless, as if you are wandering aimlessly through the seas of unemployment.

- If you take a sabbatical, be able to discuss your experience in a way that reflects positively on you and what you will bring to your next assignment.

Negotiating a favorable package. To the extent possible, you want your departure to be a "win-win" for you *and* your company. Some women who have left a job without a next step in mind have been able to negotiate a favorable separation package, even though they are proactively quitting—not being laid off. Of course, your success negotiating such a package will likely depend on your specific situation.

- **Your length and service with the company.** Melissa had been with her company for eight years when she knew it was time to move on. She wanted to leave her company free and clear, but her family relied on her benefits. Her husband was moving to a new job that would provide benefits, but they would not take effect for ninety days. Meanwhile, Melissa wanted out of her company. "My company didn't want me to leave. I told them I planned to take the summer off to spend time with my kids, and I would decide in the fall what to do next in my career. I told them I was concerned about my benefits. They needed to replace me. I was willing to stay on until they found my successor and that person was trained. I also made myself available by phone. In return, they put me on a three-month leave, which allowed me to carry my benefits through the summer. I officially resigned in the fall when my successor was up to speed and my husband's benefits were in full force. It was a win-win for both of us."

  While it may be easier to negotiate a favorable exit package if you have a long history with the company, do not be discouraged if you have only been there a year or two. See Beth's story below.

- **Your position is critical.** Beth went to her boss, the president of the company, to quit her job following her bout with "day-dream pneumonia" described in Chapter 1. The president was new. He was building his team to turn around a troubled company. At the same time, the company's day-to-day operations had to continue. Beth had been with the company under two years.

Beth went to the president and said, "You're building a team to turn this company around. You have a right to expect that the members of your team are fully committed. I have to honestly admit to you that I can't be a hundred percent committed to this organization anymore. I'm burned out. It's time for me to move on. However, I see that you need the budget completed, sales forecasts made, and the packaging project needs to move forward. At the same time, I could use some time to begin thinking about what I am going to do next. I could have just faded into my office, kept a low profile, and pretended to do my job while I looked for a new job. It probably would have taken you a few months to figure out that I wasn't really working. Instead, I thought it would be better for both of us for me to be completely honest."

Beth and the president worked out a two-month arrangement where Beth did the basics to keep her job moving—nothing more, nothing less—as she began to explore her options. "It felt so good to be honest! I realized afterward how much energy I had been using trying to make it look like I was committed to my job when I just plain wasn't. Of course, there were risks. The president could've said, 'Fine. Get out tonight.' But I figured there was a small probability of that happening. There was work that needed to get done. I was a valued employee and I was being up front and honest. . . ."

Beth continues: "I helped train my successor. And, most important, I began talking to my family, friends, and colleagues to start ferreting out what was next in my path. By the time my two-month 'job phase-out' was over, I had two freelance projects lined up—and, with the money those projects brought in, I'd bought myself four more months to figure out what I really wanted to do next." Beth's two-month agreement with her company enabled her to arrange an "interim solution" so she would not have to worry about money while she explored her options.

■ **Your organization is in transition—be it a political power struggle, downsize mania, or mass exodus by your peers.** Catherine took on a new executive-level position in a major health-care organization only to learn shortly after her arrival that she was smack in the middle of a political power struggle. The woman who had hired Catherine was fired one week after Catherine's arrival, pitting Catherine on the losing side of the battle. "Even though I had only worked for the woman for a week, I was forever associated with her. I was never able to overcome this," recalls Catherine. "I kept plugging away, trying to do my job. I eventually tried moving to another position. They were on a point system, and I earned double the points of the other candidate, and yet I still didn't get the position due to the politics. I saw the writing on the wall. I was a political football. I was a senior-level manager. They wanted me out but were worried about letting go of me for groundless reasons. But they were going to make me miserable as long as I stayed. I gave them an out. I told them what I wanted in order to leave, and they gave it to me."

■ **You experience a personality clash with your boss.** Many people have either experienced the clash of working for someone with different values or have witnessed a peer experience this destructive situation. Judi was a controller in a large division of a Fortune 50 consumer–packaged goods company. After years of strong performance reviews and a fast promotional track record, she found herself promoted to a new position. "I should have seen the signs when I first interviewed with my new boss. She said to me, 'I'm not even going to

interview you because everyone is telling me I have to promote you to this position.' That should have been a red flag to
me. No one likes to be forced to take on someone in their
group. From the get-go we clashed."

Judi tried to make the best of a bad situation but finally
reached a point where it was clear her boss would not work
with her. "I suggested it would be better if I moved to another
division. She said " 'No,' and blocked all my efforts to do so."
Judi felt she had no place to go. She knew her boss was trying
to force her out. "It didn't make sense. You look at my personnel file for over six years and it's one 'exceeds expectations'
after another. I have the accelerated promotions and raises to
prove I was well regarded throughout the company. Now, all of
a sudden, I'm working for this person, and my performance
review drops significantly."

At a loss, she sought out the counsel of a former boss and
mentor. He said, "Look, you've been thinking about leaving for a
while. Your boss isn't going to let up, so why not at least get what
you want out of a bad situation? Negotiate a package." The
thought had never occurred to Judi, but, at his suggestion, she
sought out professional assistance. She successfully negotiated a
severance package that allowed her a planned three-month sabbatical and access to a search firm. She went on to become controller of another company whose values were more in line with
her own. It was a win-win.

☑ A FEW NEGOTIATING TIPS
From Women Who Have Been There

MONEY ISN'T EVERYTHING

Melissa: "Most people think of severance packages in monetary terms
only. While money is great, it can be harder to get and may not be

exactly what you need. Be creative. Think about what you truly want. Is it money, benefits, time to interview for a new job, or time to develop a business?"

BE WILLING TO GIVE AND TAKE

Beth: "What are you willing to do for the organization? Demonstrate your willingness to give of your time, effort, knowledge, and expertise to get what you want. Negotiation is a give and take. If you do not want to give anything, you will not be able to ask for much in return."

PICK UP ON THE CLUES

Catherine: "Women need to see the writing on the wall. Be specific and succinct about what you are looking for and don't elaborate or explain. The less you say the better. Women undermine themselves by giving their opponent too much information. . . . Forget how it should be and focus on how it is."

GET EVERY DETAIL IN WRITING

Judi: "If your company is supposed to give you a pro-rated bonus at the end of the year, be as specific as possible as to what that bonus translates to in actual dollars. . . . Seek the counsel you need, but do the negotiations yourself. My negotiations turned sour when my legal counsel started doing the talking."

DO YOUR HOMEWORK

Ava: "I talked to an executive-search professional to get information on what the going rate was for severance packages." Getting settlement information is often difficult, since most people who negotiate a settlement are required to sign a document precluding them from disclosing the details to anyone. Try these sources:

Former Employee

If you know of someone who left your firm with a package, try talking with them to get as much advice as they are willing to share. Even if they cannot give you the specifics of their deal, they probably can give you information on how to approach management, what selling points worked for them, and how the whole process works at your company.

Executive-search Professionals

Many more executives are negotiating a package on their way *into* a new job in case things do not work out. Search professionals have become a wealth of information and can provide standard points to consider.

Trusted Mentor

Typically, mentors are in more senior positions with greater exposure to what has been offered to people at your level.

Do not look directionless. After you leave your job, even if you decide to take a sabbatical, you will be talking to people. You never know who might be able to help you find what is next for you. Even on sabbatical, you want to appear as though you have direction, that you are steering a ship with a purpose and destination in mind. You need to be able to talk about why you left your job and what you are up to now.

While it may be true that you hated your job and you had to get out of there, it is not going to sound very positive to people who might be able to help you on your journey. Understandably, you may feel a need to vent your frustration by proclaiming your freedom. Do it—when you are talking to close friends and family, not when you are out in your community.

"What do you do?" is certainly one of the most frequently asked questions in social and business situations. How will you answer this question? One woman said, "I used to say something like, 'I had ten years of business-to-business marketing experience when I decided to try consumer marketing. I recently decided that that wasn't the direction I wanted to take my career. At the moment, I'm taking a break and beginning to talk to people about what might make sense as the next step in my career.' I got to the point where I could say it in my sleep. I did it on autopilot. But people bought it as logical and well thought out. I looked like I knew what I was doing, even if I was unsure on the inside."

"When I first left," confides Nancy, "I think there was a conscious positioning on my part to leave doors open. I talked about it as a summer break to spend time with my kids. Most people understood that."

However you decide to respond to these inevitable questions, you must be comfortable with your answers. You may want to practice introducing "the new you" in front of a mirror or with a friend.

Taking a sabbatical. Sometimes taking time off is the best gift you can give yourself. If you are suffering from severe job burnout, a sabbatical may be the best thing you can do for your career. "The only regret I have," says Kathy, "is that I didn't take time off before starting my business. I was suffering from major job burnout that ended up lingering for nearly two years. Starting a business takes a lot of energy—energy I didn't have because I never gave myself time to replenish. Because of this, I dragged myself through the first couple of years in business. Had I taken time off in the beginning, I probably could have rested and re-energized in two to four months instead of two years."

Suffering severe job burnout is one reason to take a sabbatical. Take the time off you need *before* your job performance starts to suffer. Another reason to take a sabbatical is to identify your next step. Trying to determine a new direction for your career while you are still employed in a high-pressure, time-consuming position is difficult. A sabbatical provides the time to investigate and evaluate your options.

At thirty-five and single, Mona left investment banking for a two-year sabbatical. She called it a "retirement" because she knew she was leaving her former profession for something new. At the time she "retired," Mona did not know what she wanted to do next, so she simply told people she was retiring and left it at that. "I think it wasn't an issue for other people because I had a good attitude about it." Following her sabbatical Mona went on to pioneer fund-raising efforts for a nonprofit.

For some women, a sabbatical is truly not affordable. But in many cases, women find that they can afford more than they initially thought they could by using the Personal Financial Analysis worksheet (see page 36) to identify exactly what they were living on once taxes and work-related expenses were taken out of the picture. Your analysis will help you determine how much money to save in order to cover your basic needs for a couple of months. And, one freelance project may help tide you over until you are feeling rejuvenated and ready to make your next move.

Sylvia, a single mother, used her savings and took on a small amount of freelance work to fund her sabbatical. "I couldn't do my job anymore. It was killing me. . . . I took the summer off to be with my son. I had a couple months' savings. I rode it out. I trusted something would come up. . . , I needed the break." By the time she took a new, more collage-friendly job, Sylvia was mentally and physically renewed and ready to go. A sabbatical may seem unaffordable or somehow "not a good use of savings." If you need a break, think of a sabbatical as an investment in you—your most important asset. The investment will pay off in the long run.

Hiring managers indicate that a break in work history is becoming more and more common. There is nothing wrong with taking some time off. Even though it has become more common, keep in mind that when you return to the world of work, you have to develop a positive "spin" about why you chose to take time off.

You cannot say you have been doing nothing—even if it is largely true.

Judi handled it in the following way with prospective employers: "I was frank with them. I let them know that I was struggling with work/life issues. I was rethinking what I wanted to do. Most people I interviewed with understood that. There was only one person who didn't get it. I knew immediately that I didn't want to work at that company. I was looking for a company that valued work/life [balance]."

Delaney, a Midwestern lawyer, had a successful twenty-year law career. She was confident of her skills and proud of her accomplishments. She says, simply, "I practiced law for twenty years. I didn't dabble. I did a good job. I can balance that against one year off. Now I'm going to do something else." After her sabbatical, Delaney made a career change, moving into fund-raising for a nonprofit.

Virtually every woman faces at least one of these roadblocks at some point in her journey. Most women confront several roadblocks as they create and maintain their life collage. Facing and overcoming these obstacles readies you to explore what's next for you and your career.

four

"What's Possible?":

Beginning the Exploration

After the momentary, exhilarating liberty that accompanies the recognition that it is time for a change, comes a tidal wave of anxiety, often in the form of sharp stomach pangs or a piercing headache. Inherent in that anxiety are the questions—at the same time frightening and exciting—"What's next? What do I do now?" Rest assured, what you should do next will come to you.

There will almost certainly be uncomfortable times during the exploration. For the time being, try to accept living with uncertainty. Declare, "I am going to figure this out. I am going to create work for myself that is intellectually satisfying, financially reasonable, and still leaves time for the rest of my life." Turn this experience into a positive—view this episode as one great adventure and yourself as courageous for engaging in it. Then, be prepared to do the work to make your dream happen. Do not expect to sit down, meditate, and have it happen. You will have to work at it. And you will have to be patient—patient with yourself as you navigate uncertain waters, and patient with the time and energy it takes to investigate and implement the best option for you.

You are more likely to consider your right path once you have done the necessary introspection. Do not make a common mistake. Too many women get impatient and take a new position similar to the one they just left, only to find, six months later, that they are still miserable.

While you must be patient, there are actions you can take to prod the process along. In this chapter you will begin to take action so that the answer to "What's next?" will unfold. The first step is to create "quiet."

THE IMPORTANCE OF "QUIET"

The first, and perhaps most critical, step to determining where to take your career and your life is to create "quiet" time for yourself. Most of the women who contributed to this book used quiet, contemplative time to clear their mental clutter, to silence the day-to-day noise of to-do lists, activities, and demands. In doing so, they created a space where new, creative ideas for their future could emerge. Quiet time is meant to create a literal quiet—by journaling or doing some other contemplative task.

If your mind is racing a mile per minute, overflowing with thoughts of upcoming obligations and deadlines, there is no space for a good idea to work its way to the surface, to a place where you can recognize it, seize it, and act upon it. Quiet time will enable you to hear what your inner voice has been trying to tell you. As Catherine, a former senior executive in health care who moved on to nonprofit advocacy advises, "The body and mind have a predisposition to heal. Leave it alone and get centered. Stop looking outside for the answer. Our gut tells us things all the time that we frequently ignore. But you know what's right for you. When you go against your gut, ask yourself, 'What made me override my gut feeling here? What's driving that?'" Some women resist contemplative work. Miriam Krasno cautions, "If you are running from getting quiet, from your inner voice, ask yourself why. What message are you afraid to hear? Be open to hear anything that has to come out. It will only help you."

You will not find quiet in the context of your daily routine. For those of you who have been wrestling with what to do next—thinking you will figure it out tomorrow night between obligations or on the weekend, sitting in your car on the way to carpool—it is unlikely to happen that way. Krasno counsels, "Getting quiet is a signal to the Universe that you are leaving the chaos of your life mentally behind. It sends the message that you are open to hearing new ideas."

To create quiet, you do not have to meditate or do yoga—although both of these work for a lot of people—but you do have to break with your routine behavior. It is this break that provides access to quiet. You have to stop filling every crevice of your mind with mental chitchat. Let there be mental silence, and the space will slowly fill with ideas.

Creating quiet. How do you create this quiet in your mind? Each woman does it a little bit differently. The following is a list of techniques that helped women achieve inner quiet. Keep in mind that getting quiet will require you to dedicate some time to yourself. Block time off on your calendar now—start small, try a half hour. Do whatever it takes to keep this appointment with yourself. If you think you will have a hard time complying with this commitment, enroll a friend or family member to hold you accountable.

Read through the list that follows. See what captures your

attention. Where does your eye fall and stay just a little bit longer than elsewhere on the page? Try that "route to quiet." See what slight glimmer of an idea shows up. On another occasion, try something else. If one technique does not work for you, try another. Keep "emptying your mind" so there is space for your future to creep in. You will be amazed at the great, future-oriented ideas that fill it up!

You do not have to be a writer to keep a journal. A journal is simply a way to keep track of your thoughts and ideas. It does not need to be fancy. It can be a simple pad of paper. You do not need to write in grammatically correct, complete sentences. In fact, you do not have to write at all. Using a journal to capture those ideas that have been long buried by the pressing needs of the day can be done in a variety of ways—perhaps by recording an audiotape or by drawing. Regardless of the journaling method you use, allow your thoughts to flow uncensored. You will get the most out of this exercise if you are willing to let all of your thoughts through, good and bad. You can learn as much from your negative thoughts as your positive ones, because the negative thoughts often hold the key to what is holding you back from creating the life you want. During this step in the process, keep reminding yourself that you are not making any decisions right now. Do not worry about whether an idea is feasible, realistic, or probable. Here are several journaling techniques to try:

- **Freestyle.** Exactly as the name implies, write down your thoughts wherever and whenever they come to you.
- **Daily morning notes.** Spend ten minutes every morning writing down whatever comes to you. This is a literal clearing of the mind each day.
- **Brain mapping.** Take a piece of blank paper. Spend twenty minutes "dumping" your brain onto the page. Consider draw-

ing instead of writing, using symbols, doodles, whatever you feel the need to use to represent what is in your head. Let your creativity flow.

■ **Create a visual collage.** Flip through magazines and tear out any picture that catches your eye. Do not study why you are attracted to a picture. Simply collect pictures in a book or put them in a folder to scan through later. Once you have accumulated a sufficient pile, lay them out in front of you as if you were gluing a collage. (Consider actually making the collage. Looking at it in the weeks to come may help keep your spirits and motivation high.) Look through the pictures to see what story begins to emerge. Perhaps you find yourself cutting out a lot of pictures of water and yet you live in Arizona. Or maybe you like pictures of home offices with creative knick-knacks everywhere, which is in stark contrast to the impersonal cubicle you work in every day. This literal collage can be done in tandem with the envisioning exercise, which will be discussed later in this chapter.

■ **Audio journal.** If you are uncomfortable writing your thoughts down in a journal, perhaps speaking your thoughts out loud into a tape recorder will inspire the stream-of-consciousness, uncensored thinking needed to clear your mind.

Meditate. This may sound more intimidating than it is. When some women hear the word "meditation," they think of some solemn, holy ritual. Meditation does not need to be nearly that complicated. Sitting peacefully in a comfortable chair, lying on the floor, or relaxing in a bath are all suitable places to practice meditation. Meditation simply means to empty all thoughts from your mind.

Most practitioners find it helpful to focus on something else in order to quiet their mental noise. To get the benefits of meditation, simply relax your breathing so that it is slow and rhythmical, taking in deep cleansing breaths. Some women focus on an object to clear their mind. Others close their eyes and focus on their breathing, repeating a simple word, or counting to clear their mind. Some people combine these techniques by thinking the word "world" with every inhalation and the word "peace" with every exhalation. Try different methods to see which feels the most natural for you. Every time you find your mind wandering to your to-do list or replaying a conversation from your day, gently return to the method you are using (e.g., concentrating on your breathing). Try doing this for five minutes at first and slowly work up to longer periods of time as it gets easier to let go. Do not expect some cosmic experience to occur. Simply enjoy the sense of peace you are left with at the end of your quiet time.

Engage in relaxing exercise. Many women find a walk through tranquil scenery, along a beach or through a forest, a great way to provide the quiet space they need. For others, the wonderful stretches combined with the slow rhythmical breathing of yoga offer a respite from the noise of their day. Tai chi and Pilates are still other choices if you prefer movement to sitting still.

Change your scenery. Becky, an advertising executive, went on vacation to get the clear mental space she needed. Other women go to a favorite spot such as the beach, their local botanical garden, or their favorite art museum to gain space and time for reflection. This suggestion can be combined with the others mentioned for maximum benefit.

Engross yourself in a hobby or household task. Many gardeners swear by the mental benefits of toiling in the earth. Other women claim to do their best thinking when they are doing the dishes or laundry. The trick is to tune out your day-to-day mental clutter and focus on the task at hand. If there is something you have been meaning or wanting to do for some time, now is a good time to dive in. Have you longed to take a pottery class? Perhaps your cluttered closets are long overdue for a cleaning. Either activity will help clear your mind to make room for more productive thoughts.

Team up. Find a friend who is going through a similar quest or someone who has previously gone through it to act as a sounding board for you. Initially, instruct her to allow you to get all of your thoughts out in the open without judgment or assistance. She should listen and acknowledge you. Later on, she can help you sort through ideas and develop your game plan. Offer to provide the same assistance to her.

Give of yourself. Doing something "hands on" for someone less fortunate than you is a great distraction from your everyday mental noise. Allow yourself to become truly captivated by the task at hand, to open up creative space for your mind to prosper.

Seek professional assistance. A good therapist or career coach has helped many women by providing focused exercises to clear their minds and open them up to new ideas. Consider it an investment in yourself. Having someone who is trained to listen and provide useful direction will get you on the right path in the most expeditious way.

YOU NEED CONSISTENT, STRUCTURED, ONGOING SUPPORT: YOUR BOARD OF DIRECTORS

As you move through your exploration, you will benefit greatly from the support of your peers. Some of you may be a member of a board of directors, perhaps the board of your church or synagogue or the board of a nonprofit agency or philanthropic organization. If you are, you know that a board of directors serves an advisory and overview function—in an ongoing, structured way—for the organization to which it belongs. So why not a board of directors for you? Catherine formed a group when she was in graduate school, and she has met with them monthly ever since. She found her group invaluable as she made her way through the peaks and valleys of her career.

Everyone needs support—particularly when going through a major life change. But rather than a support group, try forming your own board of directors—with your life as the beneficiary. Your board will be available to advise you not only regarding your career, but on creating and maintaining your total life collage. The one catch: While your board of directors serves you, you serve on the board for each of the other members as well.

Here is how it works: Form a group of four or five people. Recruit people who are in a situation somewhat similar to yours. Perhaps you are all looking for a new job or are in the early phases of starting a business. Perhaps you are all working as sole proprietors in your respective professions or are working parents of young children. Or perhaps you are all aware that work is not working for you and are committed to change. Some women choose to be in groups of all women while others appreciate men's perspectives.

While your board of directors can help expand your networking opportunities by leveraging the contacts of all members in the group, what sets your board of directors apart from "a group of friends who hang out together and help one another out" is consistency, commitment, and structure.

Consistency. Your board of directors meets monthly. You set meeting dates in advance to facilitate scheduling.

Commitment. The members of the board take their responsibility seriously. They are committed to attending and participating in the monthly meetings—not just when it is convenient or when they need advice—but *all* the time, *every* month. Members need to make a true commitment to one another and to themselves. This is not an "I'll-be-there-if-nothing-else-comes-up" commitment. It is an "I'll-be-there-no-matter-what" commitment. Once a date is on the calendar, it is on the calendar. Period. If an unusual circumstance arises, the member who needs to reschedule must coordinate with the others to find an agreeable date. Note the words "unusual circumstances." This does not mean "work was busy." What is an unusual circumstance? Beth once missed a board meeting because she was snowed out of Chicago. She finds her board meetings so valuable, she once went to great lengths to attend one. Beth recounts, "I was in New Jersey on a Thursday for business and had to be in nearby Washington, D.C., on Friday night. But I flew home Thursday night for a Friday-morning board meeting, only to fly back to the East Coast Friday night. That's how committed I was to the board meeting."

Start off with your group making commitments in six-month increments. This will give the group a chance to coalesce. At the same time, six months will not seem like an overwhelming commitment. At the end of a six-month period, you each decide whether to recommit for an additional six months. People's lives change. Their needs and interests change. By committing in six-month increments, people have a regularly scheduled opportunity to opt out of the group without violating the commitment they made.

Structure. Your monthly meetings have a set, mutually agreed-upon structure. There are many possible formats from which to choose. The important thing is to agree upon a structure and stick to it. At every meeting, each member of the group should have the opportunity to be the focal point, while the other members serve as "the board."

A typical structure looks like this: Each member of the group gets twenty minutes. Who goes first, second, third, etc., rotates each month. Each person's twenty minutes is divided up roughly into the categories that follow. Your group can decide if it wants to change the amount of time allotted to each part. Keep in mind that twenty minutes is not a lot of time, so budget your time accordingly!

■ **Accomplishments.** Take four minutes to verbalize your accomplishments of the past month. Look at what you committed to do at the previous month's meeting, and report on what you actually did. Consider your accomplishments in all areas of your life—work, family, hobbies, athletics, community, charity, religion, etc. No matter how rotten a month you might have had, if forced to talk about your accomplishments for four minutes, you will be surprised at how much you have done. No matter what challenges lie ahead, it is critical not to lose sight of what you have already accomplished.

■ **Receive acknowledgment.** Following your list of accomplishments, your board of directors takes one minute to acknowledge you. As your board comes to know you and to follow your challenges and accomplishments, they will be able to single out particular achievements and applaud your efforts. They have been there with you. They know what it took for you to do what you did. Your job in this minute is to truly hear the applause. Take it in. Let it wash over you. Bathe in it. You earned it. Do not brush it off. Most people receive too little heartfelt praise. Do not shortchange your opportunity to get some. This acknowledgment will fuel you for the rest of your twenty minutes—the challenges you face and the goals you set for the coming month. Women rarely take time to acknowledge what is going right in their lives and accept praise from others. You will come to love this monthly pat on the back.

■ **Put your issue(s) on the table.** This is your opportunity to let your board know how they can help you. What are you struggling with? What issues are you confronting where you are not sure what to do? Spend these five minutes explaining what you are trying to do and what is stopping you. Give your board as much information about where you are as you can, but do so in a succinct manner. Five minutes go by very quickly when they are filled with extraneous information. Focus the information you provide toward what is relevant to the question at hand, rather than telling your whole life story. Then, it is your turn to be quiet and let your board help you.

- **Board brainstorm.** During this nine minutes, your board will brainstorm for you, offer advice, present a new perspective, suggest people for you to contact and the like, all in an effort to address and resolve the issues you presented. You will be amazed at what four brains, all focused on the same thing, can accomplish in just nine minutes!

- **Articulate goals.** In the final minute, you will articulate your goals for the upcoming month. Remember, your board will support you and hold you accountable for delivering on your commitments. This is one of the many benefits of your own board of directors—you are much more likely to keep the commitments you make to yourself when you also make them to others. At the same time, do not be afraid that they will castigate you if you fall short—your fear of looking bad by not having all of your deliverables done should not prevent you from making significant commitments. If you do not reach all the goals you set for the month, do not let that prevent you from showing up at the next meeting. If you verbalize and write down your goals, you are much more likely to achieve them. However, the world will not come to an end if you do not. So swing big—and go for it!

Remember, sometimes what you do not accomplish is as telling as what you do accomplish. Be open and willing to let your group challenge you as to why an action item continues to roll from month to month without getting done. For instance, Bonnie, an entrepreneur, kept putting off developing her marketing plan each month. After three months, her group pinned her down. One member agreed to call her midmonth to see how her plan was going and to offer assistance. Once forced to think critically about her business, Bonnie realized she really was not happy running her own firm and initiated a search for a position back in corporate America.

As you articulate your goals for the month, be specific. What actions will you take? What will you make happen in the next month? Rather than, "I'll try to have a couple of informational interviews in the next month," say, "I will make ten phone calls to people I would like to meet. I'll reach five of them. I'll convince at least two of them to see me for half an hour. I will go to each of those meetings fully prepared with a list of questions that I want to ask. I will draft that list of questions at least a couple of days before the meeting so I can ask a member of my board of directors to review it with me."

You will be amazed at what can be accomplished in just twenty minutes!

At the end of twenty minutes, it is the next person's turn. You are now on the board, advising the others in the group. Interestingly, new thoughts about your own situation will often arise even as you are listening and advising others. You will receive the additional benefit of knowing that you are helping someone else.

After each person has had his or her chance to be "the center of attention," take a few minutes to take care of the board's business—schedule meetings, discuss any outstanding issues, etc. Assuming you have five people on the board, even with bathroom breaks, administration, and a little socializing, the meeting should be over within three hours.

A few additional hints for running your meetings: Silly as it may seem, use a timer. A timer will encourage you to stick to the format and prevent you from digressing. At the same time, it is important to be flexible. If one member of the group is having a particularly rough time, you may want to allow a little extra time during the meeting for that member. Remember the old saying: "What goes around comes around." There will be a time when you need those extra few minutes, so be generous.

Some groups assign "buddies" who check in with each other midmonth, providing a "lift" as each of you lives in the trenches trying to get your action items done. Some groups make buddies optional—if in a particular month, a member feels that the structure of having a partner would be helpful, another member of the group volunteers.

You will get the most out of the board meetings if you come prepared. Some women jot down notes about their accomplishments and issues that they want to share with the group throughout the month. Others report that they simply sit down for a few minutes the day before the meeting and prepare for it as they would any other business meeting. Treat your board meeting like any other "real" board meeting, and you will reap the rewards.

Finally, as your board of directors establishes longevity, you may want to schedule some special meetings, most notably an annual meeting. While some groups have special semiannual meetings, most have an expanded year-end meeting—in effect, a ritual around the end of one year and the start of a new one. For the year-end meeting, allow each member a few extra minutes to summarize her achievements for the year, to be roundly acknowledged by the group, and to state her overarching goals for the coming year.

A FEW EXERCISES TO HELP YOU ALONG

Now that you have reduced the mental noise in your life and you have established a support network, you are probably wondering how to get started determining what is next. Undoubtedly, at times you will feel stuck as you move through the process of determining what's next for you. Take advice from Deborah, a fiftyish mother of two, who has transformed her work/life several times, from psychologist to advertising professional to business owner, and back to corporate America. "Maintain your flexibility," she says. "Just because your education prepared you for one thing does not mean you are stuck there. No one should ever feel stuck. You are never really done growing. Being an adult does not mean that you are full grown."

Sometimes, ideas will come to you that you will want to dismiss quickly with thoughts such as "Impossible!" or "I cannot afford to do *that*!" or "That would be career suicide!" The following exercises are designed to help you move forward, generating and acting on your ideas—even in the face of these seemingly insurmountable objections. Keep in mind that these exercises build on one another, so start with the Desire Gap Analysis and move through to the Trade-off Analysis. These exercises will help dispel those internal negative messages so that you can start exploring options that are tailored for you. Understand that exploring what's next is an evolving process. The exercises that follow can be updated periodically as you learn more about where you want to go.

Three exercises follow. Here is a brief synopsis of each exercise and the results you should expect:

1. **Desire Gap Analysis.** This exercise instructs you to make a list of your desires and helps you prioritize those desires and identify the level of effort you are currently putting toward achieving them. At the end of this exercise you will begin to see the specific areas of your life where there is dissonance— where you are living inconsistently with what you want.

2. **Envisioning.** This is a brainstorming exercise where you will begin to envision what your life would be like if you were living the life you want. You will describe this life in vivid detail, including those elements in your desire gap analysis that you noted as requiring greater attention. By the end, you will have a clearer picture of the life you want.

3. **Trade-off Analysis.** To make your ideal life a reality, you may have to make some trade-offs. Before you stubbornly insist you cannot, do this exercise to identify all of the trade-offs you are already making and to put any possible new trade-offs into perspective. You will distinguish the trade-offs you are willing to make and eliminate the ones that do not serve you.

EXERCISE 3

"*Someday* I'll Achieve My Heart's Desire": Desire Gap Analysis—Identifying the Gap Between What You Really Want and How You Spend Your Time[1]

Take out a piece of paper or your journal and a pen or go to your computer and do the following:

Step 1: Make four columns and put in the first column a list of the things in your life that you want to have happen. This list can include all aspects of your life, not just work goals. It can include moving your career in a different direction. It can also include moving to rural Maine, taking up gardening, taking a pottery class with your daughter, keeping a weekly lunch date with your mom, or losing ten pounds. Get all of the things that you have been saying you want to do down on the page. It is your list; you do not have to show it to anyone. Make sure the things on your list represent what *you* want—not what you should want, or what others want.

Step 2: Now, in the second column next to each item on your list, write a number from one to ten to describe how important this item is to you. The rating of one says that this item is very important to you. A rating of ten represents that this item is not very important. Rate all items on your list. Be realistic. Not everything deserves a rating of one or two. It is okay for some things on your list to earn a nine or ten.

Step 3: In the next column, write a number from one to ten that represents the level of effort you are currently putting toward making this desire happen. The rating of one indicates that you are putting a lot of effort toward achieving this goal. A rating of ten represents that you are putting no effort toward this item. Rate each item on your list.

Step 4: Now, in the last column, subtract your importance rating (column 2) from your effort rating (column 3) to see where you have the

[1]Adapted from Sheila Kimmel's workshop Get Out of Your Own Way.

largest gap between your desires and the effort you are putting forth to make your desires a reality. The items with the largest numerical gap represent the areas in your life where you are most out of sync with your desires. While there is less discord with the items that have a lower numerical gap, these items can be your "low-hanging fruit"—they may be easy to achieve with a small amount of effort. So before you discard or ignore these desires, try tackling one of them now, to give you a sense of accomplishment. This boost will give you the courage to go after the more challenging desires on your list.

Occasionally, you may come up with a negative number. This is not bad. It simply means you are putting more effort behind achieving a desire on your list than that desire may require. For instance, you may be interested in taking piano lessons. It is not high on your desire list, but it is something that you think would be fun to do. You call around to all of the piano teachers in your area. You attend piano recitals. You talk to other adults who are learning to play the piano. At some point, you have to go for it! Selecting a piano teacher and getting started may not be as difficult as you are making it.

◇ SAMPLE DESIRE GAP CHART

Desires (1)	Importance (2)	Effort (3)	Gap (3–2)
Example:			
Move to San Diego	2	8	6
Start my own business	1	10	9
Stick to a regular workout program	5	8	3
Take piano lessons	8	9	1

Desires (1)	Importance (2)	Effort (3)	Gap (3-2)
Now it is your turn . . .			

If you are like many people, you expend the least amount of effort toward achieving the things in your life that you say you want the most. Many women long for things to happen in their life but little of their day-to-day actions go toward making these things happen. How these women are living is not consistent with what they say is important. The wider the gaps and the greater the number of gaps, the more discord in their life. Women have good reasons for why the things they desire most do not happen—they are too tired at the end of the day, work is all consuming, they need the money. However, their good reasons do not get them closer to living a life that is in sync with their desires.

Occasionally, there are things on your list that you truly cannot do today. For instance, if you are a single mother, it may not be possible for you to return to school right now for that degree you want. Try breaking that desire down into smaller steps. See which steps you can take today so that you will be able to achieve this desire when the time is more appropriate. In this example, perhaps you can call for college-course schedules and applications to see what interests you and determine what you will need to do to apply. Maybe you can take an on-line course that can be done when the kids arc in bed.

Until you start making the effort to get your life back in line with what you say you want, the daily dissonance you feel now will not go away. Getting your work/life back under control goes a long way toward freeing up the time and energy needed to experience all of the other things on your list.

Now, before you get too discouraged, feeling as though you have been living by the values of others, make a separate list of the things that you wanted to happen over the last several years that you actually made happen. Your list should not be limited to career moves. It could include eating more healthfully, moving to a new neighborhood or town, volunteering your time at the local shelter, having a baby, going back to school, reaching a level of career success, etc. Pat yourself on the back. Check to see if any of your accomplishments can be built upon to close one of the gaps in your Desire Gap Analysis. When Kathy did this exercise, she had not yet left her job. Kathy had always wanted to start her own business. Before striking out on her own, she thought she should get marketing, sales, and finance experience. Several years earlier, Kathy had made a cross-functional move from finance to marketing to broaden her skills. The Desire Gap Analysis helped her realize she was in a good position to launch her business.

Use the information in your Desire Gap Analysis to do the next exercise—Envisioning. You will incorporate what you want to have happen in your life with the things that you have already made happen. This integration will enable you to see what your life would look like if you were living your conscious life collage.

EXERCISE 4

"You Mean There Really Is Life Beyond My Career and My Family?": Envisioning—What Life Would Look Like If Your Dreams Came True

This is a brainstorming exercise. Write down whatever comes to mind without censorship or judgment. If you find yourself critiquing your ideas in the middle of the exercise, gently guide yourself back to an open mind by remembering, "I'm not making any decisions right now. I'm just going to be open to the ideas that come to me."

Jump-start your journey by envisioning what your life would be like if everything you listed in column 1 of your "Desire Gap Analysis" came true. Start to describe in your notebook how your desires would play out in your life. Imagine telling the story of your life. This is not a question-and-answer exercise, but if you get stuck, use the following questions to prompt your thoughts. Be as specific as possible. When you are done, you want to have a clear picture of what your life can look like.

If your life made you completely happy, how would it look? Do not worry at this point about the specific job or job title you have. Focus on the activities and tasks that you enjoy doing throughout your day—both work and nonwork related.

Describe the perfect workday in vivid detail. For example: How would you start your day? Would you eat breakfast at home? With whom? What time? What time would you start work? Do you have a set schedule or is it more fluid? Do you go someplace else to work? How do you get to work? Once at work, describe your surroundings. What view do you have? What does your desk look like? What kind of technology are you making use of, if any? What kind of people work with you? What type of clients or customers do you serve? What types of clothes are you wearing? Continue to describe the rest of your day. What types of activities do you engage in throughout the day?

Now, describe the other roles in your ideal life. For instance: Are you a parent, spouse, volunteer, etc.? How often do you engage in each of these activities? What types of hobbies would you like to do — take up an instrument, garden, do home repair or arts and crafts? What does your ideal home look like? How would you describe your style? Is it orderly? Is it casual? Is there a particular charity or community project you would like to get involved in?

Next, start to think about what a year would look like. Think about: How much vacation would you like to take? Do you want your work evenly distributed throughout the year or concentrated with more time off? How much of your time over the course of the year would you engage in each of your life roles? Remember, it is okay to go back and add to the beginning any new discoveries or insights that come to you along the way.

Then, start to think about what you have already accomplished on which you can build. For example: Is there a hobby or a community-service activity in which you excel that you could develop further? Is there a skill you utilize that could be adapted in another setting that is more in line with your ideal day?

Finally, read over what you came up with to ensure it is as complete as you can make it. Are those desires you listed in the last exercise reflected in your work in this one? If not, why not? Do you need to add to your envisioning exercise? Or, is there a new learning coming through? Perhaps your Desire Gap Analysis has some desires you "should" want but your envisioning exercise highlights that they are not your true desires. Maybe your desire gap needs to be modified to add a desire you missed the first time around.

TIME-OUT FOR A REALITY CHECK

Did you really get out a piece of paper and do the previous exercises? Or are you planning to skim ahead, keeping any learnings trapped in your head? Are you planning to learn the inner workings of your mind by osmosis? You simply will not get as much out of these exercises without writing them down. Creating a conscious life collage takes some effort. That effort will be well rewarded by a life that makes you happy—daily.

What is stopping you from doing these exercises? Do you feel that you do not have enough time? That is an excuse. What is really stopping you? Sometimes, exploring the internal messages that stop you from engaging in activities that will help you is as insightful as the work itself. The internal screen that is stopping you from completing these exercises is probably the same screen that is keeping you from pursuing your desired life collage.

Now that you have uncovered your internal critic, set aside its message and try the exercises. What do you have to lose? You may just uncover the life you love!

Envisioning your ideal life is a great step toward making your life collage happen because you start to identify what you really want. Declaration is a powerful tool. By telling somebody or writing it on paper, you are giving it life. You inherently start to take action toward it, even if you do not realize you are doing it.

Mona, a former banking officer turned nonprofit fund-raiser, advises, "I encourage people to begin to look for the coincidences in their lives." Sometimes "coincidences" begin to occur that help you recognize the right path. For instance, Stephanie recounts this experience: "My therapist encouraged me to draw a triangle with circles at the points. In the first circle she asked me to write down everything I love about my current job. In another circle, she instructed me to write down everything I hate about it. Everything. For example, what I wear to work, what view I have, the material the desk is made of, etc. In the final circle, she instructed me to write down what I love to do in my free time. Then she told me to tip the triangle on its side so that at the bottom are the two points that describe what I love about my current job and what I love to do in my free time. This led me to what I should be looking for in my future work." Shortly after Stephanie completed this exercise, she received a call from a friend looking for a referral. Stephanie's friend was looking for someone who would be interested in moving to the nonprofit art world in a position that combined the very elements that Stephanie identified. Stephanie expressed her interest in the position and started shortly thereafter.

Keep a small notebook to record these coincidences as they occur. Where are they leading you? What is your reaction when a chance event occurs? Do you find it intriguing or curious? Does it scare you? If so, why? What fear shows up for you? If your fear came true, what is the worst that would happen? Is that "worst case" so terrible? Or is it some small embarrassment that you would get over in a day? Perhaps your worst case is not bad at all. It just is not in sync with what you are "supposed" to want or what your peers are pursuing. For instance, maybe a fear you are facing is that your career would slow down if you pursue your desires. So what? Your peer group says you "should" want your career to move as swiftly as possible, but maybe your career progression is not as important as other items on your desire gap list.

Keeping track of these coincidences, and the fears that pop up with them, will help you hone in on the issues that are standing in your way. Shining a light on these issues and on the coincidences that occur in your life will also help you recognize the assistance you can and will receive, sometimes from unlikely places.

So many women keep themselves stuck in positions that do not fulfill them because they are not willing to consider financial or status trade-offs to get what they say they want. What they fail to realize is that they are already making trade-offs; they are just not making them consciously. And those trade-offs are often far more costly than any perceived career or financial trade-offs. Since you are reading this book, it is likely that some of what you are trading off for that fast-track career is a measure of stress-free joy, coupled with satisfying relationships and personal development.

This book is not intended to drive you off your high-flying career path. Many women create a satisfying conscious life collage while continuing to successfully grow their careers. Yet these women do so by pursuing a career that is in step with the values and other life roles they want to play. They do so consciously. It is time to shine a spotlight on the trade-offs you are making, whether consciously or unconsciously.

 EXERCISE 5
"If I Do That, My Career Progression Will Stagnate":
Trade-off Analysis—Before You Think You Can't Trade
Off Career Progression or Salary, Recognize the
Trade-offs You Are Already Making

Step 1: Write down what your life would feel like if you got what you described in the envisioning exercise. What results would you experience—more peace of mind; more quality time with your kids; more personal enrichment; a meaningful romantic relationship or a better marriage; deeper, longer-lasting friendships? Be specific. For example, how would peace of mind manifest itself in your life? Or, what would you do during that quality time with your kids? If your marriage were better, what, specifically, would be different? What is the payoff you would get by pursuing a life you love? One professional laughed, and said, "I am healthier, my kids are happier, and my husband is ecstatic to have his old wife back—the wife who is fun to be around, rather than the ancient, exhausted, old woman who collapses as soon as she enters the house every night from work, turning into a shrew."

Step 2: Now, describe all that you do not want in your life. Be specific. If you hate driving for an hour to work each day, put it down. If you are frustrated by not being able to run out during lunch to run errands, write that down.

Step 3: Describe what you think you would have to give up or change to get what you want and to get rid of what you do not want in your life. Do you think you need to start all over in another career? Do you think you will have to forego that promotion indefinitely? Do not judge your responses. Simply write down as clearly as possible what you think you would have to do to get what you want.

Step 4: Now you are going to play the game "spot the assumption." In step 3, where you wrote down all that would need to change or that you would have to give up, see if you can spot the assumption(s) you are making. For instance, if you want to be the next general manager of your company, you may be assuming that you have to give up everything else in your life. Maybe you do, maybe you do not. Maybe you do at your present company but not at another. What about the timing of your goal? Maybe if you pursue other interests along the way, you will make general manager five years later than you would if you pursue your career with singular focus. If so, you may be assuming that reaching that goal five years later will lead to dire consequences in the interim. If you were to reach this goal five years later than you planned, so what? So what if peers pass you? What are you assuming will or will not happen?

The following example illustrates "spot the assumption" and may help you spot your own assumptions: Becky, former director of client services for an advertising agency, recounts, "I changed agencies to set boundaries around my work. I was a successful boundary-setter, but, because of my former all-consuming work style, I kept feeling guilty, as though I was going to be 'found out.' I knew logically I wasn't doing anything wrong. On the contrary, I had figured out a way to do a good job without making my career my life. But I still had this gnawing feeling.

"One morning I came in to my office to find one of the vice presidents sitting in there waiting for me. He asked me where my boss was. I thought, 'This is it. I'm busted. I'm going to be fired because I'm not putting in enough face time.' When my boss arrived, I was shocked to find out that, not only wasn't I fired, but I was being promoted to vice president. The reason they gave me was my 'grace under pressure.' It was such a relief to know that my company recognized that I was doing the right thing—for me and the agency."

Becky assumed that her boundary-setting would be interpreted badly by her agency. Her assumption was not based on fact. For each change or trade-off you identified in the last step, see if you can spot the assumption you are making that may or may not be based on fact. If you are having trouble looking objectively at the assumptions you are making, enlist the help of a friend who is going through a similar dilemma or seek out a career coach who can work with you.

Step 5: Start to critically assess the assumptions you have been making and write them down. Challenge them. For example, continuing with the last example, what if you reached your goals more slowly? Rather than the bleak picture you were assuming, what if you were happier along the way? What if you took the time to find your life partner? If you are already married, what if you strengthened your marriage? Took care of an aging parent? Fostered self-assured children? Made a difference at a local charity? What if you were less stressed such that you began to enjoy every day? Are these benefits worth reaching your goal five years later? Even if you get only some of what you desire, is that not better than where you are now?

Step 6: Finally, you probably already recognize some trade-offs you are making. Write these down. For instance, one woman recognized that she was worried about her ability to earn a living if she changed careers. Doing this exercise helped her realize that her worry was causing her to give up her freedom to explore what she really wanted to do with her life.

Continue to identify the trade-offs you are already making. Use your notebook to track the trade-offs you make on a daily basis for two weeks. For example, make note of every time you:

■ Leave for work early to get through paperwork rather than give your six-month-old daughter her breakfast
■ Leave early to beat the traffic rather than enjoy the morning paper the way you used to
■ Work on a task or project that you dislike rather than a project that you enjoy or from which you can learn
■ Do not call a friend or family member back because you think you are too busy
■ Work through lunch instead of meeting a friend
■ Skip a class you signed up for to work late
■ Bring work home with you at night or on weekends instead of enjoying a relaxing activity or a hobby
■ Snap at your children because you are concentrating on the work you brought home

You get the picture. If this suggestion intimidates you, then simply take out the list you made in step 2, which identified all of the things you do not want in your life. Make a check mark next to the corresponding item every time you do one of those things you say you do not want to do. Note, over the course of two weeks, how many check marks appear on the page. Keep in mind that each time you are trading off something that you want to do for something you do not want to do, you are robbing your life of one more moment of joy.

In summary, by doing these exercises and actually writing your thoughts on a page, you should have begun to identify:

■ What you want out of life
■ What you do not want

- Where your life is inconsistent with what you desire
- The assumptions you are making that stop you from building your conscious life collage
- What trade-offs you may have to make so that your envisioned life becomes reality
- What trade-offs you are already making

Look back over your completed exercises. See if there is any action you can take today—even a small one—that will jump-start you on the path you seek. Ginny, a commercial–real estate executive, says laughingly, "I made a small courageous act of rebellion—I signed up for a knitting class. It was on Wednesdays, which if you travel for business, you know is the most god-awful day of the week to plan to be in town rather than out. And, this is a ten-week knitting class! It was a personal commitment to myself that once a week I was going to be somewhere at 6:30 P.M. to learn to knit." Use what you have learned from these exercises to begin generating ideas for your future.

IDEAS! IDEAS! IDEAS!

Once you create mental space and begin to critically assess yourself, ideas will naturally begin to emerge. Review the notes you made during quiet time and the exercises completed earlier in this chapter. Pull out any ideas that you may have jotted down. As you review your notes, new ideas may occur to you. Consolidate these ideas into one list. Add to this list as new thoughts pop into your head. Do not "edit" your thoughts. The natural, human reaction immediately after coming up with a new thought or idea is to think, "That would be a waste of time." Or, "I don't have the education, training, or background for that." Then, the idea is dropped. Do not do it. Write down all of your thoughts.

What constitutes an idea? It need not be a complete thought neatly tied up in a bow. Any new thought has the potential to lead you someplace interesting, someplace that might spur the idea of what's next for you. At a minimum, your ideas may encourage you to expand your collage to include a new hobby or volunteer activity that appeals to you. Perhaps you thought of talking to an old colleague you worked with years ago, who recently changed her work situation to facilitate her life. Or maybe there is something about your current job that you really like and want to expand. Many women will not write something down because they think it is half an idea. They wonder, "What would I do with it?" Write it down anyway. You will figure out what to do with it later. There are numerous places to look for and refine ideas.

Seek counsel from the people you trust. Run your thoughts and ideas by trusted family, friends, and colleagues. Do not forget your former boss, a mentor, or your favorite professor from college. Ask for their feedback. What do they see you doing? What do they think you are particularly good at? Based on the thoughts you have, how would they suggest you proceed? Keep track of their ideas as well. Make sure the people you talk to are not the type to habitually rain on your parade. You are looking for good, objective feedback. Skip the naysayers in your life.

Remember, a good idea is not a good idea unless you either share it with someone or act on it yourself. Even if the idea you share with a friend is not right for you, it might spark an idea in her—one that works for you, or for her! Sometimes you will try things that do not work out. It does not matter. What does matter is that you learn from trying new things so that you get closer to figuring out what you ultimately want to do.

Some ideas are right in front of you. Look around where you currently work. Mandy had been with her technology firm for fifteen years when she started looking for a new challenge with more meaning. She almost left her company for a nonprofit fund-raising position. When she shared her plans with her boss, he told her about an internal position that was available—Director of Public Affairs—that controlled the corporation's giving function. It was a perfect fit. Take a fresh look. Have any policies been put into place that might help you redesign your existing job? Maybe one is under consideration. Talk to a human-resources representative about any recent changes in your organization's employee policies.

Are there other areas in the company that interest you? Do you see someone who routinely leaves on time, does not work weekends, and does not seem harried all the time? If so, there is someone who has successfully set boundaries around her work. Talking to others will help you learn how they made their change and at what cost. This review is critical, especially if you are contemplating whether you want to stay in your current organization or move on.

Appraise the strength of your relationship with your manager. You may want to approach him or her to discuss your work options. One woman stated, "I was lucky. My boss took some initiative to see how he could help me." Other women felt that if they let their boss know they were dissatisfied, work life would become untenable.

Look around your industry. Attend a trade show or conference, subscribe to an industry publication, or join your professional association to keep up with what is going on in your industry. Is there a new trend that interests you? Take the opportunity to talk to vendors, experts, and other players. What do they see happening? How are people in their company managing their work and their life? Look for a new twist in an "old" industry. Is there another area in your existing field that offers a fresh challenge for you in a better working environment? At conferences, rather than attend the workshops you "should" attend, look to the breakout sessions that really intrigue you. Bring a notebook and write down what strikes you as interesting. Ask the experts how to learn more. Chris, a successful entrepreneur of a multimillion-dollar electronics company, recounts, "I was sitting in this workshop where the speaker was asking everyone if they loved what they did. While my business was successful, it was hard for me to get excited about electronics. That workshop was the impetus for selling my electronics enterprise and forging a new firm around women's health, a subject about which I feel passionate."

Use old resources in a new way. Pull out the classifieds, but do not look at the section that lists jobs similar to your current position. Rather, scan the rest of the section to see if there is something totally different that captures your attention. For instance, Catherine, a former senior health-care executive, was in the midst of a search with several lucrative health-care offers in hand. Yet something still compelled her to check the good old want ads. There she saw this tiny advertisement for executive director of a nonprofit advocacy organization that helps former prostitutes turn their lives around. Several interviews and a cut in salary later, she landed in a position for which she feels perfectly suited. Beaming, she affirms, "I'm totally fulfilled here. For the first time, I like what I do every day."

Other women checked the curriculum listing of their local university or junior college to see what caught their eye. Still others searched the Internet for information surrounding hobby interests that could be turned into a profession. They leveraged the Internet's accessibility to research entire fields. Still other women took career-assessment tests to look for new directions to consider.

Listen to your gut. As Mandy, a professional at a large technology company, advises, "Pay attention to your inner voice." Some of the "getting quiet" exercises you have been doing may be spurring ideas that seem half-baked at first, but explore them. They may lead to some unexpected answers. For example, some women found that they were less concerned about what they did for a living. Rather, they were more concerned about creating a certain lifestyle or moving to a certain part of the world, be it near the beach or out in the country. These women looked for jobs they could fit with their lifestyle or location choice, as opposed to the other way around. Other women searched their memory for that dream they put on hold—that something that they always knew they would pursue someday or wanted to try. For some of these women, it was starting their own business. For others, it was going into nonprofit work. Still others were looking for their life's work—a cause for which they felt passionate.

EXPAND YOUR CIRCLE: INFORMATIONAL NETWORKING— MAKING CONNECTIONS

Everyone has heard the term "networking." For many women, the word is more than a little overused. It seems that a very common first reaction to networking is, "Ugh! Do I have to?" It is time to change your tune! Here is a suggestion: Begin to think of networking simply as connecting with people—for that is really all it is— on a personal, professional, religious, spiritual, or other basis. Connecting with people will make re-creating your work easier and faster.

It is particularly important at this juncture in your career to expand your network beyond your present colleagues. Too many times, women just network with peers at their company. Frequently the people around them are also "stuck." More times than not, the idea or opportunity you are looking for will come to you via an acquaintance outside your normal work group.

For those of you who hate the thought of networking, you are invited to consider that networking can be appealing, adventuresome, and fulfilling, beyond your immediate need to get control of your work life. As noted earlier, so many women come to the realization that they need to revamp their work life because their relationships are suffering. The richness of life is in relationships, the way people are connected to other people. Networking represents an opportunity to bolster and expand existing relationships while at the same time building new ones.

Some of the collagers who contributed their stories said they redesigned work without outside support, but many more found support from a wide variety of sources. You *can* go it alone, but why? It is so much more fun to garner support and make new contacts along the way. Also, the more contacts you make, the more able you are to fully consider a wide array of options, increasing the likelihood that you will choose the option that is best for you.

Of necessity, as you explore your options for re-creating your work, you will meet many new people. Rather than view this as a chore, consider what a bonus it truly is! Some of the new relationships you establish during your work transformation will endure and blossom into lasting friendships. You will see the benefits in every area of your collage—not just in work!

When the concept of networking is mentioned, women commonly have the following reactions:

1. "I hate being a bother."
2. "I don't know what I want to do, so I don't know what to ask or whom to call."
3. "I hate going to events where I do not know anyone."
4. "I hate making cold calls."

If any of these reactions reflect your own, read on for tips to get past this hurdle and on to expanding your network.

"I hate being a bother." You are *not* a bother. Most people want to help. Most people feel great that they can help someone. Of course, you will encounter some people who will be rude, short, or otherwise not helpful. Some people will be naysayers. Do not take it personally. Just move on to someone who will be helpful. That same inner critic that discourages you when you come up with new ideas may reappear when confronted with a naysayer. Instead of giving up and letting that voice discourage you, say to it, "Thanks for sharing your thoughts. Now, get out of my way. I am on a mission to re-create my work to make it work in my life." That said, move ahead to connect with the next person on your list. That next person may be the key to your work transformation.

"I don't know what I want to do, so I don't know what to ask or whom to call." You are not asking for a job. Again, you are not asking for a job. Remember that. Rather, you are calling upon people because something they do in their life attracts you. You want to learn more about it. Not only do most people want to be helpful, most people like to talk about themselves. And that is what you are asking people to do. You are asking them to share their experiences—something that you admire; something about which you are interested. Who would not want to talk about that?

As you move through your exploration, you will be continually talking with people. As you refine what it is that you want to do, people who have a job, a project, or business lead that is right for you will tell you about it, without your having to ask directly.

"I hate going to events where I don't know anyone." It does feel awkward at first to go to functions where you are unlikely to know someone. Yet, you have your best opportunity to meet someone, with whom you may have a connection, when attending a function alone. Why? Because if you are like most women, when you attend an event with a friend, you are likely to spend your entire evening talking with that friend and very unlikely to meet other people. Going it alone forces you, gently, to seek out new people.

There are several strategies that can make attending events alone a bit easier. First of all, attend events that are of interest to you.

At a minimum, you will benefit from the evening by taking in the information provided. You will also have something to discuss with the other guests. Second, if you are nervous attending the event alone, make a deal with yourself. Agree to introduce yourself to five people that you do not know. Follow those conversations where they lead. If, after introducing yourself to five different people, you want to go home, do so. Third, when you attend events alone, remember that there are other people there in exactly the same shoes. Imagine the relief another stranger will feel when you notice her standing alone and come up to introduce yourself. Relieving the discomfort of others is a great way to forget your own.

Here are a few additional hints for getting the most out of networking events: Always have an ample supply of business cards. Some women suggest wearing an outfit with two pockets. Put your business cards in one pocket. When you receive cards, put them in the other pocket. You will never fumble looking for your card to hand to someone. Next, manage your time. If you meet someone and hit it off, exchange cards and agree to call that person later to set up another meeting—then move on. You are at the event to meet people, not spend the entire time with one person.

"I hate making cold calls." For the most part, when you network, you are not making cold calls. Some of the calls may be only lukewarm, but they are not cold. Again, you are contacting people to ask them to talk about themselves and what they are doing, people you have met through an introduction by a mutual friend or acquaintance. In the course of telling you about themselves, most people will mention other people who have helped them. Follow up with a comment such as, "May I contact [that person] and use your name?" When you go to call that person, the call is not cold—you already have an introduction!

Before you begin contacting people, you may want to practice introducing yourself. If you are calling people on the phone, you have about one minute to say who you are, why you are calling, and how the person can help you. You want to be able to complete this introduction succinctly and in a way that engages the other person in the conversation.

Use Exercise 6 below to develop a list of people to call, and then call them. Start with the people you know directly. Add to your list as the people you talk to suggest others to contact. Ask your contacts if they know anyone who fits the description of the "type of person" you want to talk to (e.g., "someone who works for a nonprofit in education" in the example used in Exercise 6). Then follow up with those people. And so on and so on. Once you come to feel more comfortable with networking, you will be amazed at how generous others are with their ideas, their contacts, and their suggestions.

One final networking note: As you talk to people, always look for ways to help the people who help you. Maybe they are looking to get involved in a charity where you know someone. Maybe they need a baby-sitter for Saturday night, and yours is available. Whatever it is, always try to reciprocate. And, when someone is especially helpful, be sure to send him or her a quick thank-you note. You will ensure that the next time you have a question, he or she will be available to answer it.

 EXERCISE 6
Expanding Your Network

Look back over the list of ideas you have been generating. Begin making a list of people you want to talk to about each of your ideas. If you cannot think of a specific person, write down the type of person that you would like to talk to about this idea. What kind of job might she have? Is she likely to live in a particular area or have certain interests? Try to think of at least three people for each item. Follow these examples:

Ideas	Possible People to Contact
Nonprofit involved in education	1. Mary's friend who volunteers for an educational nonprofit
	2. John Smith (teaches in the local schools)
	3. Someone who works for a non-profit in education
Teach a junior-college course	1. Dean of a junior college
	2. Margaret Jones (teaches at an area four-year college)
	3. My cousin's wife in Omaha (teaches at a junior college in her community)
Now it is your turn . . .	1.
	2.
	3.

"WHAT SHOULD I PURSUE FIRST?":
BEGINNING TO EVALUATE YOUR IDEAS

By now you probably have a long list of ideas. You cannot pursue all of them at one time. You need to prioritize. Just because an idea does not end up at the top of your list does not mean that you are discarding it. Rather, you are simply deciding which ideas to pursue first. Exercise 7 on page 103 will help guide your exploration.

EXERCISE 7
"What Can I Do for Hours at a Time Without Getting Bored?": Skills Assessment

As objectively as you can, assess your current position. What is it about the work you do that you like? What do you dislike? Then, think about yourself and your skill set. What are your unique gifts? How do you add value? What can you do better than almost anyone? What are you good at? And, honestly, what are you not so good at? The grid below has four labeled boxes: (1) I am good at and I like, (2) I am good at but I dislike, (3) I am not good at but I like, and (4) I am not good at and I dislike. Think about your skills and what you like to do and fill in the grid as completely as you can.

"Ugh! Do I have to?": I am good at but I dislike (2)	"I want more, more, more!": I am good at and I like (1)
"Forget it!": I am not good at and I dislike (4)	"I can learn how to do this!": I am not good at but I like (3)

Use the items you listed in boxes (1) and (3) to guide your exploration. As you network, use those boxes to help you ask the most useful questions of the people you meet.

"HOW WILL I KNOW THE RIGHT MOVE WHEN I SEE IT?": DEFINING YOUR CRITERIA

Now that you have generated ideas and begun to evaluate and explore them, you will need criteria to help you select the option that is best for you. What works for one woman will not work for the next. Much of your career has probably been defined by what worked for others on a linear career path. Forget the path that others followed. It is time to define for yourself what it will take to make your career work in harmony with the rest of your life. To know when you have found that perfect position for yourself, reflect constructively on the characteristics that you are looking for in your next career move.

◪ EXERCISE 8
Defining Your Criteria

Step 1: Make a laundry list of all of the characteristics that you desire in your work environment. For instance, do you seek stability, growth opportunities, praise for good performance, a clearly defined mission, tolerance of differences, flexibility, or relative freedom from rules?

Step 2: Next, make a list of all of the characteristics that you bring to the workplace. For instance, are you flexible, innovative, careful, analytical, team-oriented, aggressive, easygoing, reflective, highly organized, collaborative, or ready to share information?

Step 3: Now circle the five most important responses in both of your lists.

The items you circled on your final list of characteristics will serve as criteria as you consider new work options. In the next part of this book, women share their experiences in redesigning work through ten different options. Keep your criteria in mind as you learn about each of these options.

Try On Change

You may find that it is hard to know what is *the* right opportunity to pursue. Career coach Miriam Krasno suggests narrowing down your list to the top two to three ideas that are most compelling and "try them on." She counsels, "There are lots of ways to 'try on' new roles. You can volunteer your time with an organization that will allow you to experience the type of position you are considering, with little risk. You can take a class. Consider doing several, thorough informational interviews with people in the field or in the position you are considering. Then, for a weekend, 'be' the change in action. Envision what it would be like to take on this new role. Walk and talk around your world as if it already happened. Surface your gut reactions to this position. Explore what comes up for you, both positive and negative, to ferret out whether this idea is a real consideration for you."

Jillian likens trying on change to trying on clothes in a store. "When you try on a dress in the store, you can stand there and look at yourself in the mirror forever. But, sooner or later, you have to make a call. You either buy it or you don't. The same is true as you envision a change. You can think about it and think about it. Sooner or later, you have to make a call. For me, sometimes I find myself spinning the same stuff in my head over and over again. I'm not adding any new insights. I call that 'overthink.' That's when it is time to make a call."

It is time to "try on" the many different ways that women are redesigning work to create a conscious life collage.

Part II

"What Else Can I Do?"

The Options—What's Worked

for Other Women and

How They Have Done It

When you picked up this book you may have scanned it for quick answers. What could you do to easily get work under control and your life back in balance? By now you realize there is no quick fix. Rather, women are carving out multidimensional lives in conventional environments and in not-so-conventional ones. They are making it happen at stodgy firms and at progressive ones.

You have many more options than you think to make your career a satisfying one while simultaneously leaving time for your myriad interests. Part I focused on helping you recognize when it is time to make a change and on opening your mind and heart to new possibilities. In Part II, women like you share how they are making their careers flourish within their collaged lives.

There are ten general ways that women are making work work in their lives. These are the options:

1. **Setting boundaries.** Women using this option generally like what they do and where they do it. They have consciously set—and enforced—boundaries around their jobs to limit the amount of time they dedicate to work. Some of these women have stayed in their existing jobs and set boundaries, while others have felt the need to make a fresh start in a new organization in order to set and maintain limits.

2. **Moving out of the spotlight.** Changing functions within their company provides some women with a career-growing learning experience while at the same time providing relief from the all-encompassing demands of frontline jobs.

3. **Telecommuting.** Technology allows some women to be employed full- or part-time while working from home, either some or all of the time.

4. **Negotiating a part-time arrangement with your current employer.** As the heading suggests, women who use this

option like what they do and where they do it but, at least for the time being, do not want to work full-time.

5. **Finding a satisfying part-time job.** Some women want to work part-time, but either do not want to stay with their current employer, or that employer is not willing to negotiate a part-time work arrangement.

6. **Job sharing.** With this option, two women share the responsibilities of one full-time job.

7. **Going freelance.** Some women prefer to work on a project or contract basis to manage the time demands of work. For some women this is a long-term solution, while for others it is a useful way to make a living while redesigning their work, using one or more of the other options.

8. **Starting a business.** Becoming their own boss—final arbiter of how their time and resources are allocated—works best for some women.

9. **Moving into the public sector.** Women who go to work for the local, state, or federal government feel that they are getting "two for one" in their collage, doing good while earning a living. Additionally, the pace is more in line with managing a life collage.

10. **Moving into nonprofit work.** Similar to the women who decide to work in the public sector, some women who move to nonprofit feel that they are fulfilling their need to earn a living at the same time that they are contributing to their community. With this "two for one," they have fewer demands on their "nonwork" time. Again, the pace is more accommodating for a life collage.

LEARNING ABOUT THE OPTIONS AND APPLYING THEM TO YOUR LIFE

The options have been labeled and grouped into categories for convenience in talking about them. This is not meant to suggest that every corporate environment can be adapted to meet your needs, that all government agencies are a dream to work for, or that all nonprofits are worthy of your contribution in time. Just as there are terrific companies to work for and there are terrible ones, the same holds true for the government and nonprofits. And, depending on the woman and the business, starting a business can be all-consuming, making a collage near impossible.

These options are not mutually exclusive. For example, some women move to the public sector or a nonprofit and work part-time. Some women work part-time and telecommute. Some women start their own businesses but still find that they use the tips discussed in setting boundaries to ensure that their work does not overpower their lives. There are any number of combinations. Truly, each woman designs the solution that works for her, using one of these options or some combination.

Do not choose an option or combination of options and then assume that you are done for life. Women often use a number of these options in the course of their career, changing options as their life needs and desires change. For example, after Delaney graduated from law school, her job as a corporate attorney consumed her. Then, realizing that she wanted a life outside of work, she changed jobs and became a boundary-setter. After she had children, Delaney negotiated a part-time arrangement with her employer. Several years later, as her children grew and Delaney wanted to be more involved in her local community, she became an entrepreneur, starting her own legal practice. After a total of twenty years as an attorney, Delaney decided that she had had enough. She has recently decided that she wants to make a larger contribution to her community and has taken a professional job with a local nonprofit. In the course of her twenty-five-year career, Delaney has implemented four of the options.

As you read this list of options, you may already be thinking that one in particular sounds good to you. Be sure to read all options with an open mind. You may discover that you want to combine two or more. You may find yourself interested in something that had not previously occurred to you. After a careful analysis of the pluses and minuses of each option, you may be surprised at where you are headed!

The purpose of identifying noncorporate options as a possibility is simply to highlight that there are many places to look in order to redefine work so that you can create a life collage. If you are currently in consumer marketing in Chicago and are only willing to consider other marketing jobs in Chicago at consumer-goods companies, your options for building a collaged life are very limited. If, on the other hand, you are willing to look at the specific skills you enjoy using and consider using those skills in a wide array of settings—the nonprofit world, the public sector, or entrepreneurship—the options you can consider grow immeasurably. This book is about possibility. Its primary purpose is to open up new opportunities for you to consider so that you have as many options as possible. The more options you have, the more likely you are to craft the solution that works for you in your life today.

Dawn Gray, a work/family consultant, says, "There are a lot of different reasons why work can be overwhelming." Gray suggests that women begin considering their options by challenging themselves with the following questions. "Look at [your existing work situation] and ask, 'Why is this work overwhelming?

- Is it overwhelming because I really have too much work to do?
- Is it overwhelming because I can't say no? Why? Can I get other people involved?
- Is it overwhelming because I'm a perfectionist and maybe it takes me too long to get certain things done or I have to review everything?
- Or, is it that the work just has to be the right way—my way?

■ Is (the work) overwhelming because my skills in some way have to be updated?

■ Is there a pattern of working into the night?

■ Is it truly the culture I work in or is it me?'"

As you answer these questions, try to distinguish how your work environment is contributing to the problem from how your work habits are contributing to the problem. You will likely need to address issues in both of these arenas as you redesign your work for your life collage.

As you embark on re-creating work and designing your own life collage, think positively. Remember that you will not get what you do not ask for. But asking means taking risks. You may be pleasantly surprised at your company's willingness to meet your needs. Then again, your company may completely reject your proposal. As you read through these options, think about the risks you are willing to take. But remember, while you are taking some risks, you are also gaining a better shot at a life that is satisfying and joyful.

As you work toward redesigning work, live as if your career is going to work the way you want it to—but have a backup plan in case it does not. Be open to the lesson you can learn, regardless of the outcome. If you submit a proposal to go part-time and it is rejected, what will you do? Your position with the organization might be jeopardized. Or your commitment might be questioned. What then? As you decide which option you want to implement, consider also what your backup plan might be. As Ginny, a part-time commercial–real estate executive, says, "There are certain points in this process where you have to be willing to lose it all because that's the only way you're going to get to the point you want to get to."

Keep in mind that staying where you are comes with its own set of risks. And these may be the greatest risks of all. If you are not currently living the life you want to live, what are you risking by staying still? Your life. And what could be riskier than that?

Altering Life in Corporate
America, Part I:
Making Full-time Work

As women shared their experiences of working in companies that comprise corporate America—big and small, in industry as well as the professions—they repeated some version of Kathy's refrain: "Before I created my life collage I felt that I had three options. I could suck it up and deal with working all the time, with no flexibility and no life outside of work. I could go part-time and be relegated to the career backwater. Or, if I could afford it, I could quit altogether. I felt like I had no real options at all."

If you currently work in corporate America and that is where you prefer to stay, you do have more options than you think. There are ways to manage your work so that both your career and your life flourish. However, the options discussed in this chapter are not limited to corporate America. They can be applied in nonprofit and public-sector environments as well as the professions (e.g., medicine and law), which have begun operating more like the business world in recent years. However, since so many women work in business, these options are discussed within the context of corporate America.

Keep an open mind while exploring your options. Do not scan the list and say, "That's not possible in my firm." Many women created their opportunities in organizations that were not previously open to alternative work options. In some cases, women who pursued their own flexible work options were instrumental in initiating company-wide alternative work arrangements.

"I LOVE MY JOB, BUT . . . ", PART I: SETTING BOUNDARIES

Meet two boundary-setting women. First, Nicole remained with her current employer but changed her own behavior to set boundaries. Second, Becky changed jobs and established boundaries from the start of her tenure with her new company. Both women have successfully trimmed their hours at work, while at the same time maintaining invigorating careers.

Nicole, thirty-five, a midlevel manager at a major technology company, has consciously moved toward setting boundaries around her existing job to enable her to pursue her many other interests. Since she is single and has no children, Nicole's career is a big part of her collage. For much of her career, her job was her collage. No more.

*   "I started to learn to say no. I did it gradually. I pushed a little harder to have my schedule accommodated. When you're single, there is a tendency for people to assume you can hop on a plane at any time, no questions asked. I can't take the moral high ground that my female coworkers with children can take, but I want a life too. I realized no one is ever going to say to me, 'Nicole, you're working too hard. Why don't you take some time off?' No one is going to pat me on the back for getting a pedicure after work, even though it is equally important to my mental well-being.*

*   "Reading* Tuesdays with Morrie[1] *taught me the power of opposites. Because work is such a strong pull, the only way to reclaim my life is to have an equally strong pull in the opposite direction. So I've started making more plans after work, which creates a 'deadline' to leave the office. Otherwise, I find myself checking my e-mail 'just one more time' before I leave the office. That's what kills you. It's not the big things your company asks of you. It's the nickel-and-diming my time away because checking e-mail*

---

[1]Mitch Albom, *Tuesdays with Morrie: An Old Man, a Young Man, and the Last Great Lesson* (New York: Doubleday, 1997).

doesn't take five minutes, it takes half an hour. Couple that with my voice mail and pager, and next thing I know, I'm starving, looking up and seeing it's nine P.M.

"The biggest challenge in setting boundaries, particularly for a single person, is that it's all so covert. You don't go into the office one day and announce, 'I'm setting boundaries.' There is no overt line in the sand for someone to honor and respect. I know that going part-time or starting your own business isn't easy, but at least you can talk about what you are doing. There is something concrete in place to honor. With this [setting boundaries], it isn't as clear. And none of [the people setting boundaries] are talking about it in our organizations. We're not sure how it will be perceived. So it's hard to find others like me so that we can support one another. New business owners have formal organizations like NAWBO [National Association of Women Business Owners] to find support. I'm doing this on my own.

"The upside to setting boundaries is that I've reclaimed my life. Because I've set boundaries around my work, I have tremendous opportunities networking with fascinating women outside of my organization. I am president of my condominium board. I sit on my company's philanthropic contributions board. I'm an overactive aunt. I work out regularly. I'm in a book club, and I have time for my friends. Life now feels a lot less frantic. The difference is choice. I'm now busy doing the things I want to do rather than running for a plane all the time."

⊠

Now a vice president at a prestigious advertising agency, Becky is married and is expecting her first child. She relates her journey to setting boundaries. "When I got out of school, the philosophy was to work hard, pay your dues, and as you rise in an organization, you get to start delegating work so you can have a life. What I found was, the more I moved up, the harder I worked. Rather than

*being rewarded [for all my hard work] with a life, I got more work
and more responsibility.*

*"In hindsight, I know there were many signs along the way
that I was headed for a change. I started to get sick a lot, cold, flu,
etc., . . . I struggled to get up in the morning. . . . I was tired all the
time. . . . I found myself routinely disappointing friends and family. . . . I had to cut back on my charitable efforts. . . . I felt like all I
did was complain about work.*

*"I tried changing divisions within my company. Then I tried
changing companies, moving into a top-management position.
Things got even worse. Finally, I took a vacation and did some
serious soul-searching.*

*"I knew I was going to look for a new job, but this time I went
in with a clear assessment of the strengths I brought to the table. I
interviewed them [the interviewers]. I explained my values, goals,
and ambitions along with my skills. I detailed the job description
of the only kind of job I was willing to take. I was brutally honest
with each company, which they seemed to appreciate. Out of the
several job offers I received, I accepted the one from a company
whose culture best fit my values.*

*"I set boundaries from day one. I was really clear that the
value I brought to the company [lay] in my problem-solving ability. I delegated the analysis and execution activities. The other
people on the team were thrilled to take on a new challenge. After
seven months at the company, I was promoted to vice president.
The reasons cited were 'my problem-solving ability and my unique
grace under pressure.'*

*"It's ironic that now that I have set boundaries, I am more
admired by my superiors, direct reports, peers, and clients. I have
not given up a thing. On the contrary, I have added even more to
my life. I take fun classes three evenings a week. I have stepped up
my volunteer efforts. . . . I'm remodeling my condo. I always have
time for friends and family. All of my relationships have improved.*

"The only hard part is to stop myself from feeling guilty. When I'm confronted with taking on a new project that I know is going to be a nightmare to manage, I say no, and then tell myself, 'If I can just stay strong for the next five minutes . . .' It is easier now because I truly understand what I will give up if I take on that project—my relationships with family and friends, activities that rejuvenate me, and, quite frankly, what my company values me for: my grace under pressure."

"What's This Option Really Like?"

Like Nicole and Becky, many boundary-setters either want or feel that they need to work full-time. For some, reducing their hours to part-time, with the corresponding reduction in income, is not a possibility. Some women are uncomfortable with the uncertainty of being an independent contractor or business owner. They need the stable, predictable income that only a position with an organization can provide. At the same time, these women want to work full-time in organizations, but they do not want to work "full-time plus." Rather, they want a life. Like Nicole and Becky, these women make conscious decisions to set boundaries around their work, preventing work from frequently bleeding into the rest of their collage.

Regardless of the other options you may consider, setting boundaries is an important skill to master in any work environment in order to create and maintain your life collage. As Ginny, a commercial–real estate executive, put it, "I said to myself, 'You know what, no one's ever going to tell you to say no. They're just going to keep giving things to you until you decide to say no. And then you say no and they'll have to deal with it. . . .'" The following are several key things to consider when thinking about setting boundaries.

"Should I stay put or find a new job to set boundaries?" Whether you are like Nicole and choose to stay put in your company or like

Becky and negotiate boundaries into a new position, it is possible to reclaim some of your free time back from work. Nicole felt that by staying with her company, she could leverage years of top-performance evaluations. Becky, on the other hand, felt it would be easier to establish boundaries by starting with a clean slate in a new company. That way, she felt, there would be no preconceived notions about what she was willing to do. Neither answer is right for every boundary-setter. Molly, a human-resources professional, followed Becky's path. She recounts, "I thought about a different job at my former company. They tried to keep me. . . . But I knew I had to leave to break the addiction of working, working, working."

You will need to evaluate your own situation and decide whether you want to stay put and establish boundaries or look for a new job and begin with a clean slate. If you are not sure, test the waters at your current company by starting to set boundaries. Leave at a normal time once a week. Say no to a new assignment. Or, suggest that if you take on a new assignment, something on your project list has to go. Whether you decide to stay put or change jobs, the strategies that follow may help you set boundaries. If you decide to find a new job, see page 134 for suggestions on finding a company culture that meshes with your values.

How do you spend your time at work? Whether they stay with their current job or find a new one, boundary setters start by not wasting time. They either minimize or eliminate chitchat in the office. When they are at work, they work. When Sheila moved from investment banking to an industry trade association and began consciously setting boundaries, she found that "I am a lot more productive during the day. It used to be that I would say, 'I'm going to work all day Sunday anyway, so I can go walk around and talk to people for an hour.' I can't. I am much more deliberate about what happens when I am at work." You do not have to be antisocial, but remember, work is not a cocktail party.

Leslie, a corporate attorney with a major insurance company, says, "I get stuff done. People tend to substitute hours for results, commitment, and productivity. I've learned time management—to manage interruptions and to understand what time of day I get the most done. I've found that if I take a break in the middle of the day, it slows me down. Find and honor your own rhythms. Don't buy into other people's paradigm of what works—long hours and all that. Women fall into the trap of fitting into other people's mold to be successful."

Setting boundaries is an ongoing process. You will never simply say, "These are my boundaries" and be done with it. Rather, your boundaries will ebb and flow with the demands of your job and the other elements of your collage. But, as a boundary-setter, you will consciously choose when to alter a boundary and when to stand firm. Leslie compares this to parenting. "It's like raising children. You choose your battles. Be accessible and supportive, and do what it takes to get a job done when you can so that when you can't, you can get away with it."

Even when you have reached a level where your boundaries are fairly well established, there will be times when true emergencies arise. That is to be expected. Just make sure that when the emergency is over, you do not regress, falling into old workaholic habits.

Sometimes an opportunity will arise that will challenge your boundaries. Only you can decide whether to make an exception. Peggy, an attorney with a nationally recognized law firm, bills the minimum number of hours required to maintain her full-time status on the partnership track. "I turn down work that I'd love to do, cases that interest me. But I know that if I took them on, I'd have to sacrifice this arrangement [my boundaries]. It's up to me what I turn down. It's hard."

You must decide if you are willing to turn down a project or if you are willing to bend your boundaries. Like Becky, at least now when you face this dilemma, you are doing it in the context of being clear about your priorities, and whether the project fits in with your long-term goals. Neither answer is right or wrong. It all depends on what you want at the time you are facing the dilemma.

Covert or overt? Most women who begin to set boundaries around their work do so covertly. As Nicole noted, when you set boundaries you do not issue a press release the way you might if you were starting a business. Even women who move to part-time positions are making a public statement. Few, if any, women, walk into their manager's office and say, "I'm setting boundaries. Period." Since there are no support groups or networking associations to assist women in setting boundaries, establishing your board of directors, as discussed in Chapter 4, may be especially important.

However, some women are voicing specific boundaries. "I have to pick my child up at day care by 6 P.M." is a commonly voiced boundary. The partners in Peggy's firm are fully aware of her boundaries. "I went in and talked to the senior partner. I said I wanted to stay with the firm, but that my outside activities were important to me. He was super-supportive. I have cut my billable hours to the very low end of what is full-time. They haven't cut my pay, but I will get a smaller bonus."

Some women who have successfully set and enforced boundaries counsel others to be up-front. Leslie noted, "When my mom was ill, my coworkers admired that I was proactive in saying that I needed to let go of something. They weren't sure they would have the courage or initiative [in the same type of situation]. I have learned that you don't commit to something you can't do. I used to over-commit and under-deliver. You either commit or you don't. Once you do, you deliver. Be up-front."

"How will setting boundaries affect my career over the long term?" The answer to this question is, of course, it depends. If you get your job done, pick your battles, and self-promote, enforcing boundaries around your work need not adversely affect your career. As Becky learned, she gained respect from her managers and was promoted after she began setting and enforcing her boundaries. When Sheila changed jobs from an investment-banking company to an industry trade association so she could set boundaries, she got a promotion and a significant salary increase.

On the other hand, setting boundaries may slow your advancement. But, as one woman says, "I have lots of years to work. So I'll get that promotion a few years later. So what?" In Chapters 2 and 3, you recognized the need for change and made a commitment to make a change in your work for the benefit of your life collage. You have to be comfortable with the pace of your career. It may slow down, it may not. As Nicole said, "If you don't make peace with the changes you're making, you're doomed. No one else will accept them."

How setting boundaries impacts your career will also depend on what boundaries you set and how flexible you are. You may want to speak with other knowledgeable people in your company or industry. Ask them to advise you on what boundaries may or may not be career-limiting in your organization. If you see yourself having trouble knowing when to hold and when to fold, take another look at the Desire Gap Analysis you completed in Chapter 4. How important is career advancement? Is the speed of your advancement an issue? How much effort are you putting toward it?

Remember, most people are living longer and as such are working longer as well. It is increasingly common for people to go through two or three careers over the course of their working life. Before you get too hung up on time lost on the fast track while reclaiming your life, bear in mind that you may not stay on the same track you are on now for the rest of your working life.

Also keep in mind that many men are starting to set boundaries as well. Ten years from now, the workplace may look very different, with nearly everyone accepting slower career progression. Finally, most organizations are getting flatter. There are fewer places on the higher rungs to go. Opportunities for promotion may be limited, whether or not you set and enforce boundaries.

All that said, some women find it difficult to watch others get ahead. As Beverly watched while one of her peers was promoted, she struggled with the devil on one shoulder whispering, "She's not as competent as you." The angel on the other shoulder chimed in, "She doesn't have it as good. She doesn't have your fabulous daughters." You may have to accept that others get jobs you might have been able to get. But, there is no guarantee that you would have been promoted if you had not set boundaries. When you find yourself looking wistfully at others, remember to look beyond your work to value your entire life collage. One woman offers sage advice: "You have to tell yourself, it's all about trade-offs. You have to look at something and say, 'This isn't as valuable to me anymore.'"

"How Do I Go About Setting Boundaries?"

Women used a number of techniques to set boundaries around their work. As with everything else, some techniques work better for some women and in some environments than in others. Try the strategies that most appeal to you. See how they work. Then try others. A word of advice: Start slow. One woman called it "weaning" herself from the compulsive work habit. Take one step at a time.

"My Plate Is Full. What Can Go?"

The first step in setting boundaries is to look at the projects on your slate. Are there too many projects? Or do you have projects with competing deadlines? Begin to think about which projects might be delegated, deleted, or delayed. The following are a few strategies to consider.

Managing your manager. Start "managing up," which means managing the way your manager manages you. The sample Project Status

Report on page 125 may help you to keep your manager and your peers informed of the status, volume, and depth of your projects. This report may help support your decision to say no to new projects with conviction when you have a full workload. Or, better yet, this tool will enable you to put a new project in perspective for your boss. This Project Status Report makes it much easier to say, "OK, I'll take this new project on. Now, let's go through my project list to see what project can go away or what deadlines can move to accommodate this new project." Encourage your manager and your peers to use the Project Status Report as well. Based on your peers' reports, your boss may determine the project would better fit on a coworker's slate.

When Kathy's manager first required her to provide a weekly report, her first reaction was, "Ugh! Not more busy work!" However, over time she found it extremely useful for managing up. She was able to keep her manager fully informed of her projects' status in a succinct way and identify how much work was anticipated. That way, as her manager came up with new projects, Kathy was able to diplomatically challenge her manager as to whether the new project took precedence over what was already in the works. Her manager could also compare Kathy's project list to that of her peers, to determine who could best take on the new assignment.

Another benefit of this report, come performance-review time, is that it provides an entire history of your accomplishments for the year. You can begin to move your manager's evaluation from a face-time orientation (e.g., one that values the number of hours you spend at work) to a results-based one.

Managing sideways: your peers. As one woman put it, "I worry that others may feel that I'm not putting forth the level of effort I used to." If you used to be the can-do gal and now you are starting to say no occasionally, your colleagues' perceptions of you may change as you set your boundaries. Self-promotion is critical to maintaining your reputation as a committed professional. The Project Sta-

◇ MANAGING YOUR MANAGER:
Sample Project Status Report

Project	Current Status	Next Steps
New-product launch	1. Shelf-life testing back; meets threshold	1. Field-quantitative testing 9/1
	2. Package design is in round of final approval.	2. Verify coupon support in remaining budget.
	3. Sell sheet designed; photo shoot set up for 9/28	3. Get industry facts to agency for sell-sheet copy.
Cost-reduction program	1.	1.
	2.	2.
Category mid-year review	1.	1.
	2.	2.
Next project	1.	1.
	2.	2.
	3.	3.
Etc.		

tus Report should help you counter your peers who might suggest that you are not working as hard. This report format is a great tool for self-promotion. You can combat their face-time comments by pointing to specific results you've achieved. Use it to fully understand and showcase the value you bring to the organization.

Managing your own attachment to "your" projects. At one point, Kathy's plate was so full, she was involved in eighteen active projects. Meanwhile, some of her peers were walking around bored because they did not have enough to do. Kathy used the Project Status Report to lobby for redistributing some of her projects. She used this report so effectively that her boss listened to her, pulled some projects off her list, and reassigned them.

Kathy was not prepared for the sense of loss she felt in giving up some of her favorite projects. "Of course everyone is going to run a project differently. I had to accept that I no longer controlled the project. Intellectually, I knew it was good for me and the team. I had a more manageable schedule, and peers were developing the way they should. But I still went through this weird phase, realizing I wasn't the only one who could run the projects effectively. I missed my projects, even though I wanted my life back. I had to learn to let go."

Ask your "customer" if there is work you do that they no longer find useful. Remember, everyone has a "customer." Your customer may be your boss or someone else in your organization, rather than an external customer. Whomever you deliver work to is your customer. Do you perform some regularly scheduled tasks that were initiated some time ago? Has it been a long time since you checked with your customers to see if they still need all that you do? Is there a task or two that could be eliminated? Becky deployed this tactic and found she was able to save mountains of work for her team by asking her client to review ongoing assignments. Celia, a marketing manager, had routinely produced a time-consuming monthly report that she felt was not being used. She was able to negotiate with her business director to change the reporting cycle from monthly to quarterly, saving her ten hours of work each month.

Create an end-of-day deadline by planning activities in the evenings. Work will always pull at you. It is easy to get sucked into plugging forward on a project. Instead, follow Nicole's advice by creating "personal deadlines," which will pull equally hard in the opposite direction to turn work off at the end of the day. For working parents, frequently the end-of-day deadline is getting home in time to have dinner with the kids or picking the kids up from day care. Sheila thought that when she hired a live-in nanny, she was stretching her budget to cover a "luxury" that would make life much easier for her family. She discovered that having a live-in nanny enabled her to be dragged into meetings at the end of the day, making her stay much later at work. Once she replaced the live-in nanny with day care, she had to leave the office by a specific time. The enforced discipline made her trim her hours. "I got much more productive. I had to."

For nonparents or empty-nesters, here are some other possible end-of-day deadlines: Sign up for that pottery class you have always wanted to take. Make a date with your daughter. Meet a friend for dinner. Order theater tickets. Join a book club. Nicole advises, "Make *firm* plans in advance because when the day arrives, impossible deadlines will always create a reason to stay." It is usually best to make plans that involve other people. For many women, it is much easier to cancel plans they made for themselves than it is to cancel plans for other people.

Consider working nontraditional business hours. Marie was responsible for running computer batches for her company every afternoon. Often, she found that she was stuck at work very late trying to get this done. Marie negotiated with her company to come in at 5 A.M. to run the batches so that they were done before everyone got to work. That way, she could leave work in the afternoon to be home in time to have dinner with her kids.

The "buddy" system. Find a friend, spouse, or family member with whom you can share your collage goals. Ask that person to hold you accountable in keeping those goals. On a weekly basis, tell your buddy what you have done to set and maintain your boundaries.

Another option is to find a coworker who will provide backup support to allow you to meet outside commitments. In exchange, agree to cover some of her work when she has personal responsibilities. Rhonda, a trader, is captive to the hours that the market is open. But she worked out an arrangement with a coworker that allowed her to drop her daughter off at school in the morning, even though that got her to work about thirty minutes after the market opens.

One creative work group took the "buddy" system to new heights. The group sat down and looked at the flexibility desires of everyone on the team. They then compared who could cover what time period so that the group always had coverage. They convinced management that the work would get done while the group met everyone's flexibility needs.

Develop a consistent, detailed process for your work. One woman shared her story: "My job is deadline-oriented, and nobody who held the position before me had set up any kind of system to facilitate the project-scheduling process. So, I met with my boss and worked out a project calendar that I would maintain, sending weekly e-mail reminders to my coworkers regarding project deadlines. That way, if someone wanted me to spend time on their project, they had to get it on the calendar; otherwise, other projects that were already on the calendar took precedence." Some women find that by developing a consistent process for their work, they can reasonably estimate how long a project will take and what the critical, time-intensive junctures are. It then becomes easier to determine how many projects to take on at any given time.

Saying no. Sooner or later, every boundary-setting woman has to say no. Dina, who set boundaries around her job in consulting, says, "By being confident, practical, and well-reasoned, you can say no to just about anything. Be non-passionate. Women are way too afraid to say no. They are afraid of the consequences. Often there aren't any."

Deborah had a client whose trade show was on the same day as her son's graduation. She said no, she could not be there on that day. But rather than just saying no, she presented several options. She could send someone else. She could be at the show the day before it officially opened or could attend on the second day. Deborah says, "Don't be afraid to say no. But don't just say no. Always look for alternatives. Present options. What else could you do? Is there some way that whatever is causing the conflict can be rearranged? Constantly remember that positioning is everything. How you position yourself, your needs, and the solution is critical. You are marketing your solution to whoever is in charge."

◇ "JUST SAY NO" FORMULA

Jill, a corporate trainer, has gone so far as to develop a "formula" for saying no. "When I need to say no, I always have an alternative proposal. So, I'll say something like:

"I understand that you feel I should _____.
    [Fill in with whatever you are saying no to.]
"I think that _____.
    [Fill in with why you think it is not necessary for you to do whatever it is.]
"My proposed alternative is _____.
"I understand that you are worried about _____.
"And we can address those concerns by _____.

I try to make sure that I can fill in the blanks with a coherent, logical position before I open my mouth."

One discouraged woman said: "My employer agreed to cut back my work a little but kept asking for exceptions to the agreement." If you face this, use Jill's formula to combat a boss who routinely pushes your boundaries. One woman who has learned to say no suggests that women not wait for projects to be assigned. Rather, lobby for the projects you want. When your plate is full of projects that excite you, it is easier to reject additional work that does not interest you.

There may be times when honoring your boundaries means saying no to a promotion. Sometimes taking on additional responsibility becomes the thing that destroys your collage. As a single mom, Beverly decided to turn down two great opportunities. She did not want to take a job that required 70 percent travel or one that would require her to relocate and thus take her daughters away from their father. Beverly realizes she is deferring those dreams, not rejecting them. "If I'm qualified for those jobs now, I'll be qualified for them when my daughters are older." If a promotion requires time and energy that is in conflict with what is important to you, you need to be prepared to say, "No thanks."

Sometimes it is important to say no when you are being considered for a position for which you do not feel ready. If you are going into a new job feeling that you are in over your head, it will take more time than normal to get up to speed and keep your head above water. Leslie, a corporate attorney, says, "I still stretch, but I don't jump. I examine. I look at what could be impacted. Am I willing to make the trade-off?" Judi, a financial vice president, is even more blunt. "Women need to speak up and say, 'I'm not the right person for this job.' Get past the flattery."

Do not bring work home, bring home to work. Some women say that long hours are inevitable at their companies. "Face time is important," say these women. If "face time" is important at your organization, try getting involved in company-sponsored "nonwork" activities. Fulfill some of the needs of your collage through your organization. For example, join the company softball team. You will get some exercise and be viewed as a true member of the team at work. Or, by joining your company's philanthropic efforts, you can be seen at work at the same time that you are fulfilling your own need to make a difference in the community.

Some companies still measure productivity by the number of hours the light is on in your office every day. Women in these companies opt for truly integrating work and life. They allow their personal commitments to cross over into "work time" since work time crosses over into personal time. They see friends at lunch. They make doctor/dentist/haircut appointments during the business day. These women do not announce to anyone what meeting they have at 10 A.M. They simply go do what they need to do—leaving the light on in their office and their jacket over the back of their chair.

Get over the perfectionist trap. If you want something done exactly the way you want it done, you will have to do it yourself. It is impossible to set boundaries and require perfection. Recognize that perfection is a myth. It is rarely—if ever—attainable or necessary. Setting boundaries often entails knowing when very good, not perfect, is enough. When you find yourself revising something for the nth time, think about the incremental value of what you are doing. Remember that clients, peers, and bosses love to add their two cents no matter how long or how hard you work on a project.

Setting boundaries also frequently entails delegating. Successful delegating means understanding that there is more than one way to get any job done, and often there is more than one high-quality end result. When you delegate, hold people to standards of quality—not your own personal version of perfection.

Successful delegating means not doing the work of others. Sometimes this means returning to subordinates work that is not up to standard. Other times, you must hold vendors accountable for delivering what they say they are going to. Additionally, do not micro-manage support groups. Quite simply, boundary-setting women stop completing work that is not theirs to complete. Too often, team members return work that is clearly unacceptable to their project team leaders. Rather than going back to the person who submitted the work and coaching them to complete the work properly, women just do the work themselves. As a manager, it is your responsibility to develop the skills of those around you. Doing others' work does not help them—and it encroaches on your boundaries.

Create an end-of-day ritual. Telecommuters and independent contractors who work at home frequently create an end-of-day ritual to indicate that they are done with work for the day. These rituals can work equally well for boundary-setters. Similar to developing a workout routine or teaching your kids a bedtime ritual, you create an end-of-day ritual that signals your brain that work is done for the day. An end-of-day ritual can be as simple as: Change your voice-mail message for the following day. Pack up your briefcase. Clean off your desk so you do not walk into a mess the next morning. Put your to-do list for the following day together and put it in the center of your newly cleaned desk. Turn your computer off. Turn the light off. Leave!

Stick to the schedule. When you convene a meeting, start it on time. Do not wait for latecomers. Set a good example by being on time to other people's meetings. A former colleague of Kathy's convened a meeting on time. Twenty minutes into the meeting, when a team member walked in late, he stopped and recounted everything that had been said in the first twenty minutes for the benefit of the latecomer. As he was about to move on, Kathy interrupted him to say, "You just taught me to be late to every one of your meetings." Start meetings promptly. Do not repeat things for latecomers. Encourage your colleagues to do the same when they convene meetings. If a colleague insists on waiting until others arrive to start a meeting, set an arbitrary deadline—"I can stay only half an hour." It prompts them to get the meeting started and focuses the discussion on issues needing your input. You will be amazed at how quickly meetings begin and end on time.

Stop being part of the problem. Stop recognizing team members for staying up all night to get a project done. Instead, recognize those people who get projects done seemingly effortlessly. Stop perpetuating the belief that the stress-monkey lifestyle is desirable. One analyst tells the story of her work group where there was so much peer pressure to be perceived as the hardest worker, as evidenced by staying late each night, that she created the "loser of the day award." The "loser" was the person in the group who stayed latest that day. This person was identified by a simple laser-printed award pinned on the outside of her cubicle. Each day, the loser of the prior day passed on the award to the loser for that day. Rather than perceiving exaggerated face-time as a superhuman commitment to work, this analyst slowly changed her department's culture to view late-stayers for what they were—ineffective. Some people may find this approach negative, but in certain organizations the workaholic badge of honor is so pervasive that it takes some abrasive language to get people thinking in a new way. The loser award motivated people to get their work done during the day.

Learn to use technology effectively. Technology can be a boundary-setter's best friend—or worst enemy. Nicole likes to tell this story, an example of using technology ineffectively: "I was paged. I responded within minutes. The caller said, 'Oh, hi. I just left you a voice mail in case you didn't respond to your page. I just wanted to talk to you about the e-mail I sent you an hour ago.'" Use technology to help set your boundaries. Do not use technology to take work with you everywhere you go.

Many people find that changing their voice-mail message daily helps let callers know how soon to expect a call back. Try leaving a message that says, "I'm going to be off-site in a meeting all day but will check my voice mail occasionally. If this is an emergency, please page me at . . ." That way, callers will know to leave a message if they can wait for your response or to page you if they need an immediate answer. Suggest using e-mail if a response is not required within twenty-four hours. Use technology to let people know you are available and responsive, but your responsiveness is related to the urgency of the message.

Look for a culture that meshes with your values. If you are planning to change companies or divisions within your company, look for one that meshes with your values. As Becky advises, "Interview them." Judi stressed in interviews that she had a Tuesday-night commitment that would require her to leave at 4:30 P.M. A potential boss said that he did not think he could accommodate this requirement. She turned down the job. She knew this inflexibility was indicative of the culture.

Molly had recently taken on a significant volunteer commitment, becoming the president of the board of a domestic-violence agency. At the same time, she was interviewing for a new job. Molly knew that not only did she want to set boundaries around work for herself, but those boundaries would be critical to her ability to meet her volunteer commitment. In each interview she went to, Molly asked, "What happens in this environment if you say no?" As Molly describes it, "I asked this question at several levels and got consistent answers. They indicated an openness to discussing priorities and resetting them, to looking at other resources, internal and external. There was a willingness to always consider the true level of urgency."

Dawn Gray suggests to her workshop participants, "Look around someone's office for telltale signs of family and other hobbies. Those are sometimes good indications of flexibility. If you are interviewing late at night or early in the morning, look around to see how many people are there. That will give you an idea of the culture. Ask your prospective boss to describe a typical day. Or ask her to describe the typical day of the person you would be replacing." If the description of that day extends late into the evening hours, this may be a red flag. Asking these kinds of questions will help you to ensure that you move into a corporate culture that meshes with your values.

Some women are afraid that if they ask these types of questions, they are less likely to be offered the job. Be polite and diplomatic, but ask. If the company does not make you a job offer because you ask these questions, do you really want to work there?

Reduce the level of conflict in your projects. Becky says one of the ways she reduced her workload was by reducing the level of conflict in which she was willing to engage. "It is pretty common in advertising for client-service people and the creative folks to fight. I just chose to stop arguing with people. Now, I state my point of view. If the creative people disagree with me, I say, 'Fine,' and let them present their idea to the client. When the client rejects their proposal, they get to hear the direct feedback, which is in sync with the feedback that I already gave them. They learn that my input can save them embarrassment in front of a client. Usually, that's all it takes for them to start listening to me. [Not arguing] has saved me a ton of time."

Beth has a similar rule. "I call it my baseball rule. When I feel strongly about a certain point, I say so. If my colleagues either disagree or don't get it, I try again, presenting my argument from another angle. If we are still at odds, I try a third time to explain my position. If, after three tries, I'm not getting anywhere, I say 'Okay,' and do it their way. I figure, three strikes and you're out." Do not waste your precious time beating your head against the wall—all you will get is black and blue.

Ask how the work will be used. Doreen, a financial analyst, had perfected the art of doing exactly what was needed and no more. She did this by asking her team, "How will this information be used?" That simple question gave her the ability to assess whether a back-of-the-envelope calculation would suffice or whether a full-blown analysis was needed.

Is Setting Boundaries the Right Option for You?

Ask yourself the following questions:

- Do you want or feel that you need to work full-time in an organization?
- Are you willing to stand apart from your peers, holding firm to your boundaries?
- Will you be able to say no and stick to it?
- It takes a combination of skill and experience to know how to meet expectations by doing exactly what is needed and no more. Do you know when work is "good enough" rather than "perfect"? Are you willing to let go of perfection?
- How will you feel if a peer is promoted ahead of you?
- Are you willing to wait a bit longer for a promotion if you have to?
- How do you currently spend your time at work? Are you willing to examine your work habits to become more efficient—even if this requires you to curtail social chitchat during the day?
- Can you self-promote within the organization? Are you willing?
- Can you effectively manage up?

"I LOVE MY COMPANY, BUT . . .":
MOVING OUT OF THE SPOTLIGHT

Emma has spent twenty years with the same technology company. For the first fifteen or so years, she moved from position to position, with each successive move bringing additional responsibility. Emma worked on the frontline with clients, generating revenue for her company. She was very successful. Eventually, Emma was promoted to manage a sales organization that, at one point, covered an eight-state territory. Her staff grew from twenty people to seventy.

Over the next several years, both Emma and her father suffered serious illnesses, bringing greater clarity to her life. She recalls an incident when one of her sales managers had been waiting to speak to her all morning because there was a long line outside her office. When he finally got in to see her he said, "You've been listening to urgent issues all morning and yet you're sitting there like a calm Mother Superior. How do you do it?" Her response: "Because I've learned to distinguish between life-threatening things and non-life-threatening ones. I haven't heard a life-threatening issue all morning. And, I doubt I'll hear one now."

Emma's illness made her a better manager. She learned to get help. She learned to delegate. She became good at helping others find their own solutions rather than taking on their problems. It empowered her workforce. Emma enjoyed managing others and found she was good at it. But, at each stage of her fast-track career, Emma lost more of her personal time. And increasingly, she found the politics within the company stressful.

Finally, in 1990, Emma's division was shaken up. She was given the option of a staff advisory position—a job that was off the firing line and out of the spotlight—or taking another line function—another job in the center of the action—that would require a considerable amount of travel. She opted for the staff job.

Emma liked not having to travel, but she missed being a part of the action. She still made an impact, but now it was in an advisory role. "Taking this staff position was a compromise, which allowed me to do the things I wanted with the rest of my life." Emma's health was still an issue; she did not want to risk illness again. Emma made a conscious decision.

Four years later, Emma was restless. She wanted to make a significant change to her work/life. "I was burned out on my old job and the corporate culture. I felt my soul eroding." She sought out "something that provided more of a giving back." She continues, "I didn't feel like I was contributing to my community in a meaningful way." Emma considered nonprofit and actually pursued a senior-management position in an agency. When she told her company that she wanted to do something more meaningful, they offered her a recently vacated position managing community relations. Emma was given free reign to revamp the group and was put in charge of their philanthropic giving, a sizable responsibility.

A couple of years later, there was another organizational restructure, and Emma was offered a highly visible position reporting to the CEO. "It was a stroke to my ego," Emma says. That position was the ultimate "spotlight" job. And yet, she made a conscious decision to say no, to remain out of the limelight. Emma knew what was involved in saying yes. She would have had to give up too much of herself by working too many hours and being available all of the time.

In her "spare time," Emma has developed a manufacturing company with her husband. This new business venture is an exciting opportunity that Emma would not have been able to pursue if she were in the line of fire at her "day job." Being out of the spotlight has enabled Emma to focus on the totality of her life, rather than just on one piece of it. Her advice to others: "Pay attention to your inner voice. It's easy to stay focused on the day-to-day. Think of the bigger picture [in your life]."

"What's This Option Really Like?"

When women, like Emma, "move out of the spotlight," they make a cross-functional move from a high-profile, high-stress, demanding (usually frontline) position to a less-pressured (usually staff) position. Moving out of the spotlight flies in the face of conventional wisdom, which suggests that if women want to reach the top, they should seek high-visibility, frontline positions. But this conventional wisdom assumes that every working woman has the same goal—to further her career in a linear fashion. Rather, Emma chose a path with several lateral and functional moves. This unconventional path has enabled Emma to maintain a satisfying and challenging career while at the same time pursuing other life activities.

Depending on your goals, moving out of the spotlight for some or all of your remaining career may make sense. One woman sums up her feelings about moving out of the spotlight in her company: "The best part is having less stress in my life. This frees up an enormous amount of mental energy that I can channel into more productive pursuits."

"A weigh station." Some women who move out of the spotlight find they prefer the pace of a less-visible position, and opt to stay for the long term. Others recognize that they want to make a change in their work/life, but have no idea what they want to do next, and opt for a position out of the spotlight as an interim step. Once off the fast track, women have increased time and energy to explore their options. At the same time, their financial situation is stable and they are able to keep their skills fresh.

Suzanne, who moved from direct client services to marketing support, put it this way: "I know I need to change companies, but I'm not sure what I want out of my career, and I don't want to make a move just for the sake of making one." Abby moved from management consulting to an internal training-and-communications job supporting her company's partners. She made a one-year commitment to her new position. Both Abby and her management agreed to re-evaluate the situation at the end of that year. Abby says, "I view this as a break. I feel like I have bought myself some time. This is a 'weigh station' while I figure out what I want to do next."

Like Abby, Simone moved out of the spotlight in her company for a period of time. Simone had two kids at home, was going through a divorce, and felt she needed more time, as well as a stable, reliable income. Previously, Simone's sales-management job had provided her with the combination of high commissioned-earnings potential and flexibility, which were great for managing her collage. But the position was demanding and her income varied. As Simone went through her divorce, she needed the security of a steady income and the reduced stress of fewer hours with less travel. She transferred to an internal training position. "I couldn't have managed my life any other way [through the divorce process]," she says. Both Simone and her management viewed her move as a transitional consideration to help her during a difficult time. As her divorce becomes final, Simone is under some pressure to get back into sales.

Simone and Abby both have an arrangement with their management that they will return to their former positions after a set period of time. If, however, you are like Emma and find that you like your life much better out of the spotlight and want to stay that way, you may face pressure from your management to return. Think through how you will respond to this pressure so that you are appropriately prepared when the questions come.

Maintain your contacts, broaden your skill set. When Simone moves back into sales management, she will bring her new training skills with her. In fact, in many cases, a cross-functional move within a company can broaden your skill set, making you more marketable. Abby is learning sales-training skills and has the opportunity to interact with partners in her firm around the world. Suzanne is adding marketing skills to her arsenal, which she notes are "new skills I can use in the future."

Camille left a position in the middle of the legislative mael-strom in Washington, D.C., to become the director of legislative affairs for a small agency. She sums up her move: "I'm making good money, I have regular hours, and I'm keeping my contacts and my skills up. I can go back [to the fast track] some day if I want to."

Hints to Help You Move out of the Spotlight

Most women moved from line to staff positions within their exist-ing companies. Staying in an organization where they have an established track record, these women were able to leverage their knowledge of the organization and its people and processes, which helped them to ramp up quickly in their new positions. Without the need to get used to a whole new company on top of a new job, women report little stress in making the change.

There is no tried-and-true way to make a cross-functional move within a company. Some companies encourage employees to get a wide variety of experiences by moving around, while others do not. The following are a few tips to help you find a new job within your existing company.

Utilize your allies. First, look around your company, at the people you work with and for. Identify your allies. Whom do you trust? Whom can you confide in? Do you have a great relationship with a boss, mentor, colleague, or human-resources professional with whom you can talk confidentially? "I spoke to my boss," says one woman. "He was kind enough to let me speak to his boss about finding me another position in the company. I made a parallel move [with his assistance]."

Be determined and assertive. Abby's experience may be typical. "I knew I wanted a change. I never entertained the thought of leaving my company. It is a global company. The people are unbelievable. I thought, 'There has to be something I can do [within the company] and be in my hometown.' I called my mentor in the company and said I wanted to move away from direct client consulting to an internal position. He said, 'If that's what you want, I'll support you,' but he did not offer any help. There was no process in the company to help you find another position in the firm. The partners did not stand in my way. But they didn't help either. I updated my resume. I interviewed for jobs within the firm. The human-resources people passed on good information, but I found the job by my own sweat. If I was not determined, nothing would have happened."

Leverage your network, your industry, and some professional help. Like every other option, leveraging your network to come up with new ideas for consideration is helpful. A friend's position at another company may be a great idea for you to pursue at yours. Setting up informational interviews with this neutral party can give you a flavor for the job before you approach your company about a possible move.

Another great place to look for options is to talk with vendors and do some exploring at trade shows tailored to your industry. You might identify an option that supports or is complementary to your existing career, fully leveraging your experience, but with less pressure.

Finally, this might be a good time to invest a little money in meeting with a career counselor. Not only can she help you answer the bigger "What's next?" question, but she can help you define and implement an approach tailored to your company to help you make a move out of the spotlight in the short term.

Find a champion. Once you have honed in on the position you desire, look for ways to bring yourself in contact with peers and managers in that group. Volunteer for projects that will put you on a team with a peer. Foster some allies in this new group. People in positions of power in that group make great champions to smooth the way when you are ready to make your move. Let your champion know you are interested in her group so that when a position becomes available she can put in a good word, increasing the likelihood that you will be seriously considered. Leverage your relationship with your champion after you move to the new group to get up to speed as quickly as possible.

Regardless of the path you choose, remember that you do have options. Simone offers this advice to those considering a move out of the spotlight: "There are lots of different options to consider. They [the company] should be able to accommodate your needs. You have to ask. Have an idea of what you need to accomplish your goals. . . . Just remember that when you are unhappy, it is the worst place to be. [By making a cross-functional move], you're not in limbo anymore."

"I've Moved out of the Spotlight. Now What?"

While arranging a move out of the spotlight may be unique to each company, you may have to overcome a common set of personal hurdles to make such a move successful.

"I miss the fast lane." Camille lamented, "I miss the adrenaline, working on big issues. . . . A small part of me regrets that my career is not at the forefront anymore." Suzanne echoes Camille: "The worst part is that part of me still misses the challenge of deadlines, high client expectations, the variety of the work." Abby offered a more colorful description, noting, "There is no crisis du jour to get high off."

Along with missing the action, some women find the work in their new position is less stimulating. Camille continues, "My job doesn't challenge me anymore. . . ." If you moved out of the spotlight with family or other activities in mind, you may welcome this change. If you use your new free time and energy to begin exploring your longer-term options, you may not mind less-challenging work.

If having less-stimulating work bothers you, you may want to look outside your career for stimulation and satisfaction. As Suzanne put it, "Sometimes I feel as though my brain is not sufficiently stimulated. I make up for it in my personal life by reading more. . . ." Abby adds, "I feel now that I'm behind the scenes [at work], less engaged. I'm going to find something else—probably a charity—to utilize my energy and time. I have to be engaged in something else not to feel like I've dropped out." Of course, these other activities can also help you with your long-term exploration.

"What will my colleagues think?" When it was announced that Alyssa, a former marketing manager at a telecommunications company, was moving to human resources, her peers were shocked. It was hard for them to understand why she would want to go from the center of the action to relegating herself to a less-prestigious support function. Her peers made veiled comments about her career sliding backward. She heard the rumors that it was not a voluntary move on her part but something she was forced to do. After all, they reasoned, why would anyone want to slow down or shift gears on her career?

Only you can attach importance and credence to your peers' comments. Remember why you made your move out of the spotlight. You had good reasons—reasons that are still valid. Whose opinion do you really care about—theirs or yours? If you have difficulties staying centered in your choice, look to coworkers in your new position for support. Also, if you feel the need, ask the members of your board of directors to provide additional support between monthly meetings.

"What have I done to my career?" How a move out of the spotlight impacts your career will depend on what your career goals are as well as whether your move is a short- or long-term one. Abby describes her move. "I am taking a detour. After all, being on the frontline, that's the crème de la crème. For one year, not being there is okay. It won't impact my career. If, after a year, I stay in this position, it will impact my career. People who make partner from internal positions are few and far between." However, Abby goes on to note that, "I don't know what my career goals are right now. That's part of what I want to figure out."

Is Moving out of the Spotlight the Right Option for You?

Ask yourself the following questions:

- Do you like the company you currently work for? Do you want to stay there?
- Do you want to make a change, but don't know what that change should be? Are you looking for an interim solution that will lessen job demands so you can figure out what you want to do next?
- Is there another function in the company that interests you? Can you acquire new skills that will serve your career in the future?
- Are you looking for a simpler way to earn a living so you can leave your work at work and focus your off hours on other interests?
- Your "out of the spotlight" position may be less stimulating. Are you willing to trade challenge for time and peace in your life, or will you be frustrated?
- If this change impacts your career negatively, will you deride yourself? Or, are you willing to re-evaluate your career goals?
- Can you handle not being in the center of the action?

"I LOVE MY JOB, BUT I HATE MY COMMUTE": TELECOMMUTING

At thirty-one, Gwen is responsible for the public-relations efforts of a trade association in the northeast. In 1996, Gwen lived about thirty miles from work. On a good day, her commute was a little over an hour each way. In winter's bad weather and in summer's beach traffic, the drive would take two hours, sometimes longer. "It started out that I had flex hours so I could avoid traffic, but that wasn't enough. I just couldn't do all that driving. I was exhausted all the time.

"I spoke with my manager about working from home. Then I wrote a proposal that explained how I would do it—how the company could measure or monitor me, how I would communicate with the office, how I would get stuff done. I identified several benefits of my telecommuting to the company. When I work from home, I have an increased ability to focus on my work. There are fewer external interruptions. In my particular job, being home makes it much easier for me to monitor the media and respond to breaking news. And, with my commute eliminated, I have much more energy to dedicate to doing my job.

"In my proposal, I asked for permission to telecommute two days a week for a three-month trial. After that, we would evaluate how it was working. If it wasn't working I'd stop. My proposal was just a few pages. I also included some research I did on the Internet about telecommuting and how it enhances productivity. I sent it to my manager and the CEO of our organization.

"As a result of my success telecommuting, the CEO made a corporate-wide policy that allowed employees to telecommute up to three days a week. At that point, there were certain caveats. You had to provide your own equipment—computer, fax, compatible software, etc. If you needed an additional phone line, you paid for it. You had to provide the infrastructure. You had to pay for calls to the office—because it is your choice not to be there. The company paid for the calls you made from home that you would have made

from the office. I already had the phone lines, the fax, and a computer at home. The cost of gas for my commute was way more than the cost of these phone calls. It was definitely worth it.

"A lot of people in the office started taking advantage of the new telecommuting policy." The program was so successful that the CEO finally said, "So many people have chosen to telecommute, it doesn't make sense to keep this office open." He made the decision to close the office. At that point, with the real-estate cost savings, all expenses of telecommuting became expenses of the company. The company provided desks, chairs, phone lines, file cabinets, software, everything. Gwen continues, "My manager lived in a small apartment and didn't have space for a home office. The company increased her salary enough to enable her to rent a larger apartment so she could have a home office.

"Since then, so many people from our New York City office have chosen to telecommute that that office is now closing. The only real office left is the company's home office, which is staying open. Those people can telecommute up to three days a week. Now, the company has a formal, written telecommuting agreement that employees sign.

"We have independent work groups. Sometimes we meet at one anothers' homes. And I talk to my manager almost every day.

"Working at home, I do have flexible hours. My manager says, 'You have a job to do. Get it done.' She doesn't care when I do it, as long as it gets done on time. At the beginning of each year, every employee and her manager agree on measurable goals for the year. We are obligated to e-mail progress notes to our manager and the CEO each week. That tells them what we accomplished toward achieving our goals.

"The CEO is very trusting. I said to one of my colleagues the other day, 'He has us forever. Where else are you going to go—with this type of opportunity, this type of flexibility, true confidence, and independence? He's got us. I don't know if I could ever leave this job. He really trusts us.'"

Through working to improve her own situation, Gwen has transformed her company. She recounts, "My boss said to me, 'Gwen, your colleagues owe you a big thank-you.'" There have been issues, but Gwen continues, "There are ways around it if you have an open mind. . . . I'm lucky, but I'm also proud of my initiative."

"What's This Option Really Like?"

By understanding her company and job requirements as well as her own life needs, Gwen was able to eliminate her commute, saving more than ten hours a week that she could then dedicate to other areas of her life collage. As Gwen initiated the telecommuting program at her company, similar programs are being developed at organizations across the country. The number of employees who telecommute at least part-time rose to nearly 8 million in 1997. With the number of telecommuters growing at almost 20 percent a year, this option is one of the fastest-growing ways to redesign work.[2] Rather than working in their companies' offices, telecommuters work from an off-site location, usually their home, either some or all of their working hours. Telecommuters communicate with colleagues, managers, clients, vendors, and others via telephone, e-mail, and fax. Although some employees telecommute full-time, more commonly, employees telecommute two or three days a week and work in their company's offices the rest of the week.

Women who telecommute reap many benefits:

■ **Save time.** If your commute normally takes an hour each way and you telecommute three days a week, you are freeing up six hours a week. That's six more hours for your collage—for family, friendships, a volunteer commitment, a hobby, exercise, or some spiritual endeavor. One woman wrote, "I couldn't [afford

[2]International Telework Association & Council (ITAC). See http://etrg.findsvp.com/prls/pr97/telecomm.html.

to] quit my job. But, working from home some [of the time] lets me be a bigger part of my own life."

■ **Save energy—your own.** Not only is commuting time-consuming, it is a hassle. Gwen's thirty-mile commute exhausted her. "I'd get home at night too tired from [driving in] traffic to do anything."

■ **Reduce expenses.** In addition to saving time, telecommuters often find that they save money. Remember, whether you drive to work or take some form of public transportation, commuting is never free. If you normally spend $3 a day on train fare and you telecommute three days a week, you will save approximately $450 a year. If you drive to work, think about the savings in gas, parking, and wear and tear on your car.

If you telecommute, you will likely save money in other areas as well. Do you buy coffee on your way to work every day? If you wear a suit or dress to work every day, what is your average dry-cleaning bill? What do you normally spend on lunch every day? You get the idea.

Since you will be saving time by telecommuting, you may be able to reduce the number of hours that you need child care. By eliminating hours of commuting time, you should be able to reduce your child-care needs. Gwen, a full-time employee, was particularly inventive: "I make a decent salary, but it is not cost-effective to pay someone full-time to watch my child. Now, I have a nanny twenty-five hours a week. My nanny comes at 8:30 A.M. and stays until 1:30 P.M. She puts my daughter down for a nap before she leaves. My daughter usually sleeps until 3:30 P.M., so I can keep working. If necessary, I go back to work at night after my daughter goes to bed."

■ **Better quality of life.** A number of national surveys have found that telecommuting has a positive effect on quality of life. A study conducted by the Radcliffe Public Policy Institute found that nearly three-quarters of telecommuters report having a better ability to integrate their work with the rest of their lives. In this same study, more than one-third reported a reduction in insomnia or some other sleep disorder.[3] As Liza, a technology manager, describes it, "My work and personal life are less in conflict. There are fewer moments of total anxiety over how to make everything work."

■ **Increase productivity.** Studies have also found that telecommuting employees are often more productive. A study conducted by the State of California found productivity increases of 10 to 30 percent.[4] When AT&T conducted a survey of Fortune 1,000 managers with telecommuting employees, 58 percent reported an increase in productivity.[5] Think about your own work. By definition, an increase in productivity means completing either more work in the same amount of time or the same amount of work in less time. Either way, as a telecommuter, you will have more flexibility in your collage.

Gwen talks about how much her commute used to affect her during the bad winter months: "When it snowed, I'd start worrying at two P.M. about leaving at four-thirty P.M. It would ruin my afternoon—I'd get nothing done. Then it would take two to three hours to get home." Gwen finds productivity increases in other ways as well. "When I used to go into the office each morning, we would have coffee and chat for a while. Now I do so much less of that. And I don't take an hour for lunch."

■ **Work objectively evaluated.** Gwen's work is now evaluated by its quality and on her ability to meet deadlines rather than on how many hours she puts in.

[3]Radcliffe Public Policy Institute and Fleet Financial Group, 1998, as cited by ITAC. See http://www.telecommute.org/surveys.htm.

[4]State of California Telecommuting Pilot Program, as quoted by June Langhoff. See http://www.langhoff.com/advice.html.

[5]AT&T study of Fortune 1,000 managers conducted in October 1995 as cited by June Langhoff. See http://www.langhoff.com/advice.html.

Can My Job Be Done by Telecommuting?

Almost all jobs have some component that can be done in a home office. Jobs that have tasks that can be done while alone are the best candidates for telecommuting—writing, analyzing data, researching, programming, drawing, number-crunching. And, of course, jobs that are done largely on the phone anyway—sales, for example—are easiest to move home. June Langhoff, a nationally recognized expert on telecommuting, cites a police officer who telecommutes twice a week, performing casework and report-writing at home. Similarly, some nurses perform case-management tasks in their home offices.[6] Perhaps your job is not a candidate for full-time telecommuting. But, odds are, you could telecommute one or two days a week. Below are a couple of things to consider.

Self-discipline is a must. Before you start thinking about selling your boss on telecommuting, remember that, first and foremost, working at home successfully requires self-discipline. While you will be in communication with your colleagues, no one will be standing over you, making sure you do your work. You must be internally motivated to produce high-quality work on time. If you need to be around others who are hard at work to get yourself going, telecommuting may not be the best option for you.

You may have to buy your own equipment. Are you willing to pay for your own computer equipment if your company will not? Compare the savings you are likely to realize in other areas with the cost of purchasing a computer and other equipment. Remember, you will save on commuting, dry cleaning, and take-out food expenses. Add it all up. How long will you have to telecommute to save an amount of money equal to the cost of your new equipment? While you are

[6]June Langhoff, http://www.langhoff.com/faqs.html.

at it, consider the other uses that your family might have for the equipment.

Hints to Help You Telecommute

It is difficult, although not impossible, to get a new job where telecommuting is part of the package. Generally, before you begin telecommuting, you will need to establish yourself with your employer for at least six months to a year. If you are a technical professional, the likelihood of finding a telecommuting position is better. As one full-time telecommuter said, "I had grounding with an employer. Trust. Getting hired into a position like this is impossible—unless perhaps you're an engineer."

Does your company have a telecommuting program? According to the Society of Human Resource Management, 24 percent of companies do.[7] If so, get a copy of the guidelines. Talk to other telecommuters in your company. It is likely you will still have to write a proposal, but it will be easier than if your company does not have a program in place.

If your company does not have a telecommuting policy, your task is harder. But, as Gwen demonstrated, it is not impossible and may yield unexpected, wonderful results. You will have to sell your company on the idea that your job can be done from home—and that you are disciplined enough to do it.

Your Proposal

Be sure to tout the benefits of telecommuting to your company:

■ **Save money.** Your company can save money on office space, especially if the organization is growing and may have to lease

---

[7]Survey by the Society for Human Resource Management in 1998, as reported by the ITAC. See http://www.telecommute.org/surveys.htm.

additional space. If you are proposing to telecommute part-time, offer to share your space with someone, since you will not be using it as often. Or offer to move to smaller quarters. You will not be needing that large office or cubicle if you are there only two days a week. Of course, if you are proposing to telecommute all, or almost all, of your working hours, then you are freeing up office space for someone else.

■ **Increase productivity.** Telecommuting often results in increased productivity. Telecommuters also tend to take fewer sick days. An irritating cold that might keep you from getting into the office will not keep you from your home office. You will also keep from getting your coworkers sick, compounding the productivity gains. As Gwen pointed out, not being subjected to the exhausting rigors of commuting leaves more creative energy for the job.

■ **Employee retention.** In a tight labor market, as Gwen indicated, telecommuting can be a useful employee-retention tool.

You will have to address several specific issues in your proposal:

■ **Who pays for home-office equipment?** If you do not already have a home office with the appropriate equipment, who will be paying for that equipment? As Gwen's story showed, commonly, when employees opt to telecommute part-time, they must pay for their own equipment. On the other hand, if you are proposing to telecommute full-time, eliminating the need for you to have equipment in the office, or if the company stops maintaining an office, then the company will normally purchase your equipment. You will also have to consider who will bear the ongoing cost of telephone lines and a cellular phone or pager if they are necessary.

■ **How will your work be measured?** As Sandra Sullivan, a human-resources consultant who specializes in helping companies make telecommuting work, says, "[The best way to answer this question is with a question.] How is the productivity measured now? The answer all too often is, 'Well, I can see them working.' Sight is not a measure of productivity."[8] As you prepare your proposal, think about how you measure your own productivity now. Include in your proposal measurable goals with established benchmarks to which you will perform. Build in periodic updates on your progress vis-à-vis these goals. You may want to use the Project Status Report on page 125.

■ **No change in compensation.** As long as you are not changing the expected output of your job, do not accept any salary reduction in exchange for telecommuting. Remember, you will be doing the same job, delivering the same value to the organization. Although you may be required to cover the cost of equipment or phone lines, you should not otherwise have to "pay" for telecommuting.

■ **Suggest a trial period.** Suggest a trial time frame, usually three to six months. If you anticipate that your manager will be apprehensive, suggest starting out telecommuting two days a week. As you, your manager, and your colleagues get accustomed to the idea, you can increase your days at home.

"I've Received Permission to Begin Telecommuting. Now What?"

There are several things you can do to greatly enhance your chances for success and happiness as a telecommuter. Consider the following suggestions.

Create your home office. Designate an area of your home as "the office." If possible, devote a room with a door to your work space. Telecommuters with young children suggest a room as far away

---

[8]Comments taken from "Frequently Asked Questions When Investigating Telecommuting as a Work Option," International Telework Association and Council, 1998. See http://www.telecommute.org/faq.htm.

from the center of household activities as possible. Whether you set aside a whole room or just an alcove for your office, it is important that this space be dedicated to work. As you associate this space with work, you will find it easier to get down to business when you telecommute.

Your home office will need appropriate equipment. If you will be on the phone quite a bit, a second phone number, separate from your home line, is a good idea. Remember, if clients or coworkers call, your children cannot answer the phone. If you will be sending or receiving faxes, or spending time on-line, a third phone line may be in order. The type of computer and other equipment you will need will depend on the type of work that you do.

Establish a routine. Most telecommuters suggest that on the days that you telecommute, have a routine. Gwen talks about her routine: "I take a shower and get dressed for work every day. I don't put a suit on, but I get dressed. I do not work as effectively in pajamas." Samantha, who telecommuted full-time for her sales job in the steel industry, noted, "Even when I work in jeans and a sweatshirt, I always have shoes on. Shoes mean work. Stocking feet mean home."

If you took breaks when you worked in the office, take breaks at home. Get out. Go for a walk. Get some fresh air. Remember, when you are in the office, you do not sit in your cubicle all day without a break. Do not expect yourself to sit in your home office all day without interruption either.

You may have to learn to shut work off at the end of the day. For many workers, the commute home serves as an end-of-the-day ritual, a demarcation between work and home. Telecommuters often need to create their own end-of-day ritual. Make a habit of cleaning your desk and preparing your to-do list for the next day. Shut off your computer, walk out of your office, and close the door. Some people go so far as to pack their briefcase as if they were going to commute home.

Switch gears between home and work. Most people recommend that at any one time you be either "at work" or "at home." This does not mean that you have to walk into your home office at 9 A.M., work until noon, have lunch, go back to your office and work until 5 P.M. If you are working for an hour before you bake cookies for your child's class, work for that hour—and then go bake cookies. Do not try to cook dinner and write a presentation at the same time; neither is likely to come out very well.

Chelsea, a telecommuter who works for a major newspaper, says, "You get good at switching gears. When you are 'in' one place, you ignore the other, even though you are physically in the same place. You are in one place mentally. You put firm mental boundaries around your life realms." Otherwise, your work and your life are likely to suffer.

Establish firm rules with your family and friends. Your family as well as your neighbors and other friends may have to get accustomed to the idea that even though you are at home, you are really at work. Says one woman, "Getting the children—ages eleven and seventeen—used to leaving me alone on the days when I telecommute has been tough. It is hard for them to understand that, although I'm home, I'm still working." Another woman adds, "Some people think that people who work from home are not on the same level as people who work in the office. Maybe they have some false impression that home workers sleep in, watch soap operas, and hang around in their pajamas all day. . . . I don't know. All I do know is that I don't fit that image at all. I'm a hard worker. I keep office hours and try to be available. I meet my goals and deadlines. And I don't hang around in my pajamas."

On managing work and family under one roof, Chelsea says, "My kids have to stay out of my office. Summers are very difficult. I do tons of work when they are asleep. I work really hard when everyone is out. My work really tanks when we have houseguests. I usually don't do much work when we have guests—and I pay for it later. My boundaries ebb and flow based on my family's needs."

Stay on top of changes in your organization. Be in regular communication with your office. This communication is not just to keep you up to date on specific job-related information, although that, too, is critical. Rather, speaking with colleagues across the organization is essential to keep you abreast of larger, company-related changes in your organization. Chelsea says, "I have to work hard at staying current on my own company's culture." Reach beyond your immediate coworkers. Staying in touch with all of your colleagues—those people you used to see at the coffee machine, in the lunch line, and on the elevator—will help you stay on top of what is going on in your company. This information will help you self-promote within the organization, a critical element to ensuring that your career continues to grow even as you telecommute.

Combat loneliness and isolation. Feelings of loneliness and isolation are one of the biggest reasons why telecommuters stop telecommuting and return to traditional commuting, traffic and all. If you telecommute only part-time, you are less likely to feel the isolation. In addition to helping you stay informed of developments in your company, regular communication with people in your organization will help give you that sociability that many people come to realize is so important. Gwen offers this tip for fighting isolation: "If I feel lonely, I call someone on the staff or a media person. I do lunch. Or I go to Barnes and Noble and read for a while, to keep on top of stuff for my job. Or I go to the supermarket to look at new products [in my industry]."

To further combat loneliness and isolation, be in communication with other people you know who also work at home or work in the area. Arrange for lunch dates or afternoon coffee breaks.

Self-promote. One of the biggest concerns that telecommuters express is a sense of "out of sight, out of mind" when it comes to the most interesting, highly visible projects and those sought-after promotions. Keep your manager—and her managers—aware of your progress. It is probably a good idea to go into the office for major presentations and department meetings. Here is some additional comfort: A Small Business Administration study conducted in 1993 found that telecommuters actually got promoted more often than their stay-at-work counterparts.[9]

If your company does not provide you with a reporting format, use the Project Status Report detailed earlier in this chapter on page 125 to send weekly updates to your boss. This status report is an excellent tool to demonstrate your value to the organization with peers and superiors. Rather than having to be there in person, your status report stands in for you.

If you are the first telecommuter in your company, you may experience some resentment. As one such woman told us, "There is some animosity in the workplace, as if I have been given preferential treatment." Do everything you can to ensure that your telecommuting does not inconvenience your colleagues. As you and your manager get more comfortable with your telecommuting, share your success with coworkers. As Gwen's story demonstrates, your success may be all that others need to get the ball rolling for themselves.

Is Telecommuting the Right Option for You?

■ Can you meet your job responsibilities without physically being in the office? If not your whole job, can you identify parts of your job that could be accomplished off-site?

---

[9]"Myths and Realities of Working at Home," U.S. Small Business Administration, 1993, as quoted by June Langhoff in "Frequently Asked Questions About Telecommuting." See http://www.langhoff.com/faqs.html.

- Are you self-disciplined enough to get work done at home? Or, will you be tempted by the newspaper, soap operas, and/or refrigerator?

- Are you a good communicator? Will you be able to understand your coworkers' needs from a distance? Will you be able to keep them informed of your needs and progress?

- Are you willing to self-promote within your organization? This will require more effort as a telecommuter than it would if you were in the office every day.

- Are you internally motivated? Or, do you need to be around others who are at work to get to work yourself?

- Will you miss having regular, in-person, social contact with your colleagues? Are you willing to reach out to others for lunch dates and other meetings to ensure that your social needs are met?

- Does your company have e-mail? Will your company support your accessing e-mail from home? While e-mail may not be essential to telecommuting, it will make your telecommuting life much easier.

s i x

Altering Life in Corporate America,

Part II: Going Part-time

Professional part-time is one of the fastest growing segments of the American workforce.[1] Part-time comes in many shapes and sizes—two days a week, three days a week, four days a week, five half-days, four three-quarter days, twenty hours a week divided among different days on different weeks— just to name a few. There are almost as many ways to construct a part-time schedule as there are people constructing them. All that part-time really means is "less than full-time." Beyond that, part-time is often a function of what you can negotiate.

---

[1]Cindy Tolliver and Nancy Chambers, *Going Part-Time: The Insider's Guide for Professional Women Who Want a Career and a Life* (New York: Avon Books, 1997), 3. (Note: This book is out of print.)

There are three major routes to part-time:

- **Going part-time at your company.** This is the part-time option women utilize most. Less than a decade ago, the women who were able to negotiate part-time arrangements with their existing employers were breaking new ground. Today, going part-time within an organization where you are established is becoming increasingly common.

- **Finding a new part-time job.** Today, women who find new professional part-time jobs are at the forefront of change in corporate America. This option is more difficult to implement. As more women who have negotiated part-time arrangements with their existing employers decide to move on to new organizations, more and more women will be pushing to bring part-time jobs into the mainstream.

- **Job sharing.** Job sharing is the one option that lets you truly work part-time, while at the same time enabling your employer to have full-time coverage in the position. While other part-timers are often called upon to work more than their usual part-time hours when work is busy, with a job share, no matter what is going on or when it is happening, one of the two sharers is "on duty," allowing the other partner true time off.

Regardless of the route you choose, there are several things to consider. See the suggestions that follow.

Make a formal written proposal. In most cases, you will have to prepare a written proposal outlining the way you would like to structure part-time. One common mistake that women make in trying to move to part-time, whether by transforming their existing job, finding a new one, or arranging a job share, is that they ask for it casually. Women often ask for part-time as if it were a favor to them, for their benefit only, rather than making a written business case. You would never casually ask your boss to change your group's budget allocation, to alter a pricing policy, or to make some other significant business decision. Rather, you would construct a proposal, in writing, explaining why you felt the request makes sense for the business. You will need to submit a similar proposal for transforming your career to part-time. Andrea Meltzer, owner of Executive Options, a company whose mission is to help people find alternative work arrangements, says, "It's an education process. You have to educate employers on the statistics, on how it works in many companies."

In her workshops on managing work/life balance, Dawn Gray counsels, "Be proactive about solving the problem. In looking at changing your work hours or your work schedule, the best advice I have for people is to go in with a plan of who is going to do the work, how it is going to get done. Don't just go in and say, 'I'm overwhelmed.' Go in and say, 'I'm overwhelmed and I've been thinking about it. This whole area is something that can be delegated to this group.' Go in with a plan that is actually written out, that states what the problem is and how you are going to solve it. Make it a no-brainer for your boss. A lot of people have the habit of going into their boss and saying, 'I'm overwhelmed. What should I do?' That's a mistake."

"What will this do to my career?" Working part-time need not negatively impact your career over the long term. "If you are comfortable with the idea, everyone else will be too. If not, not," says Andrea Meltzer. "There is nothing wrong with saying that you worked part-time. You didn't do anything wrong. It's a mind-set. Get comfortable with what you are doing. I don't think there is any validity to the notion that working part-time will hurt your career long-term. It's an issue that some women have to get over. Period." When you next revamp your resume, you will tout your accomplishments in your position. The fact that you worked part-time neither enhances nor detracts from those accomplishments. This is true whether you are looking to continue working part-time or to return to full-time status.

Part-time: "I'm betwixt and between." Working part-time is the optimal solution for a growing number of women. But many women caution that even a challenging career position structured for part-time is not a panacea. Sandy, part-time chief financial officer for a national nonprofit, voices the thoughts of some women. "I'm not a stay-at-home mom. I'm not a working mom. I don't feel like I fit anywhere." Some women do feel as if they are half at home, half at work, and not doing their best in either place.

Even though professional part-time is a growing phenomenon, there are few places to go for support and assistance, few places where part-timers "fit in" or feel mainstream. Find other women who are working in part-time positions. Help each other out. Create a place where you are "the norm."

For many women, creating the optimal life collage requires working fewer hours—so there is time to play all those other life roles. There are many ways to make satisfying, career-expanding part-time work a reality.

"I LOVE MY JOB, BUT . . . ", PART II:
STAYING PUT AND GOING PART-TIME

First you will meet Dina, who negotiated a part-time arrangement within a small, entrepreneurial consulting firm. Then you will meet Ginny, who also arranged a part-time schedule at her current employer, a large, established, "good-old-boy" commercial–real estate company. These two women navigated their way to part-time, professional, career positions in two very different organizations. They encountered different issues but both were able to make part-time work for them and for their employers.

When Dina graduated from business school in 1983, she was engaged and knew she eventually wanted a family. She had a long-range plan. "I knew even then that I wanted to work part-time eventually. I thought that the way people got to go part-time was if they'd been with the company a long time and had really proven themselves." At a small, entrepreneurial consulting firm in a big midwestern city where Dina interviewed when she was finishing her degree, there was already one woman working part-time. It seemed like a good example. "I thought five to seven years later I'd do it."

Almost five years later, Dina and her husband began thinking about starting a family. "About one to two years before I had my daughter, I began talking about working part-time. I wasn't afraid of letting my employer know that that was what I wanted. I was in an environment where one person had done it. If you've not done well in your job, talking this up would work against you, but I had proven myself."

Dina went to the owner of the firm with her proposal, in writing. "I've had so many people say to me, 'They didn't offer me part-time.' No one is ever going to offer it to you. You have to sell it. I knew I had to sell it—to lay out clearly why it was good for the company. I thought, 'It's a bargain for them, with my accumulated knowledge. My brain works on our business almost all the time.' "

Dina identified three things that she says helped her sell her proposal to management:

■ *Dina set a schedule that management could depend on. She chose three days a week—Tuesday, Wednesday, and Friday. "I chose two consecutive days so there would be some continuity, but not three consecutive days so there wouldn't be a big gap between my last day one week and my first day the next week."*

■ *While she had a set, three-day-a-week schedule, Dina also built some flexibility into her personal schedule so she could either work one additional day when necessary or switch days if a client meeting had to be on a Monday or Thursday.*

■ *Dina agreed to be in touch with the office on the days she did not work. "I said I would check voice mail every day and respond to calls as necessary."*

While she was preparing her proposal, Dina consulted with one of her career mentors. "My mentor said that the company was going to get way more than 60 percent of my value even if I were only in the office and technically 'working' three days a week. She felt that because my brain would still work on the business during my days off and because I would be in contact with the office every day, the company would still be getting 100 percent of my value. I thought it was dangerous to ask for 100 percent of my salary at the same time I was asking to reduce my time in the office. So I asked for 75 percent of my salary—and I got it!

"Eventually when I worked part-time, I was well respected, not diminished in my ability to contribute to the firm, to the big decisions. But I did feel like the outside world thought, 'If you work part-time, you'd rather be home. You're not committed.' I want to make a bumper sticker that says, 'Part-time does not mean partly committed.' The assumption seemed to be, 'If you want to be home some of the time, you must want to be home all of the time. You're

not a real career person.' That's not remotely the case. I combated these presumptions by example, by how I was."

Dina's part-time arrangement was a win-win for her and the company for eight years. During the time she worked part-time, Dina was promoted to vice president and then senior vice president. Only recently, after fifteen years with the company, Dina decided that the work was no longer satisfying to her. She left the company and is looking to move into nonprofit work. Dina expects to use the knowledge and experience she gained negotiating a part-time arrangement, working part-time, and managing her career as a part-time professional to find a part-time job in the nonprofit arena.

Now meet Ginny. Married, with two children, and the primary family breadwinner, Ginny's journey to her life collage has evolved over time. She started setting boundaries by scaling back her hours slightly and saying 'No' more. Working for a large, stodgy commercial–real estate company, Ginny informed her boss that she was pregnant only to be told, "Don't tell anybody else. I need to handle the information dissemination here because the implication will break your career." After her son was born, Ginny went to her boss with "zero expectations." She explains, "I went in with what I wanted to do and why it was good for him to let me do it. I figured that being at home one day a week—working a four-day week—was no different than being on the road one day a week. The effect was the same—you're out of the office. He bought it.

"For the longest time, my colleagues didn't even know what I was doing. When I wasn't in the office, they assumed I was traveling somewhere. The psychological constraints in that environment were such that I didn't feel like I could share that I was working part-time with the women's network in the firm—such as it existed at the time. I never let the word 'part-time' pass my lips. Today, I am much more cavalier about it. But at the time, it was so extraordinary and the reaction [from peers] would have been so negative."

With virtually no support at work, it took Ginny a while to make working part-time work in her life. "When I first started working four days a week, I felt tremendous pressure. I wouldn't go out to lunch. I would always eat at my desk. Somehow I felt I needed to enhance my productivity, still grinding out the same amount as everyone else [even though I was being paid 80 percent of my salary]. On my 'off' day I'd bring my laptop home and spend half the day working. What was the point in that? If I was working on my day off, my husband would remind me, saying something like, 'If you're working you may as well get paid for it.' I've progressed from there."

When her second child was born, Ginny took off an entire year. She thought she might want to be a "stay-at-home mom." Her year off taught her that she did not. At the same time, with two children, she wanted to work less than four days a week. Time to renegotiate her part-time arrangement.

Ginny submitted her new proposal, this time suggesting that rather than work a set schedule of days, she would simply handle one client account. "I came in and proposed that I would just do this one piece, do whatever it takes to service this one client and take a salary cut. End of story." Tactfully, Ginny let her boss know that if they couldn't work something out, she would "reassess" her situation. Ginny's boss came back with a different proposal—a schedule that Ginny liked, but a job description that didn't thrill her. They negotiated back and forth a few times and worked it out. "Looking back, it's staggering to me just how easy it was. Thinking about doing it [negotiating part-time] was dramatically more difficult than actually doing it."

Ginny continues to work part-time at the same company— three days a week, two in the office and one at home. Her advice? "You have to ask. You have to be prepared, but if you spend too *much time negotiating with yourself, it's ridiculous—and you don't get anywhere."*

What Is This Option Really Like?

While there are no firm numbers, perhaps one of the most significant workplace trends of the past decade is the growth in the number of women working in professional part-time jobs. The vast majority of these women have crafted part-time positions at their current company. If you truly like—or love—what you do and the company you work for, this may be the option for you.

Generally, the women who choose this option have been at their companies for at least a few years and have proven themselves within the organization. These women like their job and company. Consequently, they look there first to craft an alternative work arrangement. These women also do not want the pressure that often accompanies the first few months of a new job or the anxiety that is commonly present at the beginning of a freelance practice. As Ginny put it, "I was thinking about freelancing. I sat down with a friend for whom I have a lot of respect and she said, 'You know, you're doing this the hard way. If what you really want is some kind of part-time paid work and the psychic energy involved in family is so high, particularly when children are young, your best path is to come up with something at your present employer. You won't have the stress of proving yourself again or the stress of finding new business from scratch. It's the low-key way to get what you need.' That friend really turned my thinking around. After that, I thought to myself, 'She's right. I've got a lot of sweat equity at this company. I've got a certain reputation that will tide me over.'"

What if you do not love your current job and/or your company? If you truly hate your current full-time job, you are unlikely to suddenly love it just by going part-time. On the other hand, if your job is "okay" and you like your company, and if a predictable schedule and income are important to you, this option may still be for you. While part-time often grows to consume more hours than it is supposed to, most part-time arrangements offer a greater degree of schedule predictability than most other options. Women who negotiate part-time arrangements can also count on a predictable income, where those who choose to freelance or start their own businesses cannot.

Hints to Help You Go Part-time

The key to negotiating a part-time arrangement with your current employer is to thoroughly understand the environment in which you work. It is not enough to just know your job. Understand how the business or the business unit as a whole operates. What are critical elements of its success? How does your job fit into the whole organization? What need do you fulfill? Pretend for a minute that you are a vendor selling a service to your company. Negotiating a part-time arrangement is similar to renegotiating the terms of a vendor agreement.

Can you imagine if one of your vendors walked into your office and said, "It's no longer convenient for us to provide this service to you this way. I want to provide it part-time"? Be honest. You would look at that vendor as though they were from another planet. You expect your vendors to do what you need when you need it. However, if that vendor could propose an alternative way to deliver their service in a way that was beneficial for you and the vendor, you would likely approve that proposal.

The same is true of negotiating a part-time agreement with your existing employer. You have to craft a proposal that takes into account all of your employer's needs as well as your own. As Dina said, no one will come to you and offer you part-time. You have to sell it to your management.

Your Proposal

Your proposal need not be a lengthy treatise, but it must address the central issues:

Do not try to do a full-time job in part-time. "The quickest way to sabotage a move to part-time," says Andrea Meltzer of Executive Options, "is to try to condense a full-time job into part-time. The job has to change. You can't do a five-day job in three days." Do not confuse going part-time with working a "compressed" week such as four ten-hour days, or with telecommuting from home one or two days a week. If your job description does not change, then you are still working full-time.

Sandy, the chief financial officer and head of Information Systems for a national nonprofit, made this mistake when she first went part-time. "My mistake was that I didn't ask for a reduction in responsibility. I proposed thirty hours, three days a week, at 75 percent of my pay. I ended up working more than thirty hours. I went back to my boss. My pay went back to 100 percent, but I still wasn't working part-time." Part-time did not work for Sandy until she and her boss agreed that she would remain the CFO, but that one of her colleagues would take over Information Systems.

Change your job description to fit the part-time hours you are proposing. Think about the needs of your particular job and company. How will you reduce your workload? Who will pick up the rest of your workload? Who will ensure that all of the work is done on time and at high quality? Try to structure this reallocation of work in a way that will minimize headaches for your manager. The easier it is for her, the more likely she is to accept it. As Lynn Martin, former U.S. Secretary of Labor, counsels, "Think through the impact your part-time arrangement will have on your peers. If they will be expected to pick up some of your work, there may be resentment. You must think of the total team dynamics when crafting your part-time solution."

If you are having difficulty trimming your existing job description to fit a part-time schedule, look around your organization for a need that could be filled on a part-time basis. Write the job description for the part-time job that you want. You may be able to create a new job for yourself within your existing company. Ginny knew that her department had one particularly difficult client. Rather than redesigning her existing job to make it part-time, Ginny proposed that her part-time job would encompass handling this one client. The client was delighted to have someone dedicated to his account, and Ginny knew that she could handle the client on a part-time basis. Her manager and peers were satisfied with the arrangement because it took the responsibility of handling a difficult client off their plate. Ginny found a solution that was good for all parties involved.

If you propose a new part-time job within your company, include a plan for how you will transition out of your existing job. Be willing to help hire and train your replacement. Be willing to be available to help that person get up to speed.

There are many ways to go part-time. What is part-time to you? Commonly, part-time means three or four days a week, but not always. Eve, a lawyer, works 60 percent of full-time. The full-time attorneys in her firm are required to bill 2,000 hours per year. Eve is required to bill 1,200 hours per year. She has developed a niche as a brief writer in her firm. Her weekly hours vary. Sometimes, in a crunch, she works more than full-time in a given week. Then she has other weeks when she does not work at all.

Some people work full-time for part of the year and then work far fewer hours for the rest of the year. One accountant, who loves to mountain-bike, works crazy hours during tax season, from December to April, and then works one day a week for the rest of the year. Of course, the seasonality of the accounting business supports this kind of schedule. Look at your company and your industry and consider what will work.

Even if you opt for one of the more conventional part-time arrangements such as a three-day-a-week schedule, there are still some questions to answer. Will you have a set schedule or simply work whichever three days the company needs you that week? If you have a set schedule, how flexible are you willing to be to alter that schedule when the need arises?

In some professions, full-time means a lot more than forty hours a week. Between seeing patients, making rounds, and handling administrative duties, many full-time physicians often work sixty hours a week. So do many lawyers and consultants. Working part-time in these professions can mean working forty hours a week—what used to be considered full-time. Vickie, a primary-care family physician, works for a group practice owned by a hospital in her community. Full-time doctors in her practice must see patients thirty to thirty-two hours per week. Add hospital rounds and other duties, and these physicians work between fifty and sixty hours per week. Vickie has negotiated to carry eighteen patient hours per week. With administrative duties, hospital rounds, and on-call time, she works "part-time" at thirty-five to forty hours per week.

In proposing a structure for your part-time job, consider what type of part-time arrangement is most likely to meet the needs of your firm. Will that arrangement work for you?

What are you willing to do on your "days off"? What will happen when something comes up and you are not in the office? Are you willing to check your voice mail on your days off? Are you willing to return calls? What about e-mail? Will you participate in a conference call from home? Attend an occasional meeting in the office? You get the picture.

Andrea Meltzer says, "Talk about what you are willing to do on your days off up front so it's not an issue when it comes up— because it will come up. Make sure you and your boss have the same expectations. There are also personal issues you will have to deal with. What are you going to do when something comes up? How will you handle day care or other obligations if you have to do something on one of your days off? Anticipate these things and be proactive. You don't want to be on the defensive. You want to appear in control. Present all of this up front to your employer. Say, 'In the event that this occurs, this is how I will handle it.' Make a list. There is a much better chance that your employer will buy in." For instance, Ginny's company was most concerned about Ginny's availability when her client needed her. While the client's needs could be met part-time, these needs did not happen at regularly scheduled times. Ginny negotiated compensation that enables her to have full-time child care to accommodate the company's need for maximum flexibility.

Being clear about what you are willing to do on your days off is particularly important when you manage people. Dina said, "I was a manager at the time. I set expectations with my employees. I never wanted progress slowed because I wasn't there. I said, 'If you need to call me at home in order to move forward on a project, then call me. If it can wait until the next day when I'm in the office, let it wait.'"

How will you be compensated? How much will you be paid to work part-time? Commonly, women earn a proportion of their full-time salary based on the number of days or hours that they work. For example, women who work three days per week typically get 60 percent of their salary. Often, women will get a proportionate share of bonuses as well. But what happens if you work more than the set number of part-time hours? Just as there are numerous ways to structure part-time work, there are as many ways to structure compensation

Dina was able to negotiate being paid 75 percent of her base salary, rather than 60 percent, in exchange for being in the office three days per week and being available as required on other days. Laura found a new part-time job in public relations. When she began working more than the agreed-upon hours, her boss offered to pay her. She said no. The reason she went part-time was to gain more time. She did not want more money, she wanted the time. She went on to negotiate compensatory time when she works more than twenty-five hours a week.

Eve, the 60 percent attorney, is paid a flat salary to bill 1,200 hours per year. It is her responsibility to track her billable hours. She is not paid any additional amount for any hours she bills over 1,200 in the year.

Leslie, a health care–marketing consultant for a biotechnology company, is supposed to work three days per week, or 60 percent of full-time. Yet she negotiated to be paid by the hour. "I fought hard for that. When I work, I get paid. When I don't work, I don't get paid. We're all targeting sixty percent, but if it's more or less, no one gets upset. I like that. There is ebb and flow to consulting. Sometimes there are no projects. Sometimes there are a lot. I don't sign on to a project where I can't do the hours. But, then, I don't get paid. I have a lot of flexibility to manage the time-versus-money trade-off. If I didn't have this arrangement, I would get resentful. I'm a professional, and I would work until everything got done, even if that meant full-time, but I would only be getting paid part-time."

Many women, eager to get some flexibility into their work/ life, are too quick to accept less pay for the same work. Kelly, an entertainment-industry manager, adds, "We are total suckers for doing that." She was adamant about maintaining her salary when she began working four days per week because her responsibilities did not change.[2]

There is also more to compensation than just money and time. What about benefits? Vacation? Tuition reimbursement? All of these should be covered in your proposal. Most companies require you to

[2]Reed Abelson, "Part-time Work for Some Adds Up to Full-time Job," the *New York Times,* 2 Nov. 1998: 1.

work a minimum number of hours per week to receive benefits. Check with your company to see if they have such a policy in place.

Can you be promoted as a part-timer? What does going part-time mean to your promotability? Can you still make partner or are you off the track? Will your career growth be delayed—or derailed? As a 60 percent attorney, Eve accepts that she is not on the partnership track. To remain on the partnership track she would have to work at least 80 percent, a trade-off she has elected not to make. In your proposal, lay out any promotions you would like to be considered for and a possible timetable.

Suggest a trial period. Suggest to your management that you implement working part-time as structured in your proposal for six months. Build in regular reviews during the trial period. During these reviews, rather than discussing your performance, talk about how part-time is working for the company and for you. Identify what is not working and make some changes. Tailor part-time to work in your organization.

Selling your proposal. "Presell" your proposal. Let your manager know that a proposal is coming. Indicate that you are giving your proposal a lot of thought and are structuring something that you think will work well for the company as well as for you. Present your proposal as good for the business. "Don't apologize for wanting to work part-time," says Andrea Meltzer. "Companies are benefiting. Everyone can win." Lynn Martin echoes Meltzer's comment: "Don't treat your part-time arrangement as a favor your company is doing for you. Why? Because the minute the business climate goes south, guess what gets cut? Rather, show your manager how it is good for them, and then demonstrate that as you work part-time."

Remember your company does not want to lose a high-quality employee. It will cost your company money to recruit, hire, and train a replacement. These costs will entice management to at least listen to you. Do not threaten, but be clear that you want to work part-time. You are willing to work something out, but if the firm demonstrates absolutely no willingness to talk about part-time, you may need to reconsider your options. Remember Ginny's advice—"There are certain points in this process where you have to be willing to lose it all because that's the only way you're going to get to the point you want to get to." You cannot reshape your work without taking some risks. Only you can decide how firm you want to be with your management. Reassure them that you are still committed to your job and company. You will be there in a bona fide emergency.

Possible Obstacles to Going to Part-time

A brief or unproven track record. Unless you have been a high-performance employee, going part-time is almost impossible to arrange. The longer you have been with the company and the more valuable you have proven yourself, the easier negotiating part-time is likely to be.

What if you are single or childless? Most companies that allow part-time do so on an ad-hoc basis, without any formal policy. Often the need to care for children is considered a "valid" reason for working part-time, while other reasons are not. One notable exception is the professional services company Deloitte & Touche, which is on the forefront of developing part-time arrangements for its employees. Ellen Gabriel, the partner in charge of the Women's Initiative at Deloitte & Touche, says, "Our employees submit a proposal. We don't ask why. Flexible work arrangements are needed for many reasons—not only child-care-related."

If there are other women in your organization who have moved to part-time, ask them if they have a sense of whether the company will ask about your reasons for wanting part-time, and, if so, what reasons are "okay."

Management resistance. As much as you try to cover every angle in your proposal, management may argue that the company needs you to be available every day. Client needs, they argue, are five days a week.

Management may also resist letting you go part-time because they are afraid that once one person goes part-time, everyone will want to. This is known as the "floodgate theory." There is ample evidence from peer companies who offer part-time that the floodgate theory is a myth. Do your homework so that you can appropriately reassure your management. Remember also that, with communications technology and clear job accountabilities, many people within one organization could work part-time. Managing many part-time employees is likely to become commonplace over the next decade.

What if they say no? When your proposal is drafted, you may want to "test the waters" by showing it to a mentor or colleague inside your organization. Keep in mind, no matter how great a proposal you write, management may say no. And, despite any precautions you might have taken, management may question your future commitment because you asked about part-time. As a result, your request may impact your career within the company. You may end up feeling like you must leave the company to continue growing your career while having your needs met. These negative ramifications are becoming less common, but they are not unheard of. It is a good idea to have a backup plan in mind, in case management outright rejects your proposal.

Your own psychology. If you are working less, you may not be "on the fast track." If most of your peers are on that track, will you feel left out? If you are working 60 percent and your peers are working 100 percent, all else being equal, it is only fair that they will be eligible for promotions before you. For your part-time arrangement to work, you may have to be willing to accept a slower career progression.

Ellen Gabriel describes the reactions of some women in consulting who have tried reducing their annual billable hours to 60 percent. "We haven't found the magical formula yet. Employees tend to come back and say, 'This isn't working.' The peer environment doesn't lend itself to it. Employees are uncomfortable. They say things like, 'Everyone is in the fast lane. I'm in the slow lane.' They feel like misfits."

Eve, the 60 percent attorney, also commented on the psychology of being different from the prevalent corporate culture. "I know that I'm not going to run cases. I'm not going to make as much money. I'm consciously doing that. It makes it easier to say, 'No, I won't work that way. I made a different deal. I pay my price. You pay yours.' I have had to resist the values of this place. Some women can't value themselves separately from the value system within the firm. I'm not hung up on fitting in." Eve goes on to encourage women "not to be dependent on other people's assessment of your success. Don't use an outside standard to value yourself. Women seem particularly vulnerable to this. Instead, ask, 'What matters to me? How do I measure up against what I think matters?' Ask those questions rather than, 'What does he or she think of me?'" If you go part-time, how will you value yourself?

Management Says Okay. Now What?

Perhaps the biggest issue for part-time women is sticking to part-time. Many women report that they end up working more than what their agreed-upon part-time arrangement calls for. One women aptly calls this "job ooze." Many women report that they end up working 3.5 to 4 days a week when they are supposed to be working three days. Often, these women are getting paid for only three days. As one woman, whose sentiments were echoed by others, said, "That is a price I am willing to pay to have some flexibility." While Dina and Laura demonstrated that you may be able to get paid or get compensatory time for those hours, getting these benefits is challenging.

Often, working overtime is part of the price for part-time. Discuss with your employer up front how overtime will be handled.

Even though you have a stellar track record as a professional in the company, people may question your commitment. "I had to prove myself again in a way," says Dina. "I had to prove that I was still committed, still valuable. I was flexible, and occasionally I took some work home with me. I did not self-promote enough."

At first you may be taken less seriously. Your peers may feel that they are "picking up the slack for you." You will have to show that part-time does not mean "partly committed." Refer back to the Project Status Report introduced in the section of Chapter 5 called "Setting Boundaries." Use this report to regularly convey the value you bring to the firm.

You may feel some resentment on the part of your peers. Particularly if your company does not have a formal part-time policy or if you are the first (or one of the first) professionals to go part-time, your peers may perceive your part-time status as a perk that they cannot have. This resentment may manifest itself in petty, demeaning comments. One woman described how, when she was scheduling a meeting with a coworker, he said with pointed sarcasm, "Now, when are you in?" Other women tell of coworkers who specifically suggest scheduling meetings on their days off.

Finally, part-timers often find that they are not "in the thick of things." Leslie says, "There is a bit of segregation between part-timers and full-timers. Part-timers have other stuff going on. I do my job and I leave. I'm much less involved in firm development. The people who work full-time are much more into firm development. I come in. I do what I have to do, maybe a little bit more. And then, I'm outta there." Eve, the attorney, echoes these sentiments. "Within the law firm, I'm a little bit of an outsider. I don't know the scuttlebutt. I'm focused on getting stuff done. I'm different." You have to be certain you can handle being a bit of an outsider. Being outside the mainstream may hinder your advancement. To combat this, take time to self-promote.

The bottom line. By negotiating a part-time arrangement with your current employer, you are staying in a job and/or with a company that you like with a schedule that works for you. You have reduced hours, even if, in reality, they are not as reduced as you might like. You have a guaranteed salary. Once negotiated, moving to part-time is generally a less-stressful option. You are not changing jobs or starting a business, but rather staying in a comfortable, familiar place. You know how to navigate your way around the company. You know the people. And, you are moving forward, albeit for the time being at a slower pace, in your profession. If you want to resume full-time in the future, you will be welcome.

Is Staying Put and Going Part-time the Right Option for You?

Ask yourself these questions:

- Do you like your job and/or company?
- Do you desire a relatively predictable schedule? Can you be flexible about your schedule?
- Do you need or want a predictable income?
- Have you done the math? Is a part-time income enough? Don't forget to factor in the savings you will realize from not working full-time. You may want to look back at the Personal Financial Analysis in Chapter 3.
- Are you willing to accept slower progression up the ladder, even as your peers working all around you may remain on the fast track?
- Are you willing to prove yourself again? Are you willing to self-promote within your company to ensure that management and peers remain convinced of your value to the company?

"I WANT TO WORK PART-TIME—IN MY CHOSEN FIELD": FINDING A SATISFYING PART-TIME JOB

At thirty-one, Laura tried several options in her journey to create a meaningful career that works in her life. Laura worked for a public-relations agency for seven years, rising to the level of vice president. "I loved it. It was such a good fit for me. But it was also very demanding, very time-consuming. . . . After seven years, I was burnt out. I was disillusioned. I was working sixty hours a week. The client always came first. One day I just said, 'This is costing too much.' I was out of town for Valentine's Day, my husband's birthday, and our anniversary. I missed Mother's Day. I [was] constantly calling to say, 'I'll be late for dinner tonight.' I never [cooked] dinner. I [was] not proactively in touch with friends and I [had] no time with my husband."

Laura began exploring her options. She knew she did not want another full-time job. Laura was interested in academia, so she went on a series of informational interviews with public-relations directors at colleges and universities. Eventually, one of Laura's former colleagues, who was the director of public relations at an area college, got a job share approved and invited Laura to apply. "My husband and I talked about it. We were in the middle of infertility treatment. I knew I couldn't do this job [be a vice president at the agency] and be a mom. I applied for the job share and got it.

"I was scared to quit. The agency was shocked. They tried to keep me. They offered me part-time. But I knew myself. I couldn't say no to clients. That was the culture I created for myself. I needed to get out. I had to go. And I wanted to see what higher education was all about."

At first, Laura thought the university setting and the job share combined to form a good option for her. But, as the months went by, she admitted, "I missed the sexy stuff." *One day, Laura received a call from the president of an agency that had tried to recruit her four years earlier. He wanted Laura to work for his agency full-time.*

Although she knew she would not work full-time, Laura agreed to meet him for breakfast. "I thought I'd go and lay down all my rules and then he'd laugh at me. I was really empowered to say what I wanted. He had interviewed me four years earlier. He knew my work. He'd tried to steal me from my old agency. I thought, 'If this is going to work out, it'll be on my terms.' I was afraid that I couldn't get the charge out of the things that energized me without paying the cost of what sapped me.

"At breakfast, I was so proud of myself. I had my key messages. I would work three days a week, preferably Monday, Tuesday, and Thursday. No half days. And three days in a row doesn't work either. Working a job share had given me enough experience to know how to structure a part-time job. I had to pick up my daughter at 5:15 P.M. so I would have to leave by 4:45 P.M. I spoke about my 'former life' at the old agency. In my 'former life,' when there was a conflict between family and client, I always chose the client. I was done with that. No more."

The agency hired Laura part-time, three days a week. Laura negotiated a full-time salary and then was paid 60 percent of that. She received pro rata vacation and benefits. "It was great to be back with 'my people,' where I belong."

But all was not smooth sailing. Shortly after Laura started with the agency, one of her peers quit. The agency was scrambling to ensure that clients and projects were not affected. "After my first four weeks on the job, I realized that I had worked an average of four days per week. My husband was nervous. So was I. My boss said, 'We'll compensate you for that.' I said, 'It's not about money. If I work extra time, I want time back.' I started taking comp time. I wanted him to know that I wouldn't become full-time. Since that time, I have stuck to three days.

"I have a new client. I haven't told them that I only work three days. I want to establish the relationship first. I do check my voice mail once per day. I change the outgoing message—so that on days off, the message says, 'I'm not in the office today.' People

think I'm traveling on business. The person who works for me takes care of stuff and calls me if she really has to—if it's an emergency. I don't want them to take advantage of it."

There are other adjustments Laura has made. "Things happen when you're not there. You have to let go. You can't go to all meetings and still get stuff done. I work sixty percent of the time. I go to sixty percent of the meetings. I got an e-mail requesting a meeting on a Wednesday. I started to e-mail back, 'Sorry, I don't work on Wednesdays.' I had to redo it. I just say I'm not available. No one will be the keeper of my schedule except me. I don't apologize."

Now that she has been in the job for several months, Laura is thrilled to be in a challenging, growth position in her field. At the same time, she has time for her family and her outside interests. "I've brought running back into my life. I accepted a three-year commitment to be on my church council. I read the newspaper. I have opinions! I am able to think about what is going on in the world and talk about it intelligently. I'm on the committee to plan the annual fund-raiser for a substance-abuse treatment clinic. And I handwrote all of my Christmas cards and remembered my friends' birthdays with cards and gifts. I look back and I say to myself, 'Working so hard is too one-dimensional. I will never do it again.'"

"What Is This Option Really Like?"

Women who want to enter an organization as a part-time professional are on the forefront of change in corporate America. Consequently, this option is often difficult to implement. But women like Laura are leveraging their experience and contacts and marshaling their confidence and courage to find challenging, career-expanding part-time jobs.

Much of what was discussed in "Staying Put and Going Part-time" also applies here. As you consider this option, be sure to read that section as well. Typically companies accept a part-time schedule from an employee they are trying to retain, rather than from a prospective hire. In negotiating a part-time schedule with their current employer, women are able to leverage their proven high performance to persuade their employers to structure a part-time arrangement. Moving to a new firm means that you lose this leverage. However, you can still leverage your reputation as presented on your resume and conveyed by your contacts and references.

Hints to Help You Find a Satisfying Part-time Job

There are unique tips to consider when looking for professional part-time work.

Your contacts are critical. Developing and using your contacts is important in any job search. In the search for a professional part-time job, it is critical. Seemingly, the most common way that women are able to change organizations and move directly into a part-time job is that they have previously worked with someone who is currently working in their new organization. This person can vouch for them and their work from firsthand experience.

Cheryl is a good example. For nearly eighteen years, Cheryl, forty-two, worked for a major bank in human resources and training. For almost nine of those years, she worked part-time, with a number of different work schedules and in several different positions. When her last assignment within the bank ended, Cheryl felt she had done much of what there was to do in the bank. It was time for her to gain fresh experience in a new place. In the course of her years at the bank, many of Cheryl's coworkers had moved to other companies. Cheryl began to contact these people. She explained that she was considering leaving the bank and wanted to pursue other opportunities. And, she absolutely wanted to continue to work part-time.

One of Cheryl's former bosses was now a senior manager at a national consulting firm. He knew firsthand the value Cheryl would bring to his organization. There was very little risk—and great opportunity—for him to go to bat with his managers to bring Cheryl in on a part-time basis. Someone who was less familiar with Cheryl's work would be less likely to go out on a limb for a part-time hire. At the same time, through discussions with her contact and others in the organization, Cheryl was able to impact the description of the job she eventually filled.

Use your contacts to create your own job. Using your contacts to establish links with new organizations exposes you to job opportunities that will never be advertised. Indeed, you will likely be in discussions with companies regarding their needs and be able to contribute to drafting the job description for the position you wish to fill. When you are involved in designing your part-time job, you have a much greater likelihood of success and satisfaction in the job.

Freelance work can be a way in. Sometimes doing a project for a company as an independent contractor is a useful way to "get in." In the course of doing a project for a company, you have the opportunity to prove yourself. Like women who leverage their solid performance to negotiate a part-time schedule with their existing employer, you may be able to leverage the success of your freelance project into a permanent part-time job. In addition, as you complete your freelance project, you have the opportunity to get to know the organization and its needs. This additional knowledge puts you in a better position to propose a part-time job that will work in that organization.

Leslie, a part-time health-care consultant, used this strategy: "I wanted part-time, a challenge, and a good career move. I was hired to do a project for the firm where I now work. I liked the project and they liked me. There is a good cultural fit between me and the company. One project led to another. I was able to work out a part-time arrangement that works for them and me."

Should you apply for full-time jobs? There is no clear answer to this question. A few women have had success applying for a full-time job and then transforming the position into part-time during the interview process. Going this route is not impossible, but it is more difficult. You may want to consider proposing a job share, particularly if you have a job-share partner in mind.

Remember Andrea Meltzer's admonition against trying to do a full-time job in part-time hours. If you negotiate a part-time schedule for what was originally billed as a full-time job, you will need to revise the job description to fit that part-time arrangement. Revising the job description to fit part-time may be especially difficult, given that the company has already identified a full-time need prior to commencing its hiring effort. Also, as an outsider, unless you have a solid contact within the organization, it may be more difficult for you to propose a part-time arrangement that meets the company's needs.

Even if you are successful in negotiating a part-time arrangement from what was billed as a full-time job, the company is more likely to expect you to make exceptions to your part-time schedule. You are more likely to be compelled to work more than part-time but for part-time wages.

If you do decide to interview for a full-time job, when should you introduce part-time? Some people suggest interviewing for a full-time job, getting an offer, and then negotiating part-time. While this may work for some, using a "bait and switch" strategy is a bad precedent to set. If you interview—seemingly in good faith—for a full-time position and then broach part-time at the last minute, what are you saying about your own integrity? Is that how you want to begin to establish your relationship with a new employer?

If you apply for jobs that are billed as full-time, you do not have to shout "part-time" in your cover letter. Perhaps you need not say anything about part-time in the first interview. If you have "wowed" the employer and are called back for a second interview, you should broach part-time at that time. If the employer is absolutely unwilling to consider altering the job to fit part-time, and you are sure you want part-time, there is no point continuing the interview process. You will only waste their time and yours—time that could be spent pursuing a more viable part-time opportunity.

Should you be willing to start full-time with the understanding that you will be able to move to part-time later? Consider your willingness to start a job full-time with the understanding that you will work full-time for a few months to learn the ropes, then move to a pre-established part-time schedule. This "way in" is not unheard of, but be wary. Despite assurances when you are hired, you may encounter resistance to implementing such an agreement when the initial time is up.

You should also be concerned about a change in management. Unless you have a written agreement, a change in management might bring a change in the rules. Agreements made by one boss might not be honored by the next. You may find yourself in a permanent full-time situation.

Are professional part-time jobs ever advertised? Occasionally, professional part-time jobs are advertised. It is rare for organizations to think in terms of part-time when structuring jobs. They think full-time. So most companies do not generally post or advertise for part-time professional help. More likely, you will have to identify opportunities that interest you and for which you are qualified, and sell a prospective employer on you and on part-time. When you look for a full-time job, you have to sell yourself. When you look for a part-time professional job, you have to sell yourself and sell part-time.

Is a part-time job really a part-time job? If a company advertises a professional part-time job, it is still important to make sure the employer is being realistic. Be wary of companies that are out to save money and think they can get a full-time job done at part-time pay. As Andrea Meltzer says, "Everybody has to define their needs realistically. Some companies want to save money, so they say, 'This is a part-time job.' But really, it's a full-time job."

Remember, when you are in a job interview, you are interviewing your prospective employer as well as being interviewed by that employer. You may want to ask some of the following questions to evaluate whether the job you are interviewing for is truly part-time:

- Is this job currently being done on a part-time basis? If not, how has the job been restructured to make it a part-time job?
- If this is a new position, why has it been structured as a part-time job?
- What contingencies are in place if it becomes clear that the job really requires more than part-time? You may want to put these contingencies in writing before you start the job.

Executive-search firms. There are a few executive-search firms that specialize in finding professional part-time work. To help get you started, ask around to see if your company has hired professional help to work on a project basis. Companies typically hire contract professionals to cover a maternity leave. If your company hires contract help and uses a recruiting company, find out what firm they use. Contact that firm. Often firms that place professionals in contract projects also fill permanent part-time jobs.

"I Did It! I Found a Part-time Job. Now What?"

When you first start your new part-time job, you may find it hard to maintain your part-time boundaries. Any new job, whether full-time or part-time, tends to be demanding and consuming. At the same time that you will want to go the extra mile to establish yourself, you will want to be careful not to establish a precedent of working more than part-time. Be sure to have a clear understanding with your new employer. If you work more than part-time, do you get paid overtime for the extra hours worked? Can you get compensatory time?

Is Finding a New Part-Time Job the Right Option for You?

Ask yourself the following questions:

- Have you considered trying to negotiate a part-time agreement with your current employer? Remember, it will be easier to move to part-time with your existing employer than it will be to find a new part-time job.
- Are you willing to exhaust your personal network? Are you willing to engage in an all-out marketing effort to find a professionally satisfying part-time job?
- Are you a high-quality performer? Do you have a reputation in your industry or functional area in your community?
- Is it a good time in your career to be changing employers?
- Are you willing to make a fresh start, to go the extra mile to establish yourself in a new organization?
- Do you have the persuasive skills to sell a potential employer on you and on part-time simultaneously?

"I WANT TO *REALLY* WORK PART-TIME": JOB SHARING

Prior to their job-share arrangement, Anna and Marybeth both worked for a major technology company, each in her own job. Anna tells her side of the story first.

"I was beginning to feel 'supermom' burnout. I had to fire people at work. . . . We were downsizing. . . . My son was exhausted, commuting with me one hour each way, twice a day. When I had my second child and was on maternity leave, I reduced my son's day care from five to three days a week. The difference in him was dramatic and immediate. I knew I couldn't go back full-time.

"While my goals were not the same as when I got out of college, I didn't want to be relegated to an insignificant staff position after having been an integral part of doing deals for the company.

"I tried a couple of other options. I moved out of a management position. That gave me some relief, but not much. I managed to negotiate a part-time arrangement. I was officially on the books at twenty-four hours per week, but I worked quite a bit more. I was feeling undervalued and overworked. . . .

"I finally got on the project from hell. We were working on a big opportunity for the company. I was the lead support person. I was working sixty to eighty hours a week. My youngest was an infant [whom] I was still nursing. My baby turned one year old, and I realized I had missed it [the first year]. We closed the piece of business, and I got my bonus, but it wasn't worth it.

"I had talked to Marybeth (my future job-share partner) about job sharing many times. We were already backing each other up on projects. We had common personal goals, a common standard of quality, and a common perspective on evaluating people. We knew we could work together. Marybeth was coming back from maternity leave, so we decided to try to sell the company on a job-share position."

Marybeth adds her perspective: "Because I knew Anna so well, I had seen all she had been through trying different options. Rather than re-create the agony she went through, I decided to learn from her experience. I jumped at the chance to job-share with Anna.

"We identified members of senior management [who] we thought would be supportive of the idea and sold them on it first. We also chose a group within the company that was growing and more willing to try new things. We put together a proposal for the position we would fill, how the work would get done, etc.

"Our job share has worked out so well because we are both great communicators. The quality of the work is seamless between us. Our manager can assign us a project, and we will determine between the two of us how it will get done. We have made career moves within the company together."

Anna picks up the story: "Job-sharing bought me a life outside of my job—time for friends, family, and me. This isn't for everyone, but when it works, it's terrific! It takes a tremendous amount of trust and communication. It allows us to pursue professionally challenging positions that would be tough to negotiate on a part-time basis."

"What Is This Option Really Like?"

As Marybeth and Anna demonstrate, job sharing can help you maintain your career trajectory while still enabling you to work part-time. In this option, two people share the responsibilities of one full-time job. Each partner in the job share works part-time. Together, the team works full-time. No two job-share arrangements are exactly alike. Each team will put its own imprint on the concept. In practice, some teams structure their job share so that each partner works three days per week and there is one "overlap" day. In other job shares, each partner works half-time and there is no overlap time. Regardless of how the job share is structured, the partners work closely together to ensure that the entire job gets done.

In some cases, the job-share partners split one full-time salary and benefits allowance. In other cases, particularly where there is an overlap day and the team can demonstrate enhanced productivity, each partner may earn more than a strict 50 percent of a comparable full-time salary and benefits. Also, some teams consist of a more experienced person and a less experienced person, in which case each partner's compensation may be individually negotiated.

Job sharing is on the rise. A survey conducted by Hewitt Associates, a consulting firm specializing in human-resource issues, found that of 718 large corporations, 258 offered job sharing in 1996, compared with 161 five years earlier.[3]

True part-time. For many women who are already considering part-time, job sharing is one step better. Part-timers often feel pressured to be available on their days off, to respond to voice mail and e-mail. Many part-timers bring work home with them and end up working closer to full-time but for part-time wages and benefits. Job sharing is the answer to this "job ooze." Job sharers are truly off on their days off. Says Brenda, one-half of a job-sharing team, "I don't feel the pressure on my days off. Someone else is there to handle whatever comes up."

Job sharing makes it possible to create part-time opportunities out of jobs that cannot easily be reduced from full-time. As Andrea Meltzer of Executive Options says, "Some jobs can't be done part-time. An equity trader, for example . . . [or other] very client-oriented businesses that need coverage. These kinds of jobs are better suited for a job share." By job sharing, you get part-time while the company continues to have full coverage in the position.

---

[3]Steven Ginsberg, "When Half a Job Is Better Than One," the *Washington Post,* 26 Oct. 1997: H4.

"And the two shall be as one." As long as you share a job, your career and your partner's are married. Job sharers progress in their careers as a team. You are evaluated as a team, promoted—or not— together. Partners lobby for raises and choice assignments together.

Accordingly, you must be able to trust your partner's judgment. When a decision needs to be made, it is made by the person who is working that day. When the other partner returns, she must support that decision as if she made it herself, even if it is not the decision she would have made. Job-share partners cannot second-guess each other.

Most job-share partners agree that both partners rarely attend a meeting together. Of her arrangement with her job-share partner, Laura said, "Always one of us, never both of us. That was our rule. Meetings were scheduled. Whichever one of us was working that day went to the meeting. Sometimes that was hard for me. I'd say to my partner, 'Should I come in for that?' She would remind me of that rule. It worked."

Some job-share partners come up with a combined name to sign correspondence.[4] "Mary" and "Jane" sign all correspondence "Mary Jane" to indicate that it comes from the two of them. Whether you opt for a work pseudonym or not, all correspondence is from both of you, even though only one of you actually prepared it. It is a good idea to include both names on all correspondence. Again, you must trust your partner and believe in her abilities.

Because job-share partners' work lives are so closely aligned, many teams find that it helps to share some of their personal lives as well. Some teams, for example, go so far as to pick up each other's kids from school on their days off.

Opportunities to learn new skills. In addition to being able to work "true" part-time, job sharers are often in a unique position to learn

---

[4]Steven Ginsberg, "When Half a Job Is Better Than One," the *Washington Post,* 26 Oct. 1997: H4.

new skills. Many job-share pairs bring complementary skills to the position. This wider breadth of experience is a boon for the company and for the two team members. Job sharers often have the opportunity to learn skills from each other that they might not otherwise develop. Sometimes teams are able to take on projects because one person has the necessary skill set, providing the other partner a fabulous learning opportunity that she might not have been given on her own.

Hints to Help You Arrange a Job Share

Perhaps the biggest hurdle to job sharing is selling the idea to management. Job sharing is still a foreign concept to many. You will have to educate and persuade. As with the other part-time options, you will want to prepare a written proposal, spelling out how your job share will work, what your contingency plans are, and what you are seeking in terms of compensation and benefits.

Leverage your star quality. You will have greater success negotiating a job share if you are a known entity at your company. Usually, at least one of the job-share partners already works for the organization and has an established reputation. In that case, you will have to sell the idea to management and then find the right partner. If both you and your prospective partner already work for the company, you are one step ahead and should present your proposal as a team.

If you are a high performer that the company would hate to lose, you will likely have an easier time negotiating a job share with management. But do not dismiss the idea of a job share if you have not been a star performer. Recognizing that burnout is sometimes the cause of shoddy work, some companies, such as the Montreal-based Royal Bank of Canada, have stated that they are specifically willing to consider job sharing for poor performers when it can be determined that burnout is largely responsible for the poor performance.[5]

Job sharing is advantageous to the company. Job sharers offer the following hints to help you convince management that job sharing is not only a viable concept, but also to the company's advantage:

■ **Full coverage.** Unlike in a job in which an individual takes vacation and has sick days, there is *no* downtime in a job share. An employer has full coverage because there is a team member who can fill in, if necessary, while the other member is out. This is a particularly great selling strategy to use if you are proposing a job share that may cost the company additional expense (either in overlapping hours or in benefits). Royal Bank of Canada determined that the additional $450 a year they incurred per job-share team was outweighed by the savings they realized in recruitment and training and the cost of coverage during vacations.[6]

■ **Motivated employees resistant to burnout.** Because the company is meeting the job sharers' personal needs, the company gets two employees who are totally motivated to make the arrangement work. The job sharers are also unlikely to suffer from burnout, since they are getting the necessary downtime needed to attend to their other commitments. Due to the downsizing of the last decade, many employees are asked to manage larger-than-life workloads that take their toll. With a job share, this workload is more manageable.

■ **Greater breadth of expertise.** The company benefits when there are two talented, capable heads with complementary

[5]Bibi S. Watson, "Share and Share Alike," *American Management Association* (October 1995): 50.
    [6]Ibid.

skills working on projects. This combined brainpower will often yield better and more refined ideas. There is truth to the old adage that "two heads are always better than one."

■ **Better response to a department's workload peaks.** In a job-share situation, there are two people to call on to help out during unusually busy times. In a true emergency, the company has more resources to draw upon.

■ **Potential for reduced-training costs and better succession planning.** By pairing a pro and an amateur together in a job share, companies can improve their succession planning and reduce training and development costs. The more experienced team member trains the "amateur." The company saves salary expense, paying the less experienced employee less. In total, the team is paid less than a full-time experienced employee would be paid. At the same time, the company is grooming the junior team member.

■ **The halo effect.** By considering a job share, a company sends a message to the rest of its employees: "There's nothing sacred here. We can try new ways to work." When a company wants to retain its high-performing employees, demonstrating an openness to alternative ways to work is an effective tool. Ellen Gabriel noted that by increasing the availability of alternative work options in the firm's accounting/auditing division, Deloitte & Touche had unexpected success retaining women in their consulting division. The fact that the options were available and being used in the accounting practice persuaded consulting women that the company was serious about helping employees manage work/life needs.

Overcome employers' common objections. Despite your best efforts to tout the advantages of job sharing to your company, your employer will likely throw up some objections that you need to be prepared to answer.

■ **A job share will cost the company more money.** Employers frequently cite an increase in cost for benefits, salary, and office space. Job-share teams need to think through not only how the work will be shared, but also how the salary, benefits, and office space will be handled. Some teams share office space. Others negotiate telecommuting for all or part of their workweek schedule.

Salary and benefits can be negotiated. Are you willing to split one person's full-time salary? Job sharers who want additional salary and/or benefits, particularly if there is an overlapping day, must justify the cost. Show management that there will be productivity improvements to make up for the additional cost. Hillary and Faye, a team with a high-tech firm, took on extra projects to justify the cost of their overlapping day.

Anna and Marybeth convinced their company to switch from a head-count system to a full-time equivalency system that appropriates expenses based on the number of hours worked instead of the number of people working those hours. Similarly, a pair of marketing consultants proposed that management staff them based on 120 percent of one consultant's billable hours. Yet another team pointed to the cost of hiring and training a new employee to combat the cost of overlapping time.

■ **Problems evaluating as a team.** What if one employee shines and the other does not? Most teams encourage managers to evaluate them as a team, rather than as individuals, and to let the team handle any inequities.

To assist management in evaluating them and the job-share arrangement, Hillary and Faye sent out a questionnaire to their colleagues, subordinates, and managers after their job share had been in place for six months. Based on the responses, Hillary and Faye were able to capture what was working and what needed improvement in their job share. They had time to tweak their working arrangement long before their annual performance review. Hillary and Faye were also able to use the survey results as a tool to manage up, letting their manager know that people affected by their job share felt the arrangement was working well.

■ **Personality conflicts within the team.** Many employers are concerned they are going to find themselves in the middle of personality conflicts should the team hit bumpy times. Some teams have a plan in place, a sort of prenuptial agreement, should the team reach "irreconcilable differences." Such a plan often makes management more comfortable that even in the worst case, the team has thought through what to do—and the job will get done. Hillary and Faye's management wanted them to think through what would happen if one person wanted out of the arrangement.

Finding the right partner. Finding the right partner is critical. Anna and Marybeth had worked together before they became job-share partners. They knew they had similar work styles, similar standards of work quality, and similar views of evaluating people. They trusted each other completely. In short, remember that no one will be the perfect job-share partner. Look for someone who mirrors you in areas that are important to you, such as work style and quality of work, yet complements you in skill set. Look for someone you trust.

■ **Compatible work styles/complementary skill sets.** Do not necessarily look for someone with the same skill set and background as yours. Rather, find someone whose skills complement your own. Look for someone whose ego is similar to yours, someone who will be comfortable in a collaborative relationship, rather than a competitive one. Your partner should manage deadlines and handle criticism as you do.

Anna and Marybeth advise taking the Meyers Briggs or a similar assessment test, which they found to be a good indicator of compatible work styles.

■ **Trust is imperative.** This cannot be overstated. You must be able to trust your partner completely—trust her to be fully committed to the job share, to do her best work, to promote the team, not herself, and to fully communicate with you at all times. Without this trust, the team will be rendered ineffective from the start.

"Management Said Okay. And I Found a Partner. Now What?"

What does it take to make a great job-share team? Job sharers offer the following tips for crafting a successful job-share arrangement.

Communication is key. Communication is paramount to the success of the team. Without detailed, full communication between partners, the job share is doomed. Developing a communication process that works to keep both partners informed is the most critical system the team must work out. Job sharers warn that, at least in the beginning, full communication between the partners is time-consuming and requires a level of detailed effort that many did not expend when they held their own individual jobs. Job sharers offer the following strategies to make the communication process work.

The weekly handoff. Some teams structure weekly overlap time, when both partners are in the office. During this overlap, the job-share partners review the status of all projects and agree on who is going to do what and by when in the week ahead. To ensure that there is no confusion, during the weekly handoff, partners review all decisions made and communicated to colleagues. Rather than overlap time, some teams simply maintain a detailed computer log of projects with places for status reports and comments. This list usually includes a "hit list" of critical upcoming tasks. Teams that do not overlap usually have "handoff phone calls," when one partner is finishing and the other starting.

Some teams divide the workweek such that one partner works Monday, Tuesday, and half of Wednesday and the other partner works the second half of Wednesday, Thursday, and Friday. Sometimes both partners work a full day on Wednesday. Alternatively, some teams divide work such that each partner works two days one week and three days the next. Regardless, each partner hands off to the other only once per week.

Take copious notes. You will attend meetings for your partner and she for you. You may attend a project-launch meeting, and she may end up attending the follow-up meeting. It is critical that both of you know what transpired at meetings that occurred on your days off. Some team members go so far as to make notes of body language to help the other person fully participate in meetings they did not attend.

Office nuts and bolts. You and your partner should agree on a filing system, what to do with mail, who reads what, etc. Determine whether you will share an e-mail address and voice mail or whether you will each have these and will copy each other on everything. Several teams use a joint voice-mail box so that peers and clients can leave one message for the team. On any given day, the member who is working picks up messages left in the joint mailbox. The partners also have separate boxes so that they can leave frequent, detailed messages for each other and so that family members can leave private messages.

Regular "partnership" meetings. Build in a time to meet monthly to talk about the job share. What is working? What needs improvement? Where do you each see yourself in the future? Anna and Marybeth regularly ask each other, "Is this still working for you? What interests you next?" Luckily, they have both wanted to move their careers in similar directions. They have been able to move to new positions together. But that is not always the case. Job-share partners must share changing career aspirations so that each team member can adequately prepare her next move.

Do not be attached to your own ideas. Just as when you are a member of any effective team, you cannot be attached to your own ideas. As Laura said of her job-share experience, "You have double the ideas but only single time. While it is a real advantage to get the benefit of two heads, you can't spend too much time collaborating and brainstorming. Otherwise, it defeats the purpose of the job share because the job becomes too labor intensive. Therefore, your partner must have ideas of her own that you respect and are willing to let represent you."

In many cases, the shared job originally belonged to one of the team members prior to the job share. That person must be willing to give up some control and be open to the idea that there is more than one way to get the job done.

Create a self-managed work team. Job shares work best when they are self-managed work teams. Partners fill in for each other and resolve any disputes within the team. Managers assign a project to the team, much as they would assign a project to one individual employee. The team decides how the project will get done. Hillary and Faye make things as easy as possible for their supervisor. Hillary says, "Our job share should be no more difficult to manage than any other personnel."

Each team must figure out how to divide job duties and responsibilities—what works best for the team members and the job requirements. Some job shares virtually split a job into two part-time jobs, each with different responsibilities. More frequently, both team members are involved in nearly all projects. The work is "seamless," with only the team members themselves knowing who did what.

Check your ego at the door. You cannot compete with your partner. If you compete with your partner, you will kill all trust that exists between you. You may find this hurdle hard to get over, especially if you are an overachieving fast-tracker accustomed to competing with your peers. All of a sudden, you have to stop competing with one of them.

Not only must job sharers stop competing with each other, they must be able to share the spotlight. You cannot focus attention on your contribution by saying, "*I* did that." The focus must remain on the team's efforts—"*We* did that." If you are not confident that you will be comfortable promoting the team rather than yourself, this option is not for you.

Both partners must understand that there may be a variance in compensation between the team members, particularly if one partner brings more experience to the position.

Be okay with the spotlight. Job shares are often unique, and therefore, watched closely. Teams are sometimes held to a higher standard than an individual employee. If anything falls through the cracks, management may blame the job-share arrangement. An error that would normally be okay may be magnified and manipulated to show why job sharing does not work. Most teams work even harder than they did as individuals to ensure that the work is top-notch.

Do not let people pit one of you against the other. Like small children who hear "No" from one parent and immediately run to the other, some employees and clients will try to pit one partner against the other, depending on the answer they are looking for. Job-share partners must be prepared to back each other up even if they do not always agree with the other partner's response.

Develop a plan for how you can move on as a team. Job sharing is a great way to keep your career on track because you can share a challenging position on a truly part-time basis. But your career mobility may be limited. Changing jobs as a team requires selling a new management, peer, and subordinate group on the feasibility of a job share. If the new group is unwilling to consider this alternative, your career movement may be limited for the duration of the job-share arrangement.

Is Job Sharing the Right Option for You?

Ask yourself the following questions:

- Do you want to work part-time? Can you live with the reduced pay and benefits that accompany working part-time?
- Are you well-organized? Are you a good communicator? Are you detail-focused enough to ensure that someone else can make sense of what you have done?
- Can you work collaboratively as a team, putting the team's needs ahead of your own?
- Can you trust someone else to make decisions on your behalf without second-guessing? Once a decision is made, can you support your partner even if you do not fully agree with the decision?
- Will you feel comfortable letting someone else handle a meeting or a presentation on your day off?
- Are you able to diplomatically help managers learn how to manage you and your partner as a team?
- Are you committed to making the job share work?
- Can you let go of your competitiveness if an intriguing project comes in or an exciting meeting is scheduled on your day off?
- Are you open and flexible about how things get done? Will you welcome your partner's input or bristle when it differs from your own ideas?

seven

"I Want to Be My Own Boss"

There are nearly 9.1 million woman-owned businesses in the United States today.[1] These range from sole-proprietor independent consultants to multimillion-dollar enterprises. More than half of the small businesses being started in this country today are owned by women. For many women, even though they may work as many hours (or more) than they did working for a corporation, having flexibility and control over their schedule enables them to create and manage their life collage. Owning a business serves women's collages on many fronts—it provides them the ability to earn an income and allows

[1]National Foundation for Women Business Owners (NFWBO) study, "1999 Facts on Women-Owned Businesses: Trends in the U.S. and 50 States," 11 May 1999. See http://www.NFWBO.org.

opportunities for personal development. At the same time, these women can give back to their community by providing jobs and/or high-quality products and services. Many entrepreneurial moms also get the benefit of bringing children to work or basing the business in their home to be near their children.

There are two avenues to self-employment:

- Freelancing, which is also known as working as an independent consultant or contractor
- Owning and running a business, including starting a business, purchasing an existing business, or buying a franchise

Historically, freelancing was reserved for the creative fields— graphic designers, writers, photographers, and the like. In the last few years, driven by a combination of corporate downsizing and the desire to have more control over their schedule, business and professional women have adapted the freelance model and christened it "independent consulting." Today, there are successful independent consultants in nearly every field, from computers and systems to accountants, marketers, human-resource professionals, doctors, and lawyers.

There is no hard-and-fast distinction between independent consulting and owning and running your own business. For the purposes of this discussion, the distinction stems from what is planned for the business long term. Women who start their own business plan to grow it beyond themselves, eventually hiring employees and moving into office or retail space beyond their homes. They may envision creating a sellable entity or a legacy to pass on to relatives. By definition, independent contractors work on their own and do not have employees, although they may subcontract specific projects or parts of projects. Usually a freelancer does not have a sellable entity, because without her, there is no business.

GOING FREELANCE: BECOMING A SUCCESSFUL
INDEPENDENT CONTRACTOR

Meet two women: April, who is freelancing while she figures out what is next for her, and Megan, who has adopted freelancing as a permanent way of life.

At forty-five, April had built a successful career with a promotions agency. Over nearly twenty years, she had risen to the vice-president level managing a team of people. She had helped nurture the company from infancy to prominence in its field. By all outward standards, it was a plum job. Everyone thought April had arrived. And yet, she was miserable.

In thinking about her career path, April reflects on her childhood. "My dad had only daughters. He grew up poor and rose to affluence. He wanted us to have nice things. He said, 'Career, career, career.' My dad died when I was in my mid-twenties. He would have relished my accomplishments, savored them." Her hand motioning like a plane taking off, April adds, "He taught me 'Zoom—Tycoon!' "

Forever trying to prove something to herself, April climbed the corporate ladder. "When I got out of college, I went straight to work. My view of success at the time was warped. A salary meant I could acquire things. I had a healthy dose of materialism. At the same time, I didn't think I was good enough. I lacked courage and had self-esteem problems. But, I fought my insecurities and forged ahead."

As she climbed the ladder, April was outwardly very successful, but inwardly she was pained. "I got used to the running— being frantic. I was totally focused on work. It was my life. I was still trying to prove myself. I didn't have a full life. I was a commodity to the company. I was a creative director. I managed other creatives. And yet, I felt robbed. What about my own creativity? At the same time, I felt like I couldn't leave. I so identified with the company and the job and the salary. I didn't have the courage to quit."

April began to think about what she might do. She attended a career workshop and joined a group whose members were all in career transition. At one point, April had to have foot surgery. "I was on the couch. I had to sit still, which is so unlike me. Someone suggested that I use the time to read The Artist's Way by Julia Cameron. That book really spoke to me, got me thinking." At that point, April knew she had to do something.

Before leaving her job for freelance work, April tried another option. She negotiated a part-time arrangement with her company where she worked on special projects that nurtured her personal creative side. April changed functions within the organization. She initiated the firm's first training department and got involved in the company's development. But one day she came to a realization: "There wasn't anything else for me to do in the company and still be me. The truth is, it took there being nothing for me to do for me to finally get it. I had to go."

A single, self-supporting woman, April had to figure out how to pay her bills without her salary before she could quit. She decided to do freelance work while she took some time to think about what she wanted to do next. She figured that the freelance work would pay her bills, but at the same time she would be able to relax and take life slower than she had been. April was determined to recalibrate her life, to bring new elements into her life collage and rearrange things a bit. Freelancing would give her the freedom to do that.

Before formally leaving her job, April let her colleagues within the company know that she was looking for contract work. She contacted many of the people she had worked with over the years who had moved on to other companies. And she let some of her clients know that she was leaving but would be available for any projects that were too small or otherwise not appropriate for the company to undertake. Of her last day as an employee, April *says, "I couldn't wait to leave. I rolled all the windows down in my car and hollered all the way down the highway on my last drive home."*

Four weeks after leaving her job, April got her first project. In the ensuing six months, she made enough money to cover her expenses, but left enough free time to think about what she really wanted to do next. Looking back on those six months, April says, "There were some very dry spells. I got anxious. But mostly I'm okay. Now, I have a coach to help me through the transition. She challenges me, asks me the hard questions. I'm learning to tune everything else out when working at home."

April is rebuilding the other aspects of her life. "I'm in aerobics classes. I work out with a trainer. I've enjoyed a summer for the first time in years. I'm volunteering with children in my community. I take piano lessons, go on walks, and enjoy cooking. I never had time for any of these things before. My freelance work fuels my dream. I'm comfortable living with the question of what I really want to do next."

Meet Megan. At thirty-two, Megan has been freelancing for nearly three years. Her work is concentrated in two areas—computer training and database development. Based in New England, Megan has a number of her own clients, both for profit and nonprofit organizations. And, she has relationships with several companies that place training professionals in temporary assignments. "On average, I have about twenty-five to thirty-five billable hours a week, plus about five hours of nonbillable administrative stuff. Sometimes I have a couple of fifty- to sixty-hour weeks, and then I have a couple of weeks that I take off. It varies."

When Megan resigned from her last full-time job, with a management-consulting company, they offered her a part-time option to keep her. "I just didn't want to do it. [My concern] was that I felt like I could always convince myself to stay a little longer.

But the core of the work wasn't interesting to me. If I didn't force myself to go figure out what did interest me, I figured I could hang out there [in limbo] forever.

"When I quit, I had no idea what I was going to do." Of the first few weeks after she quit, Megan says, "I felt anxious. I remember I did a lot of knitting. I did go through the help-wanted ads just to see what was out there. I did yank out a couple of career books and go through those. I went to the university where I had gone to school and took some interest tests and stuff like that. I don't remember what else I did. There was a lot of nothing time in there. I think I watched more than my fair share of soaps. The answer emerged. I think there may have been stuff going on in the back of my mind that I wasn't aware of because somehow I came up with a good answer for me. [I wasn't] conscious of that happening. I needed to vegetate for a while. That was what I was consciously accomplishing.

"After a few months, my husband began asking, 'Are you ever going back to work?' He asked that several times. We definitely had some very vocal discussions. Some of it was me whining and saying, 'I'm not ready. I don't know what I want to do. I'm still looking.' I was scared. I was thinking, 'Oh my God, it's been months, and I still don't know what I want to do. How am I ever going to figure this out? I'm going to have to go back and work someplace that I don't like.'"

Slowly, Megan began to take steps. She began talking to people. She responded to ads in the newspaper that caught her eye. She went to talk to a company that hired freelance computer trainers. One of them hired her for a few days. Slowly, Megan figured it out, saying to herself, "Hey, this isn't bad. I like this and can do a pretty good job at it." She adds, "I sent out letters to several other training companies in my area." Megan's freelance practice took off. Looking back, Megan likens her experience to getting into cold water at a pool. "It always takes me a long time to get into the pool because the water's cold. But once I get in I realize, 'Wow! This is nice.' There's no fear anymore."

One of the challenges that Megan faced was how to talk about her career change during interviews or when trying to sell new projects. "You have to explain why you have reinvented your work/ life—in my case, several times—to someone who might not ever make significant changes in their own career. You have to explain your choices to someone who might not accept [them as] a normal part of life.

"I think you have to know yourself. If you don't really know why you made the choices you did, it will be very hard to explain to someone else. I think some of that comes down to if your convictions are strong enough. If you really believe that what you did was the right thing, and it helps you in what you are planning on doing next, then that goes a long way toward paving over the bumps."

Megan knows now that she is in the right place. "I'm someone who needs a lot of feedback. I receive a course evaluation at the end of every class I teach. I may be tired in the morning going to work, but I never dread going to work. I always feel more energized at the end of the day than at the beginning of the day. Occasionally, when I see old business-school friends (who are making tons of money, but working mega-hours), I compare myself to them. Sometimes I think about the money. But then I remind myself that I really like what I am doing."

Megan offered a parting thought: "The fears that are holding you back are just fears. They may not be grounded in reality. It was easier to find business than I thought it would be. It has also been easier to say no to projects I don't want. Initially, [I had to get] over the fear of, 'If I say no, they're never going to call me again.' Or, 'Gosh, I really should do this because it would be nice to have the income.' Getting over [the fear] and being able to say no was easier—and had fewer ramifications—than I expected.

"I always knew that I wanted to do something other than work. Early in my work life, all I really had time for was work." *Today, Megan enjoys her flexibility and has brought some of her childhood loves into her adult collage. A competitive figure skater*

as a youngster, Megan has returned to the ice. She is also an accomplished chef. Freelancing provides her the flexibility to be able to handle many of life's errands during the week so that she and her husband have more quality time together on weekends.

"What Is This Option Really Like?"

April and Megan used freelancing for different purposes. April became a freelancer as a stopgap measure to take care of her financial needs while she determined her next career move. Megan has made freelancing a permanent career choice. But both women found that the flexibility that freelancing provides has enabled them to create and manage a diversified life collage, even if the anxiety of not having enough work—or having too much work— is sometimes difficult to handle.

As April and Megan demonstrate, rather than being a permanent employee, freelancers move from employer to employer— client to client—on a contract basis. As independent contractors, freelancers must continually find new business, but they can also decide which projects to accept and which to decline.

Many people think of freelancing as "doing temp work"—and in a way it is. Temporary work used to be limited to administrative or secretarial functions. Today, women are doing temporary work in virtually all professions. Freelance marketers, trainers, social workers, engineers, accountants, doctors, and lawyers contributed to this book. Here's what you can expect as a freelancer.

Control and flexibility. Many women say that freelancing offers them more control over their lives. One happy freelancer said, "Once you think out of the box that your title and place of employment define your position in life, it opens up vast new horizons to achieving whatever goals you have for meeting your definition of success and ideal work/life scenarios. It's more about taking control of your own skills and deciding what projects are the most profitable use of your working time and doing them as opposed to having someone else define those things for you. It's wonderfully liberating."

Another successful freelancer spoke about her choice. "My husband and sons really wanted me to quit my job because all I did was complain about it. I wanted an opportunity to take charge of my life while still working and still having time to be with my sons. So, [this] seemed a good way to go. I originally planned to work about half-time. I felt I could afford to earn less as a consultant than I had in a full-time job. The irony is that I make a lot more money now, while not working any harder, and have more control over my hours and calendar."

As a contractor, you always have the choice to turn down an assignment. Of course, when you turn down an assignment, you do not get paid. You also run the risk that the client who offered you the assignment might not offer you another. Most women cannot afford to turn down many projects. However, the choice is yours. As Claire, an educational-publishing freelancer, said, "Increasingly, I found myself working seven days a week for months at a time, twelve to fourteen hours a day. It just became too much. I loved the work I was doing, so rather than switch to another field, I decided to freelance. This has enabled me to work as much—or as little—as I want and to take the projects that interest me."

In addition to having flexibility to accept or (politely) reject a particular job, freelancers also often have flexibility to decide where and/or when the work gets done. Some freelance assignments will require you to be on-site at the client organization during business hours, but many will not. Many projects will have deadlines, but the work can be done at home and done when you want, provided it is completed by the deadline. Claire continued, "I don't have to wear business suits every day to make a living. I do just fine with my computer and home office, wearing shorts and T-shirts. I can even go outside whenever I want, or take a day off whenever I please."

Another woman said, "I have control over my time and how it is spent. I wanted to be able to take care of myself and be available to my child, which is very difficult for single working mothers." Still another commented, "If I want to be with my sons or husband on a weekday, I can. I can take vacations to suit their calendars. I can work when they are in bed or off with friends."

One single woman loves to travel. She works on projects for several months, then travels for one or two months. She works through a company that specializes in matching professionals such as herself in temporary positions. The agency introduces her to prospective clients and helps her close the sale. When she returns from a trip, she lets the agency know she is available. It may take a few weeks, a month, or sometimes longer before she is reassigned. She then works for several months before taking off on another trip.

Uncertainty and anxiety—the other side of control and flexibility. If freelancers routinely cite control and flexibility as the best things about the way they work, they just as routinely cite uncertainty and the anxiety it creates as the worst things about freelancing. A freelancer's income and workload are on a perennial roller coaster. If you need to know exactly how much money you are going to bring home each week or month, freelancing is not for you. This up-and-down income will always be the case, no matter how long you are a freelancer. It is simply part of the job description. Says one woman, "I still have times when I become overwhelmed with worry about where my next paycheck will come from. So far, these worries have been needless, but when I am between assignments, I do not always remember that."

Many women can deal with this uncertainty in the short term, if they are using freelancing as a stepping stone to what they really want to do. However, if you are thinking of building a freelance practice over the long term, understand that the uncertainty never goes away. You have to learn to live with it. Marcy, who recently left a marketing job with a consumer food company, does not like the uncertainty. She is freelancing to pay her mortgage, but recognizes the uncertainty is not something she can handle on a regular basis. She hopes to be hired by one of her clients.

Bobbie, a freelance marketer serving the financial-services industry, put it this way: "There are days when I get up and think I'll never get another client. Then the phone rings. The hardest part is to keep a level state of mind. Managing the ebb and flow is difficult. Sometimes I have nothing to do, then out of the blue. . . ! If you do a good job, it does work out. Some weeks I work twenty hours, some weeks sixty hours." She goes on to add, "It's hardest to walk away from the office. I try to do that if I'm in a funk. Then I come back and the phone has rung. Sometimes you just have to break away. That's why God made answering machines!"

It is natural to be anxious. The trick is not to let it paralyze you. For Bobbie, that means getting away from the office. For Deborah, it means staying put in the office and making more phone calls. "When I first started, there was a flurry of projects. Then a dry spell hit. I panicked. I would make phone calls to hear prospective clients talk about projects that might happen in the future. It was somewhat comforting. I would hang on to the possibility." If you can make calls to prospective clients or contacts even when anxious, do it, especially if it makes you feel better. If, however, you are so anxious that you simply cannot make a phone call, or do not feel like you can sound confident on the phone, then take a break. Get out of your office. Do not languish, staring at the phone and willing it to ring. You will only make yourself more anxious than you already are. Look to Chapter 9 for additional tips on handling your anxiety.

A fluctuating income. The revenue roller coaster does not mean that you will earn less money as a freelancer, although you may. Some women are able to earn more money as freelancers than they ever made as full-time employees. Others report earning the same amount of money, but in fewer hours. Regardless of whether you earn more, less, or the same money, your income will likely be uneven. Some months are great, while others may be as dry as the desert in summer. As one freelancer put it, "The worst thing about freelancing is the periodic money worries—when I have no income and no immediate job prospects." Another says simply, "This is not for the faint of heart." If you do not already have the skill, you need to develop the ability to manage your cash flow to carry you through the dry spells.

Your schedule is not routine. Not only will your income ebb and flow, so will the amount of time you work. If you are someone who likes a regular routine, working certain days and certain hours, freelancing is probably not a long-term solution for you. As Peggy, a full-time, boundary-setting attorney, says, "I wanted routine and control. Am I in control of my life or is my life in control of me? When I have a routine, I feel in control." Peggy freely admits that freelancing is not for her. There are two things you can do to make your unpredictable schedule palatable.

■ **Learn to enjoy your time "off."** Successful freelancers learn to enjoy the time when there is little work. Most women report that, over time, they are able to take advantage of slow times to pursue hobbies or personal interests or to catch up with friends, rather than sitting at their desks fretting over when the next project is going to come along. Jillian, a single mom and freelance marketing consultant, says, "At my first slow time, I felt panic. But I used the time to put a brochure together. I made some phone calls. That made me feel like I had some control—with emphasis on feel. I did question myself. Was this going to work? No one was paying my bills and I had a child. But then the phone rang. Everything was okay for a while. Then there would be another hiatus. Now, I try to enjoy the hiatus. It's an opportunity to update files, clean up, get organized, etc. Now, six years out, in the last one and a half years, I finally feel I can make it through the lulls to the other side." After going through the cycle of work a few times, many women report that they have gained the confidence during slow times to know that the busy times will come again.

■ **Be prepared for the crazy times.** Just as you will have slow times, you will also have periods when you are working like crazy to meet a tight deadline. When there seems like there is too much work and not enough time, Barbara says, "I try to remember that nobody's going to die here. I ask for support from my husband and kids. I let them know what I need. The kids feel good that they can contribute." These crunch periods do not last forever. Keep your eye on the light at the end of the tunnel and forge ahead. Also, if you choose, you can subcontract work to other freelancers.

Assignments come in all shapes, sizes, and colors. Some projects last for days, others for weeks or months. Sometimes assignments will be part-time or do-at-home. Sometimes the client will want you on-site, full-time for the duration of the project.

Freelancers are rarely bored. Says one freelancer, "I became an independent contractor, which allowed me to pick the assignments I would accept. I was approached by several different agencies. I chose the one that would allow me to have the broadest scope, to do multiple tasks." For some women, these multiple experiences help expand their skill set, giving them more to offer future clients or employers.

You may occasionally end up on a project that you do not like. You may have a difficult or hostile client. But no matter how bad the situation might get, the end is in sight. When it is over, you start fresh on a new assignment with a new client. You do not have to work with that hostile client again. And many freelancers work on more than one project at a time, so even if one project turns out to be unpleasant, you may be working on other projects that you enjoy.

Constant newness can get old. Freelancers are constantly walking into new situations. Each time you start a new project, it is like starting a new job. Each time you meet with a prospective client, it is similar to a job interview. While some women thrive on constantly taking on new projects, other long-term freelancers find this challenging. Says one woman, "Getting past the fear of doing new things, of taking risks, was very hard for me, but it resulted in my feeling much more confident about myself." Says another, "I really hate changing jobs, so I do find the transition between contracts quite trying. Luckily, my people skills carry me through those rough first days. And I've been called back to most of the companies I work at!"

Rejection is part of the game. When looking for a job, you do not get an offer after every interview. The same is true of freelance work—you will prepare and present proposals to prospective clients only to have them say no. The "no" may have nothing to do with you. The client may simply decide they do not need the project done. But no is still no. You may have invested several hours in that proposal—for naught. Of course, you never know when that prospective client who says no today may call you back in a month for an entirely different project.

On your own and by yourself. Many work-at-home issues, such as the isolation and the self-discipline required, discussed in the "Telecommuting" section of Chapter 5, hold true here. Often these issues are magnified for the freelancer. One woman laments, "I feel lonely at times and need to reach out to counter that." While telecommuters have a regular set of colleagues with whom they communicate every day, freelancers—especially those whose projects are completed almost entirely from their home offices—often find that they are isolated and alone on a daily basis. Says another freelancer, "The worst thing for me is the isolation from intellectual stimulation on a daily basis."

Once your freelance practice is up and running, you may want to look into subletting an office from a company with extra space. Sally, a freelance nonprofit consultant, sublet space from a public-relations firm. She liked getting out of her house and enjoyed having others around with whom she could bounce around ideas.

Sheila thought freelance marketing was what she wanted. "I had been bitten by the entrepreneurial bug. In fact, that is one of the reasons I went to work for a consulting firm. I wanted to get some experience on the consulting side because I didn't know what I was doing. I thought if I worked for a firm for a year or two, I could figure out how to structure engagements and contracts so I could do it on my own."

Sheila did freelance work for about one and a half years before deciding it was not for her. She returned to a management position in an organization where she is now an ardent boundary-setter. "I felt so isolated [as a freelancer]. I think one of the things I do best is gather people together to work toward a common target, to get everybody moving in one direction. I'm not that good doing it all on my own. When you are on your own, you can influence your clients, but it's not the same as working with the teams of people I have in place now.

"The other thing is that I got so attached to my clients, it made me crazy. I remember one client. I just loved those people and we were on this roll with these great things. The work I had done was materializing, but I had to hand it off to them to implement because you have to manage the size of these engagements. At some point they will say to you, 'Okay, you've done what we need. Now, move on to your next project.' I had separation anxiety, big time. I knew I needed to get back into an organization as opposed to being on my own." One advantage of freelancing is you will no longer have to deal with intra-office politics. You will no longer be competitive with your coworkers. But the downside is you may miss being part of a team.

Another aspect of being on your own is that you will rarely get the verbal feedback that is common in some work settings. You will know you did a good job when clients hire you for another project, but you may miss hearing, "You did great work. Thanks." Here is how one freelancer deals with this issue: "[Time] spent chatting with coworkers, hearing their ideas, and receiving direct encouragement and praise, is missing. I make up for this by patting myself on the back for work well done. I spend quality time with friends I have chosen, not just people I have to work with because the company hired them."

Successful freelancers say it is critical to know other freelancers. It does not matter whether these other freelancers work in your field or an entirely different field. Freelancers, regardless of their area of expertise, face common dilemmas. Develop a cadre of freelance "colleagues" you can call on for ideas, inspiration, and feedback—not to mention lunch dates and "morning coffee klatch" conversation. As one freelancer complained, "Sometimes I miss the social aspect of working in an office." Happy freelancers create their own "office social network." If you have not already established your board of directors, as suggested in Chapter 4, get going!

You're the chief, the cook, and the bottle washer. When you freelance, you are responsible for everything—you are secretary, furniture mover, computer specialist, bookkeeper, etc. Some freelancers hire part-time secretarial help or an information-systems contractor to assist with their computer setup. But it is difficult and costly to hire someone to take care of all the miscellaneous tasks associated with running your practice. Some freelancers indicate that they are able to barter with other freelancers for some of the help they need. One computer maven, for example, needed help marketing her practice while a marketing expert needed computer assistance. They made a deal.

More often than not, you will have to do most of these business chores yourself. Beth remembers when her first file cabinet was delivered. "When I worked in a company the cabinet would come already assembled, ready for me to hang my files. Not so when you work on your own. The office-supply store delivered my cabinet. I had to put it together. It's not that it was difficult, it wasn't. But it took time—time that I could have spent selling and delivering business."

On another occasion, the hard drive in Beth's computer crashed, rendering the machine useless. "I cannot afford to be without my computer for a minute. There was no way I could wait for someone to make a house call. And the computer-repair stores wanted to keep my computer for weeks! I had no choice but to figure out how to replace the hard drive and reload the software myself. I am a bit of a technophobe, so it was exhausting and emotionally draining. I did it, but it took the better part of two days before I was up and running again."

You don't work, you don't get paid, and other "benefits." One freelancer voiced her primary lament this way: "When I get sick, there is no sick time, no vacation time, no company benefits." Furthermore, health insurance, retirement planning, and other common company benefits do not come with freelance assignments. If you are married and can be covered by your spouse's company health insurance, you may be all set. If not, you will have to find and pay for your own insurance. If you are looking for insurance, ask other freelancers what they do. Some trade associations and professional organizations offer group plans.

Retirement planning is a necessity. Freelancers can take advantage of tax savings when saving for retirement. Ask your accountant or financial advisor to help you understand your retirement-savings options.

While as a freelancer you do not get common employee benefits, there are some benefits you do get. As a self-employed person, you can deduct many business expenses from your income when you file your taxes. To take full advantage of these deductions you must keep detailed records of your expenditures and activities. Talk to an accountant to fully understand how to best keep your records so you can optimize your tax savings.

An interim solution—and a foot in the door. Many women freelance to pay their bills while they explore their options and decide on their next career move. Accepting a freelance project with a company can be a great way to "get your foot in the door." Leslie, a health care–marketing consultant, did freelance work for a firm for several months. She liked them and they liked her. She was able to negotiate a permanent part-time job. Many other women made similar moves: "I took a contract job so I could work in different companies before I made a decision about where I wanted to work permanently," said one woman. Said another, "I quit my job and did contract work for about six months until I found the right job and the right boss."

Freelancing is an ongoing journey. Unlike other options that have a sense of permanence—negotiating a telecommuting or part-time arrangement, for example—the journey to freelancing is an ongoing one. Successful freelancers are always looking for their next project. As Sally, a management consultant to nonprofit organizations, puts it, "When a project ends, there is the feeling of, 'Oh God, where is the next piece of business going to come from?' The greatest challenge is finding time to market yourself while you are delivering on existing business."

Hints to Help You Find Work and Manage Your Independent Consulting Practice

There are three ways that women typically take on freelance assignments:

1. Sell projects directly to the end client through former colleagues, friends, and other networking.
2. Find projects through a company that specializes in placing professionals in temporary-work situations. These agencies will identify consulting opportunities, introduce you to prospective clients, and help you sell the work. Occasionally, these companies will have a firm agreement with the client to complete the project and will be able to simply place you in the assignment.
3. Act as a subcontractor for a company in your field. In this situation, the company sells the business to the end client. The company then hires you to help them deliver the work. Consulting and other professional-service companies sometimes find that they have more work than their permanent staffs can deliver; at those times, firms will hire freelancers on a subcontract basis. Also, you may find that occasionally your peer freelancers have more work than they can handle or they may require a specific expertise to complete a project.

Many women, especially those who want to work freelance in the short term while they explore their options, will secure their first assignment before they quit their job. Some women quit their job and gain their first assignment simultaneously, by converting the company they work for from employer to client. Says one such freelancer, "I actually do most of my freelance work for the same company [I used to work for], but I feel much better being able to be at home and in charge of things here as well as contribut[ing] to the family income."

Advance planning—how much is enough? Many people will tell you that you should have an organized, written plan of how you are going to market yourself, deliver work, and manage clients. Most of the successful freelancers interviewed did not follow that advice. Many of these freelancers insisted that none of their colleagues had either. This is not to discourage you from planning. In fact, some planning is a good idea. But do not get caught up in planning, forever thinking that you are not quite ready. Do not let planning become another roadblock to change, your own conveniently created excuse for inaction.

At the very least, you should clearly review your financial situation. Can you support yourself for a month or two until that first project comes in? Have you figured out how to reduce your living expenses while you are developing your freelance practice? Some women experience significantly reduced earnings during their first freelance year. Others do not. Some women said, "I made a lot more money without working any harder," while others said, "My income tumbled the first year I was a freelancer." You will not know into which camp you will fall until after you get started. It is a good idea to assess your financial situation and lifestyle flexibility.

It is also a good idea to establish a time frame for developing your business. For example, you might say, "By the end of six months, I will have sold x dollars' worth of work. If I do not reach this goal, I will reconsider working on a freelance basis." That way you have a specific target in mind from which to assess your progress as a freelancer. This assessment takes into account your needs and expectations in developing business.

Your office. Perhaps the first step to becoming a freelancer is designating a place as "your office." If you are planning to work at home, read the "Telecommuting" section in Chapter 5 that addresses this issue.

You will need some basic equipment. Unlike telecommuters, whose companies often provide the equipment they need, you will have to equip your own office. A computer, printer, and telephone are absolute musts. A few years ago it might have been okay to send and receive faxes from your neighborhood copy store, but today you should be able to fax directly from your office. Similarly, clients will assume that you have e-mail and Internet access.

Given these requirements, you will need at least two business-phone lines.

How do I get work? This is the number one question would-be free-lancers ask. There is no absolute answer to this question. The following are suggested next steps to take, with some hints from successful freelancers. No two freelancers work in exactly the same way. As you proceed, you will develop your own style.

1. **Inventory your skills.** What do you have to offer? What services are you selling? Who is likely to buy what you are selling? What benefits will you be able to provide to your clients? Why should they hire you? If you have ever sold any product or service, you know that a successful salesperson knows the benefits and value of what she is selling. If you haven't done so already, you may want to complete Exercise 7, which is entitled, "What Can I Do for Hours at a Time Without Getting Bored?" (see page 103), to help identify the skills that you want to use in your work. Use the exercise's grid to begin defining the kind of services you will offer to your clients.

   You do not have to limit yourself to the skills you were using, or the job you were performing in your most recent position. If you have hobbies or other interests that could be sold and delivered on a freelance basis, you could center your free-lance practice around them. A word of caution—most women find, at least initially, that it is easier to secure freelance business in the industry and functional area where they have recently worked—where they have a demonstrated track record and a cadre of contacts. As you develop your freelance practice, you may be able to segue into new fields that interest you.

2. **Be able to articulate your capabilities.** Not only do you have to fully understand the value that you bring to a client, you also have to be able to convey those benefits in a succinct way in order to persuade a client to hire you.

You should be able to describe the work you do in a few different ways. If you are calling someone on the phone, or meeting someone in a social or informal business setting, you must be able to introduce yourself and your work in a brief, one-minute introduction. The objective of this brief introduction is not to land a contract. Rather, the objective is either to be invited to a lengthier meeting where you can present your capabilities more fully or to have the other party refer you to someone who may need your services. See the section of Chapter 4 titled "Expand Your Circle," for more information on developing this "one-minute commercial."

If you meet with a prospective client in a more formal setting, you should be able to make a ten-minute presentation, introducing yourself, the services you offer, and your qualifications. Be prepared for this presentation to be interactive— prospective clients will often interrupt. Also, be prepared to ask questions yourself. This will be as much an opportunity for you to learn more about the client and her needs as it is an opportunity for her to learn about you and your services.

You will need a business card and should create a written statement of your capabilities and qualifications. These materials should look professional, but they need not be expensive. Many freelancers opt to have their cards printed by a professional printer, but print their statement of capabilities on their own computer and laser printer so that they can continually update it as they complete projects.

3. **Use your network.** Your network is essential to finding your first project—and it is critical to every project after that. All of the freelancers interviewed secured their first project as a result of a previously established relationship. Contact people in your network and share your capabilities. Let people know that you are looking for project work. "It was a challenge to get clients," Bobbie says. "You have to go find them. Network with people from your past." As you contact people in your

network, use the capabilities statement you prepared to tell them about you and your services. Listen and offer to prepare a proposal that will address their needs.

Your network will naturally expand as you complete projects. After you complete a project or contract—after you have done a superb job—do not be afraid to ask your client to refer you to others who might be able to use your skills. Also, ask your clients for feedback on your work. This will help you do even better next time.

4. **Contact companies that place professionals in temporary work.** Many of these companies specialize in certain types of professions (e.g., social workers, marketers, or finance professionals). Others may specialize in certain industries, such as information systems. Using a placement company offers the added benefit of letting you focus on what you do best—delivering work—letting someone else do the selling. Particularly if sales is an area where you lack experience, this suggestion allows you to develop your practice and your network while you develop your selling ability.

5. **Identify subcontract opportunities.** Contact companies that provide services similar to those you are offering. If you are a trainer, contact training companies. They may be able to use you on a subcontract basis. The same goes for engineers contacting engineering-consulting firms, marketers pursuing marketing-consulting firms, etc. Consulting firms in many industries and functional areas will use subcontractors to manage the ebb and flow of their businesses. Contact those firms that work in your area of expertise. Felicia used this technique when she launched her freelance practice. "I thought I had better learn how to be a consultant. I talked to a few firms. I realized that they really needed help when they have a lot of business. It was a way for me to learn—and I wouldn't have to work full-time for someone else."

6. **Show the client that you understand her needs.** Part of that understanding is to determine which benefits are most important to her and convince her that you will deliver. When you put together your proposal, tell her how you would propose to go about meeting those needs. What steps will you take? How long will it take? Clearly show the client why she should hire you to complete the project. What benefits will she realize as a result of your work? For instance, as an external resource, one benefit is your objectivity. Or it might be your approach. Usually it is a combination of several things. You have to convince the client of the benefit to her of using you. Include a tentative project schedule, your fees, payment schedule, and any additional expenses that will likely be incurred. Present that proposal. Sell yourself. You may not get the project from the first proposal you prepare. But you will learn from the process. By the second, third, or fourth proposal, you will get a project.

7. **Put it in writing.** *Always* put the terms of your agreement with the client in writing. Most freelancers write a letter to their clients, confirming the details of the arrangement after they have reached a verbal agreement. This letter should include a description of the work to be done, a list of fees and expenses, and a schedule for project completion and payment. In the project schedule, be sure to include any steps that the client must take to move the project along. Make it clear that to keep the project on schedule, both you and the client must meet the target dates. Some freelancers, particularly those in highly technical fields or in areas where the potential liability is substantial, use formal contracts.

8. **Keep up the sales process.** Remember, every project is your last—until you find another one. Successful freelancers deliver on one project while simultaneously marketing themselves for another. The hardest part of freelancing for her, says one woman, "is having to sell myself over and over and

over. . . ." Your credibility and reputation are key. Do not commit to delivering something that you cannot. Deliver on every commitment. Be realistic about how much time each project will take so you do not take on more than you can handle. Just as you can subcontract work *from* other freelancers, you can also subcontract work *to* other freelancers.

If you choose to sell your services directly to clients, be aware of the possible pitfalls of accepting a full-time, on-site engagement. While working full-time, on-site with a client, it will be difficult to continue marketing yourself for your next project. A full-time assignment may pay well in the short term, but, when it is over, it may be some time before you are able to sell your next project.

If you are planning to do freelance work while you look for what is really next, try to avoid projects that require you to be on-site with the client on a full-time basis. Otherwise, when will you interview with prospective employers or with others who can help you explore your options? Many clients do realize that as a freelancer, you have other responsibilities and may need to be gone several hours a week. As in other negotiations, be honest. Let the client know what you need. As long as the work gets done, you may be able to build in the time you need to continue marketing yourself for your next project or to explore your future options.

9. **Form alliances with other freelancers who do the same type of work that you do.** When they have more work than they can handle, they will refer it to you. And when you have more than you can handle, refer it to them. The old saying, "What goes around, comes around," is true. You should also form alliances with people who do work related to, but different from, the work that you do. Sometimes one of your clients will ask you to do a project that falls outside your bailiwick. You want to be able to refer that client to someone you trust.

Alliances will also help you keep your sanity when you are between projects. "I have a fair number of informal alliances," Felicia says. "They help a lot. The alliances are with other people who work on their own. It is about support. These are people who understand how I feel when I call and say, 'I haven't worked in a month.' They've been there. They can relate."

How should I set my fees? The second question would-be free-lancers ask is, "How do I determine how much to charge?" And, of course, everyone wants to know, "How much will I make?"

How much you should charge and how much you will earn depends on you and the type of freelance work you do. If a project is worth x amount of dollars, you can be paid all of it if you have a direct relationship with the client. If a placement company has the relationship with the client, that company will get a portion of the fee, leaving you with less. Similarly, if a company, or another free-lancer, sold a contract to a client and wants you to help fulfill the contract, you will be paid less than if you sold the contract your-self. Think of it as if you are paying someone a sales commission for selling your work.

Before you think to yourself "If I can make more money finding my own work, then that's what I want to do. Who needs a recruiter?" note that finding freelance work takes time—a lot of it. Generally, people freelancing through agencies make less money per billable hour, but are often able to bill more hours. Freelancers who market themselves directly to clients bill more per hour, but tend to bill fewer hours because they have to spend considerable time on marketing and sales efforts—time that is not billable. While no true study has been conducted, many believe that over time, it averages out to the same thing—free-lancers represented by agencies and those who market themselves directly end up making the same amount of money per working hour.

If you work through a placement company, the recruiters will be able to give you an idea of what the client is willing to pay for each project or contract. You do not have to accept the initial figure they give you. If it sounds low, make an effort to negotiate.

If you are cultivating relationships with clients directly, the best way to figure out what—and how—to charge your clients is to ask others who do similar work what they charge. If you or people you know have hired independent consultants to do work similar to the work that you want to do, ask them what they are accustomed to paying. Do they generally pay freelancers by the hour? The day? The project? Use your network to garner this information.

Just when you think you have things all figured out, something changes. You may be working on a project that is estimated to be a six-month assignment. Two months into it, the project may be canceled. What happens to that additional four months' worth of income that you were expecting? It is gone. Many freelancers negotiate a cancellation fee up front. Whenever possible, structure your projects with defined deliverables and due dates. Arrange with the client to be paid a portion of your fee up front, with the remainder paid as project milestones are achieved. That way, if the project is canceled midstream, you are paid for the work completed.

Sometimes a client will not cancel a project but will want to drastically change the project parameters or schedule. Perhaps the original project called for completion in eight weeks, and now the client wants it in six. Or maybe the project was designed to address one business issue, and now the client wants to expand it to cover an additional issue. In either case, review the letter of agreement you prepared at the beginning of the project. If the client wants to change the schedule, before you agree to jump through hoops to meet her new deadline or risk losing the client by saying no, ask a few questions to determine what the client really needs by the new deadline. Perhaps you can adjust the project schedule to meet her needs by postponing other elements of the project. If the client is asking to broaden the project scope, you can renegotiate your fee. As you become an experienced freelancer, you will learn to expect—and handle—the unexpected.

Is Freelancing the Right Option for You?

Ask yourself the following questions:

- Can you repeatedly sell yourself? More importantly, do you want to? Will you enjoy selling yourself? Even if you are aligned with a placement company, you will have to continually present yourself to new prospective clients.
- Are you self-disciplined enough to get the work done—on time? Remember, there will be no boss hovering around, asking for daily status updates. You will have to be able to stick to a work plan on your own.
- Do you want maximum flexibility? Can you handle the uncertain income—emotionally and financially?
- How will you handle the dry spells? Will you be able to confidently reach out to prospective clients, looking for work without sounding desperate? Will you be able to enjoy the time when you are not busy? Or will you be sitting at your desk, staring at the telephone, willing it to ring, and fretting? Conversely, can you handle working at full throttle to meet a tight client deadline?
- Are you comfortable working independently? Can you be proactive, reaching out to others when isolation gets the best of you?
- If you are thinking of freelancing to cover your living expenses while you explore your options, are you willing to deal with selling yourself, the uncertainty, and other issues inherent in freelancing even for a short time?
- If you have small children who require day care, how will you handle the fluctuating demands on your time?
- Do you have proper space at home to work without interruption by other household members?

"FORGET CLIMBING THE LADDER, I WANT TO *BE* THE LADDER!": STARTING A BUSINESS

Ruth, thirty-eight, grew up with a family business. Her father owned and operated a jewelry business. Almost by osmosis, Ruth learned about the risks, opportunities, and responsibilities of being a business owner. She knew from her father that owning a business can be all-consuming. Still, Ruth thought that running her own business was the best way for her to have a career and a life. She wanted to control her own schedule as well as the kind of work she did and for whom. And she wanted to "build something" that she could leave to her children.

Ruth's road to business ownership has been bumpy. As Ruth tells the story, "About five years into my interior-design career, I was working for a small firm. When the owner was ready to retire, I expressed an interest in buying the business. My boss, the owner, agreed to teach me about the business. Because my boss's health failed, I ended up buying the business more quickly than I had planned—perhaps before I was ready. The day I signed the bank loan to purchase the company, my husband initiated divorce proceedings. What an up-and-down day!"

She continues, "When I bought the business, revenues were around $7 million, and there were about twenty employees. We were located in office space just off the financial district in our city. In the first year after I bought the business, the economy went into recession. In a matter of months, both my largest client and my largest vendor went out of business. I was facing bankruptcy if I couldn't get things turned around."

Needless to say, it was a tough time for Ruth. Her determination and lifelong desire to be a successful business owner pulled her through. "I had to let most of the staff go. Those that stayed began working on straight commission. I couldn't pay salaries anymore. I had to renegotiate payment terms with my remaining vendors so that client orders for furniture and other materials would be accepted. I gave up our office space and moved the business—me and several employees—into the basement of my home. In the next three years, I built the business back to profitability."

Even as she rebuilt the business, Ruth rebuilt her life. She remarried and had a baby. "Even though it may seem odd to have several employees in your home, our basement has its own entrance. My employees were all client-service people, so they were on the road most of the time and worked out of their own homes. They came to my house for meetings. [Having the business in the basement] also provided separate space from my home life so that I could shut the door at the end of the day and leave work behind. And because I had no commute to work, I could go upstairs and lie down during my pregnancy."

Even after her daughter was born and the business returned to profitability, Ruth has kept the business in her home. "With my daughter and her nanny upstairs, I can be there if I want to or need to. We always have dinner together as a family. Sometimes I put my daughter to bed and then go back to work. It's very easy—work is in the basement. I can readily move back and forth between my three major life roles—mother, wife, and business owner."

While her business is now very healthy, Ruth has allowed it to be less profitable than it might be, hiring more people to help her so she can manage her career, her family, and her life—in other words, so she can have a life collage. As she describes it, "I am very active in the National Association of Women Business Owners and at my synagogue. These are important aspects of my life as well."

Her words of advice to women thinking of becoming business owners? "The business must suit who you are. Owning a business is more than a hobby, more than a job. It's a lifestyle. It becomes part of your family. In the end, you're the only one who can make sure that everything gets done in your business. It often requires a huge sacrifice of time. You have to have passion for your business.

*Be committed. Have a plan for both success and loss. In my busi-
ness, we don't have failures, we have 'situations' and then we figure out what to do about the 'situation.'"*

In the final analysis, Ruth says, *"I never thought my life could
work out so perfectly! I love my company. I love my child and my
child-care arrangements. I love the balance I have struck with all
of the areas of my life. I have time to enjoy my hobbies (cooking
and gardening). And most of all, I love feeling that I have control
over how my time is spent!"*

"What Is This Option Really Like?"

As Ruth's up-and-down path to business ownership shows, owning
your own business is perhaps the riskiest of the ten general options
for redesigning work. But, owning your own business also offers
the greatest potential return. There are no limits to your financial
success, except the ones that you put in place. In corporate America, when it comes to raises, promotions, choice assignments, and
the like, you are at the mercy of others. When you own your own
business, you decide how high you are going to reach, how hard
you want to work. To a large degree, you control your own destiny.
Owning her own business enabled Ruth to realize considerable
financial and professional success. At the same time, Ruth has a
high degree of control over her life, enabling her to manage her
business, family, and outside interests.

Most women business owners are driven to entrepreneurship
either by a need for greater control over their work/life, a passion
for the content of their business, or, most commonly, a combination of the two. As one woman said, "[I was] banging my head on
the glass ceiling." When Kathy left corporate America to start her
first business, a neighborhood coffee store, she said to herself,
"I'm not going to play by their [corporate America's] rules anymore. I'm going to create my own game. Forget the old boys' network, I'm joining the new girls' network!"

Some women "graduate" from working as independent consultants to owning their own business. Simone, for example, left an accounting position at a financial-services company to begin providing accounting services to individuals and small businesses as a freelancer working out of her home. A couple of years later, Simone rented office space and hired administrative staff as well as additional professional personnel to support her growing business.

Some women who choose to start a business are driven as entrepreneurs from childhood; they have a long-standing desire to be their own boss. As one woman put it, "I always knew I could never work set hours and be at the same place every day all day, five days a week. I also knew I could never be happy working for someone else." These women often speak of wanting to leave a legacy to their families and/or making a difference in their communities by providing jobs.

Flexibility, but . . . Some women choose to become business owners specifically to facilitate their life collage. Keep in mind that just as there are corporate jobs that encroach substantially on personal life, a business can as well. Therefore, many business owners are also boundary-setters. But they have the freedom to set their own boundaries without concern for what a boss or coworkers might think.

Karly, a teacher, became a business owner to better manage her life collage. "I was on maternity leave from teaching. My first child was five and my second was almost two. I had to return to the workforce but did not want to leave my two children. I solved the problem by utilizing my teaching skills [in business]. I bought an existing nursery school. I went from a classroom teacher to also being a director and owner of a business. I was able to work the hours I wanted and had my younger son with me, while my older child was in kindergarten."

Like independent consultants, business owners control their daily schedule, but they also must pay the price of saying no. As

Moira, who is co-owner of a television-repair business, says, "The best part is the flexible schedule. If one of my children is sick, I stay with him. If I want to work at night instead of in the morning, I do. If I want to take a two-hour lunch break, there is nobody to stop me! I don't feel tied down, guilty, and looked-down-upon all the time [the way I did when I worked for someone else]." On the other hand, she continues, "Nothing is steady. Income varies by month. Schedules change according to what suits the customers. I miss the stability of a job but not enough to make me go back!"

At the same time that business owners tout their flexibility, most say that building a successful business is not a part-time job. Dana started as an independent contractor, managing market research–data collection for her own clients as well as on a subcontract basis for research companies. She moved on to build her own data-collection company. Dana's company now has several employees and a healthy client roster. "My friends say that I am calmer, less intense than I was when I worked for somebody else. Before, I was working hard, but not necessarily working smart. Now, I work smarter. When I worked for somebody else, I worked ninety hours a week. Now I work fifty or fifty-five." Dana's hours are more manageable, but she could not have achieved the level of success she enjoys working part-time. The flexibility of her hours has allowed Dana to exercise and to forge many, and more varied, friendships than she had previously. And, unlike when she was an independent contractor, Dana's business has a stand-alone resale value.

Madeline, owner of two restaurants, warns, "The first few years in the restaurant business are all-consuming. There are so many details to manage. Too many things can go wrong. As the owner, you have to be there. Sure, there's flexibility. But you better plan to give it your all in the beginning if you want your business to succeed."

While, with proper planning, it is possible to take vacations as a business owner, extended leaves such as maternity leave are very difficult. As Ruth puts it, now that her second child has arrived,

"Maternity leave is a joke [if you have your own business]. My office manager is out sick today. I have a new salesman starting next week [that I have to train]. One of my customer-service representatives has called me five times today with problems at a customer installation." All of this is going on while Ruth is dealing with the sleep deprivation that comes with new motherhood. She is managing work situations around her breast-feeding schedule.

You control your work environment. Karly speaks of other advantages of owning her own business. "I am my own boss. I can set my own hours. I choose the materials to be taught. I also have a closer relationship with the children and their families. I am less formal. In a public-school setting, it was extremely formal."

Sally, who has her own nonprofit consulting business, values the control she has not only over her time and work environment, but also over the type of work she does and with whom. Frequently, as an employee, you are assigned a project and/or teammates. When you own your own business, you make the hiring decisions. You decide what business to go after, how, and for how much. Your business may pay a price, but you can "fire" a difficult client. The choice is yours.

You only have so much control—uncertainty comes with the territory. You need to learn to expect the unexpected. Independent contractors have to learn to live with uncertainty, to accept it. Business owners must learn to embrace the unexpected, to make uncertainty a friend. As Dana describes it, "I have fewer occurrences of insomnia since I started my own business. The uncertainty of having my own business is somehow more comforting than working for someone else." Chris echoes, "Business owners have to have the ability to be scared out of their wits and handle it. You need a high-energy level and optimism—you'd slit your wrists otherwise. You need spiritual peace—the understanding that no matter what happens, you'll learn from it."

There is a downside to being in control—you, and only you, are responsible. As she assessed her situation, Karly also described some of the disadvantages of being a business owner. Business owners are plagued by many of the same fears as women pursuing other options. But there are some very real day-to-day fears that are unique to new business owners. "There is always the fear that we will not have enough students to pay the bills, salaries, etc." For many entrepreneurs, even as their businesses become successful, this fear looms. Businesses reach critical junctures at different points in their development. Rather than propel her business forward, a woman may watch her business crumble due to insufficient capital and business-owner inexperience.

Almost all of the business owners we spoke to made the following comment: "No matter how many employees you have, the buck stops with you." In the end, if the customer is expecting something from your company, and an employee has the flu, it will often be you who has to fill in. You will find yourself doing just about everything at one time or another. As one owner of a retail store says, "I have to take on a lot more tasks now that I work for myself. Things such as buying products, hiring new employees, and managing the whole affair is a lot more than just the one set task that I used to do all day [in a job]." Another entrepreneur is a bit more colorful: "You wear a lot of different hats when you're in business for yourself."

You will make mistakes. If there is one guarantee about owning your own business, it is that you will make mistakes. Successful women entrepreneurs say, "Just accept it. Do not beat yourself up." As one woman said, "[If I had it to do all over again], I would have learned how to go easy on myself many years before I did."

Challenge your own thinking. Often, as part of making those inevitable mistakes, you will be forced to challenge your assumptions about yourself and how you have always thought things should be done. Cindy nearly lost her business because she kept doing things the way she had always done them in her father's business. When she started her business, she emulated him. Unfortunately, what worked for him did not work for her. "I had to break out of my father's mode of doing business. Like my father, I had fancy, and expensive, office space downtown. I dressed up for work every day, just like I had always seen him do. Only his was an established, profitable business that could afford these things. My business was just getting off the ground. The overhead was killing me! I finally realized that some of the business skills I had inherited from my dad were great. But I also had to let go of some of his practices that did not suit me and my business."

Ask for help. Cindy continues, "Successful entrepreneurs are not lone rangers. Once I knew I couldn't operate the way that I was, I had to open up and ask for help. I almost lost my business until I admitted that no one can do everything themselves. I went on to find other women who could relate to my predicament. They helped me—and they rooted for me!" Chris says it more succinctly: "Lose your ego."

An ability to contribute to your community on a larger scale. Some women business owners feel that they contribute to their community by providing jobs. Chris, who recently sold one company and is now launching another, consciously located her business in an area of her city where jobs are hard to find. Chris's business benefits from tax credits for providing jobs; her business has the employees it needs; and Chris enjoys a sense of satisfaction from her contribution. "Many people would consider the women I employ unemployable. These women aren't stupid. They just need a chance. A *real* chance, where someone actually takes the time to train them rather than throwing them into a job and magically assuming they can produce. Some of them have not worked in quite a while. You can't assume they know how to operate in an office setting. There is tremendous satisfaction with knowing I'm making a real difference in their lives." Other women business owners note that, as a company, they can contribute products or services of greater value to charitable organizations than they could as an individual.

Hints to Help You Start Your Own Business

Before you jump into business ownership, consider shadowing an entrepreneur for a few days. Or volunteer your time at her business to see what it is really like to own a business. Just as you would do informational interviews if you were changing jobs, do informational interviews with women business owners to determine if this is really right for you. You may want to attend a National Association of Women Business Owners (NAWBO) event and listen to the issues that women confront.

While there are undoubtedly successful women business owners who are not passionate about the subject of their business, many women feel as Ruth did when she said, "Choose something you love because you will put a lot of your time into your business." Make sure you like the work you will be doing. As one woman shop owner says, "I had always dreamed of owning my own little business, a shop of some sort. I sat down and listed some things that I really enjoyed doing and picked out my favorite, which was easy. Then, I had to go through a lot of steps [to make it happen]. But it was worth it." Says another woman, "I used my talent for writing and a hobby that involved collecting [videotapes of] old TV shows. I started a small-budget magazine and built it into a full-time living for my husband and me."

Three routes to business ownership. Generally, there are three options for becoming a business owner: buying a franchise, buying a business, or starting your own business. Within each of these paths, women's experiences vary greatly, depending on the industry and products or services they are offering.

Buying a franchise. There are thousands out there, in nearly every business. When you buy a franchise, you are buying use of a name brand and a way of doing business. The best part of buying a franchise is that you gain instant name recognition for your business, and you get a built-in franchisee peer group from which to learn. This peer group is made up not only of successful business owners, but business owners who are successful in the very business you arc in. Thcsc pccr franchisccs do not compctc with you so thcy are willing to share their knowledge. Generally, the franchiser owns a business concept that has been tested, proven, and replicated in several locations. When you buy a franchise, you are getting a model to follow for your business. Usually, along with the concept, the franchiser will provide you with the training and support you need to make your franchise a success. Most well-run franchises will help you find a good location for your business.

Because you are working from a proven model, when you buy a franchise, you will have fewer of your own decisions to make, and more support in making them, than if you launch your own business. Franchises carry a greater likelihood of success. As a result, buying a franchise often requires more up-front capital than starting your own business. When you become a franchisee, you will pay an initial fee and ongoing franchise fees, usually a percentage of your gross sales, for the duration of your business. And, you will not have total control over your business. The franchiser may require you to adhere to certain policies, to abide by established pricing, and to offer only certain products and services. In addition, the franchiser may set the standard hours of operation and decide on all of the business's physical characteristics. During business start-up, there are so many decisions to be made that it is great to get assistance in making some of them. However, for many business owners, making these types of decisions is the fun part of owning a business. By relinquishing the ability to select hours of operation and determine which products/services to offer (among other decisions), some of the excitement of owning a business may be lost as well.

Not all franchisers are the same. If you are thinking of buying a franchise, take a good look at what the franchiser is offering. Will you get the support and training that you need and that you are paying for? How will that training be delivered? How much help will you get after initial start-up? Will the franchiser be there for you long term? Will you get support selecting your site? If the business is a product business that requires inventory, does the franchiser offer a good system for managing inventory? If not, you should be paying a lower price for your franchise. Additionally, ask the franchiser how many stores closed in the last year. Keep in mind, franchisers will be reluctant to tell you outright, and their answers can be misleading. Some franchisers do not count stores that were in trouble and sold through fire sales as actual store closings. Find out what percentage of the franchiser's income comes from initial fees versus royalties. It is a good sign if a significant portion of the franchiser's income comes from royalties, indicating they have been in business awhile and the concept is well tested in the marketplace. Otherwise, the franchiser may be too inexperienced to provide the support you need to ensure your business's success.

Talk to a dozen people who are operating a franchise that you are considering buying. And do not just talk to the franchisees whom the franchiser recommends. Find as many locations near you as possible. These franchisees will be able to talk about how well the business concept is received in a market very similar to yours. Ask them to recount their experiences in getting up and running. How long did it take them to turn a profit? Ask them about what it is like working with the franchiser. Did the franchiser meet their expectations? Did the franchiser provide the support that was promised? Ask these franchisees what their average store sales are. You will not get them to tell you what they are personally making, but you can say to them, "I would like to be making x thousand dollars at the end of two years. Is this realistic?" Ask about and learn from their mistakes.

Remember, franchising increases your likelihood of success, but it is no panacea. It does not guarantee success. It just minimizes some of your risk. Many times, the franchise purchase process sets you up for disappointment. Because the franchiser is selling you on the concept, you are likely to go in with high expectations, assuming you will be a star operator. The reality is—by definition—more than half of all operators are performing at or below average. Less than half are performing above average. Not all can be stars. Additionally, in the first three years in business, your royalty fees will be well worth their cost because you will be working your way up the learning curve. Unless the franchiser continues to add value (e.g. improved systems), three, five, and ten years into operation, your learning slows, adding a level of frustration each month when you write your royalty check for little additional value.

Buying a business. If you buy an existing business, by definition there is an operating structure in place, and there is an existing customer base. You will not be starting from scratch. It will likely cost you more up front than starting a business from scratch, since you are paying for an ongoing enterprise. But you are likely to see a quicker return on investment as well. Ruth had the advantage of working for the company she eventually bought. By working there first, Ruth had a good working knowledge of the business and was able to provide a smooth transition with employees, vendors, and clients when she took over. There was no ramp-up time.

There was a downside for Ruth: "I was emotionally involved with the company, so I wasn't as objective as I should have been during negotiations. While working for my former boss, I was responsible for bringing in business. I unwittingly increased the value of the company, so it cost me more in the end to buy it. In hindsight, I overpaid for what I got. My attorney kept saying to me, 'Why are you doing this? You have the reputation with the clients. Why don't you go out on your own?' But at the time, I was scared. I wanted business as usual. It was an expensive price to pay. Once the recession hit, it wasn't business as usual anyway." Most women who purchased a business found "unexpected skeletons in the closet" after the deal closed. For some women, "the books were cooked." For others, like Ruth, vendor relationships were weakened near breakage, and a major customer was near bankruptcy. When you buy a business, you are inheriting someone else's problems. If you are considering buying a business, get expert assistance in examining and evaluating the operation. The more you know in advance, the less likely you are to be surprised. Ruth offers this advice: "Get a *good* attorney. Be prepared to walk away from the deal. Know as much about the business as you can. Plan for the 'what ifs.' Separate the emotion from the financial decision."

Starting a business. Starting your own business from scratch is the riskiest way to become a business owner. Roughly half of all new small businesses fail. But that means that half are successful. While this avenue to business ownership is the riskiest, it enables you to design and control your own organization, and it offers the greatest opportunity for financial rewards if you are successful.

Regardless of which option you choose, there are some hints for becoming a successful business owner:

Have a plan. If you will need to borrow money or raise capital, you will have to have a business plan. While planning for a freelance practice is helpful, when starting your own business, planning is essential.

- You must be able to define your business—clearly. What product or service do you provide? Who are your customers? What value do you provide to your customers? What is the benefit to them of doing business with you? Do not just answer these questions. Ask your would-be customers what they want. What is missing for them? How might the product or service you provide be improved? The answers to these questions will change over time. Even after your business is up, running, and successful, you will want to continually ask these questions. Getting and biding by the answers is what keeps a successful business successful!

- You must know your business—intimately. How will you deliver the product or service you offer? Will you need employees? If so, how many and to do what? How will you manage these employees and compensate them? How will you find and secure customers? How will you service customers? What about all of "the details"—those support functions—administration, insurance, equipment, technology, bookkeeping, etc.? You cannot be an expert on every aspect of your business, but you will need to know enough to be able to ask pertinent questions of experts and to understand their responses.

- You must know your competitors—intimately. Who are your competitors? What do they provide that you do not? What do you provide that they do not? Why do customers choose to do business with you rather than with your competitors? How successful are your competitors? Is their business growing? Are other potential competitors on the horizon?

- You must know your industry—intimately. What are the trends in your industry? Is it growing or shrinking? How is it changing? What is likely to be in demand in the industry in the future? What aspects of the industry are fading? Where does your business fit in the industry?

■ You must have a detailed, step-by-step action plan and time line for launching or acquiring your business.

■ You must have a detailed financial plan. How much capital will you need to launch or acquire your business? When will you need it? If you are borrowing capital, what time line do you have for repaying it? If you are raising capital from investors, what return do you project and when? One of the biggest reasons cited for new-business failure is insufficient capital. If you are planning on starting a service business, you will not have much in the way of assets for a bank to use as collateral. While you may need less financial support in a service business, you will need to think through how you will raise the money you need.

If a bank will not lend you the money you need to get up and running, consider Madeline's advice: "Get creative. Can you find ten friends who can each loan or invest $10,000?" Madeline sent out query letters to 200 friends, family, and acquaintances to raise the money she needed. Some of her friends did not want to invest in the business but were willing to lend her money for less than she could get from a bank. By locating her business in an empowerment zone, Madeline was able to get additional financial support from the government. Empowerment or enterprise zones, as they are frequently called, are impoverished areas designated by city or state government. Government encourages revitalization of these districts through a combination of tax credits, exemptions, deductions, and loans to businesses who move into the district. Businesses receive a variety of incentives for employing local residents, making capital expenditures, and renovating real estate in the area. Businesses who participate are able to lower operating expenses, thereby increasing profits. Contact your local Small Business Administration office to find out more about these zones in your city.

To complete your plan, you will need to be able to answer these questions and more. By preparing a thorough plan, you dramatically enhance your chances of success in building a profitable business. If you skip this step, you nearly guarantee failure.

Your board of advisors. Chapter 4 included the suggestion that you create your own informal "board of directors" to support you as you explore your career options and create your life collage. If you decide to own your own business, a more formal board of advisors is essential. In building this board, make sure that you have people whose professional expertise complements yours, people who have the ability to understand your business, your customers, your industry, as well as people who know you. At a minimum, your board of advisors should include an accountant, a banker, and a lawyer, among other professionals. Once you have drafted your plan, share it with your board. Revise it as they suggest. You will need your board throughout the life of your business.

Chris, who is in the middle of launching a new business that provides wellness products to middle-aged women, talks of her board: "I formed my own advisory board, with an attorney, accountant, finance manager, marketing professional, writer, a woman who had firsthand experience serving my target market, an alternative-medicine professional, and a woman business owner who had struggled and succeeded in launching her business. We meet as a group once a month. I don't pay these people, but when I need the professional services they offer, I always use them."

Review your finances. Unlike freelancing, where an initial project or contract can often be secured fairly quickly, it commonly takes much longer to turn a profit when you launch a business. You will need to be able to support yourself in the interim. As Chris, who has both acquired an existing business and started a new business, offered, "If you are launching a business, it will take four times the money and four times the time that you think it will. If you are buying an existing business, it will take four times the time and two times the money."

Service-based businesses—where the customer is paying you for a service (e.g., accounting, legal advice, management consulting, communications, etc.) and where a significant investment in equipment and inventory is not required—are sometimes profitable in the first year. In contrast, product-based businesses—where you will likely have to invest in equipment and inventory—usually take three to five years to turn a profit. This three-to-five-year projection is based on the real experiences of millions of businesses. Do not think you can fund your business and your own salary by beating the odds and turning a profit in your first year. It may happen, but most likely, it will not. If you cannot fund the growth of the business for three years, you are setting yourself up to fail.

Before you jump in and say, "Then I'll go start a service business," keep in mind there are pluses and minuses to both. While a service business has the potential to turn a profit far sooner and requires little in the way of start-up capital, it is harder to build a saleable service business because so much relies on the owner's client relationships. Often, without the owner, there is not much of a business to sell. Where the service provided to clients involves knowledge transfer—consulting, for example—the business growth may be limited by the hours the owner can work. Typically, employee recruitment and retention in knowledge-transfer businesses may be more difficult and costly because you have to pay more for professional employees than you do for laborers, and these employees are scarcer. In a new or small enterprise, it is difficult to compete with the big salaries and benefits that a larger firm can offer.

On the flip side, a product-based business requires more start-up capital and takes longer to turn a profit, but it is more likely, if the business becomes successful, that you are building a saleable entity. Business growth is not limited by the hours the owner can work, but rather by the number of products the business can sell. If the business owner gets sick, it does not impede growth of the business, at least in the short run. Weigh your long-term goals against your short-term goals as you determine which business— product or service—is right for you.

Know your tolerance for risk. Along with reviewing your finances and the financial needs of your fledgling business, you should also reflect on your own tolerance for risk. Owning and operating your own business is generally the riskiest of the options for redesigning work—at least financially. Freelancers usually have to make relatively small financial investments. If you buy a business, a franchise, or start a business of your own, you will have to make a greater financial commitment. Recent statistics show that there are as many small businesses started today with the assistance of personal credit cards as are begun with traditional bank financing. Either way, you will be personally responsible if the business fails.

Moira, along with her husband, started a television-repair business. He had the technical skills. She was an accountant and bookkeeper by training. "We auctioned off everything that wasn't nailed down and started the business with no money in the bank. It was hard at first, but there was not one moment that either of us felt we had made the wrong decision." Are you willing to cut it that close? Critically assess your feelings about risk.

Know your skills. Michael E. Gerber, author of *The E-Myth Revisited: Why Most Small Businesses Don't Work and What to Do About It,*[2] writes that entrepreneurs must be able to balance three roles to be successful: technician, manager, visionary. Many business owners are great "technicians." They know the subject matter of their business. Karly, for example, went from teaching young children in the public schools to owning a nursery school.

---

[2]Michael E. Gerber, *The E-Myth Revisited: Why Most Small Businesses Don't Work and What to Do About It* (New York: Harperbusiness, 1995).

But many would-be business owners have never run a business. They are not experienced managers. Yet, as a business owner, you must be able to handle all of the elements of management. You must be able to market and sell business. You will be your business's primary advocate. You must be able to structure the work and your employees to ensure that the work gets done—on time and at high quality. And you must also be able to manage the "business" aspects of the business—financial, human resources, legal, equipment purchases, maintenance, and technology, among others. Reflecting back on when she became the owner/operator of her nursery school, Karly says, "If I had to do this all over again, I would find out more about what is entailed in the management part of operating a business. I have had a lot of 'learn as you go' experience, which has tended to make me unsure if I am making the best decisions."

Moira's television-repair business is growing. "Just recently, we moved our business into a large commercial building." Even though she had some business training, neither Moira nor her husband had ever managed an operating concern. "What would I do differently?" she asks herself. "I would keep better records and stay more organized. Now that we have been in business for a year and a half and are opening new markets, I would like to send out flyers to all our past customers. Well, I realized that I hadn't kept our customers' addresses! Also, records for over a year get really out of hand if they are not organized and updated often."

You also need to be the company's visionary—forever looking to the future so that the business is appropriately set to realize its long-term potential. Can you imagine your business in one year? In five years? In ten? What does it look like? Can you see a path to getting there?

You will have to balance all three of these roles—technician, manager, and visionary. Many people are drawn to start a business by the sexy "visionary" part of the job. They become disillusioned when mired down in day-to-day technical and management duties. As your business grows, you may hire people to do some of this work for you. But, even with a crackerjack staff, you will have to "get your hands dirty." Conversely, if you like the technical aspects of your business—the actual providing of services—then significantly growing your business may frustrate you because you may be forced to aggressively market your business, which means someone else in your organization is doing the technical work. You may find that much of your work becomes managing others while they do the work you most enjoy.

Both Ruth and Chris indicated that they got involved in their local chapter of NAWBO to help them learn these skills. Other women sought help from the U.S. Small Business Administration and from the Women's Business Development Centers that have sprung up in cities across the country.

Is Starting Your Own Business the Right Option for You?

- Are you a risk taker? Can you live with constant uncertainty?
- Are you open to asking for help and sharing your business situation with others to allow them to help you?
- Do you have the financial resources to start a business? If not, do you have access to the capital you will need?
- Can you check your ego such that you can perform any task your business needs?
- Are you good at managing others, willing to develop and coach them to be all they can be?
- Are you prepared to be the chief salesperson for your business? Are you a savvy networker who can create opportunities for your business in most networking situations? Are you prepared to be "on" all the time, willing to talk about your business with interested friends in social situations?
- Are you good at juggling multiple roles? Do you have what it takes to be a technician, manager, and visionary all in one? Or, do you only like the actual service-delivery piece of your business? Do you like only the visionary component?

eight

Looking for Purpose in Your Work

Relatively few women choose to move from the private sector to public-sector and nonprofit work as an option for redesigning their work/life. Most women choose to stay in the business world. However, women are increasingly looking for more meaning in their work and turning to the nonprofit and public sectors as viable options. Public and nonprofit work is worth considering because both offer challenging, interesting work, often with greater responsibility and authority than is commonly available at equivalent levels in corporate America. Both options are more likely to offer "normal" hours, respect for personal time, and a less frenetic pace. Unlike most corporate jobs, public-sector and nonprofit positions tend to provide the personal satisfaction of knowing you are making a difference as well as a living.

"IT'S NOT JUST A JOB, IT'S AN ADVENTURE!":
MOVING INTO THE PUBLIC SECTOR

Roberta graduated from a leading law school with a heavy student-loan burden hanging over her head. The big salaries offered by large law firms were appealing. "In school, you hear the horror stories about the hours and how bad it is, but I was in denial. I thought, 'I'll rise above it.'" In a new city, at a prestigious law firm doing litigation work, she quickly realized the horror stories she had heard were not just stories. "I looked around my office and saw that everyone was miserable. But they were hooked on the money. . . . Everyone around me had bought into the lifestyle. They became so dependent on it that they couldn't give up the money. I didn't want to be like that."

Roberta's breaking point came when her father visited for a week. "I was so busy at work that I was only able to meet him for dinner one evening. When I told the partner that my father was in town, his response was, 'Well, I hope you know where your priorities are. The law firm comes first.' On Sunday, my father's last day in town, he had to pick me up from the office and rush me to the hospital because of stress-induced hives. I knew something had to change. I started to ask myself, 'Did I make a huge mistake [going to law school]?'"

Roberta found a group for lawyers who were reassessing their careers. This group helped her come to a realization: "It wasn't law that I didn't like. I just didn't like the environment [I was working in] . . . the pressure for billable hours, the partnership-track grind. . . ." The group opened her eyes to a whole new set of career options within the legal field. One of those alternatives was going to work for the government. It turned out to be the perfect solution for Roberta. She could still practice law, but without the law-firm madness.

Using her existing network of friends and business associates, and building new collegial relationships through this group of attorneys, Roberta was able to find a position with a federal agency involved in international trade. She recognized the trade-offs. "I gave up the big dollars I was making with the firm and the prestige that accompanies working for a 'name' law firm. In addition, I had to give up the perks that came with firm life—luxurious travel, extra support staff, etc."

For Roberta, the trade-offs were a nonissue. "I gained my life back. And, the subject matter [at work] is one thousand times more interesting. . . . It's great! There is so much satisfaction that my work is having a positive impact on society. The people that I work with are happy. They're well-rounded, interesting people who don't want to be slaves to their jobs. It's a big change being in an environment where people like their jobs." Roberta also gets other perks like international travel, which offset the perks she lost leaving her previous firm.

In Roberta's agency, both men and women take advantage of alternative work schedules such as flextime, telecommuting, and part-time. Currently, Roberta is taking advantage of flextime, working nine nine-hour days instead of ten eight-hour days in a two-week period. Roberta takes every other Monday off, which means she gets three-day weekends twice a month.

Roberta has no regrets. She does challenging work that she loves—work that allows her to contribute positively to her community. And Roberta notes one more benefit of moving into the public sector: "You can really pick up marketable skills in the government. So if people want to go back to the private sector sometime in the future, they are really sought after."

"What Is This Option Really Like?"

Historically, with the exception of a few plum assignments, working for the local, state, or federal government was perceived as "less attractive" than working for private companies. With news stories documenting ghost payrolling schemes, backroom dealings, and government waste, the public sector had a blemished reputation. The story is quite different today.

The government, like any corporation today, has been pressured to eliminate waste and increase productivity. Roberta's story is but one example of taking private-sector experience and applying it to public work to yield a more challenging and satisfying career that is less demanding than many private-sector positions. And it is not just for lawyers. Talented businesspeople are equally in demand. Government agencies are as interested as any company in recruiting talented people to bring efficiency to the workplace. As in the business world, there are great agencies to work for and agencies that are behind the times. The diligence you would apply to finding the right company to work for is equally important in finding the right government agency.

More opportunity—sooner. "You are given as much opportunity as you can handle," says Lois, a former corporate executive who is now head of a $400 million division of a major city government. "If you are talented and ambitious, your work will be recognized and rewarded." Many women say they have been given the opportunity to take on challenging projects earlier in their career than would generally be the case in the private sector. Unlike private corporations where there are often artificial hurdles to advancement—a minimum number of years before an employee can be considered for partnership or a promotion—there are fewer established criteria in the public sector. Patricia, a specialist in estate tax, who works for a federal agency, says, "I have an amazing amount of responsibility and independence here."

Great support of your collage. While there are government jobs that demand numerous hours, most do not. The women we spoke to raved about the "normal" hours and respect for their personal time. Most women indicate that they have evenings and weekends off, without constant pressure to work. Many agencies make extensive use of flextime and telecommuting to help their workforce manage personal needs. Other agencies allow employees to take compensatory time following peak work periods.

Patricia takes advantage of her agency's work-from-home policies. "I work from home most days, which saves me a good three hours a day. I don't have to be exhausted every day. I'm so much more productive. I don't have the interruptions. I can really focus. . . ."

Two for one: making a living and a difference. Lois says, "I love being able to do my civic volunteerism through my work." Lois does not have to carve out separate time during her nonworking hours for community involvement. She contributes through her work each and every business day, creating a two-for-one benefit. Patricia adds, "I really enjoy working for the people, the taxpayers. I love to be able to answer their questions. This really affects their lives. I can contribute to my community and make a good living."

Interesting work. Roberta shared how her government work is significantly more interesting than the work she did in private practice, which she found boring. Patricia says, beaming, "I love to be able to focus on a specific area of law and really become the expert in it. I have a tremendous opportunity to learn new things."

Workplace diversity. Unlike many corporations that pay lip service to diversity, government agencies truly honor diversity in their workforce. Public-sector managers tend to be held more stringently to equal-employment and affirmative-action regulations. "They [the government] believe employees shouldn't all be alike," says Lois. "It's the different perspectives that people bring to the table that make it interesting, keep people learning. . . . I get to interact with people on every level," she says. During a normal business day, she interacts with folks who use the services of her agency, the first-level employees who service them, all the way up to the mayor and visiting dignitaries.

This diversity supports a broad range of opinions—and the freedom to express them. Patricia describes the atmosphere in her agency. "I can be an individual here. I can have an opinion. It's okay to challenge the boss. No one is staying within the lines. We are free to give our opinion."

Perks of a different sort. What government work lacks in financial perks it can make up in the form of other perks, depending on the job. Roberta gained international travel. Lois's division receives free passes to all city museums and events. Most government agencies recognize more national holidays than the average corporation, which translates into more days off for employees.

Hints to Help You Move into the Public Sector

Finding a job in government is much like finding a job in the private sector. Your best bet is to use your contacts. Even if your contacts are mostly in the private sector, ask them whom they know in the public sector. Then follow the leads.

If there is a particular agency you would like to work for, write directly to managers in that agency. Express an interest in moving your career into public service. Many agencies are eagerly looking for talented people. And, many current public servants want to encourage people to move from the private to the public sector. You will likely find people willing to speak with you, even if their specific department is not currently hiring. As Lois put it, "I always make time to talk with talented people who are interested in my department. I want good people working with me."

In most cases, public agencies are required to post job openings. Unlike the private sector, where only a fraction of job openings are ever advertised, most local, state, and federal jobs are posted on government Web sites, at state unemployment offices, and in a variety of government publications. You may have to be patient and persistent, as applying for government jobs can require filling out unwieldy forms. Often these jobs must be posted for a set period of time. The interviewing and hiring process can be lengthy. Depending on the government agency, hiring may be subject to the political winds.

While finding a job in the public sector is not unlike finding one in the private sector, to make this option work, you will have to get over some unique hurdles.

Get over the stigma: Working for the government is not a step down. Similar to the roadblocks to change discussed in Chapter 3, some women resist moving to the public sector because of a preconceived notion that government is a "step down." Just as there are some companies that are poorly run, there are some government agencies that play true to stereotypes of "no-show" jobs and bureaucratic paper-pushing. But, more often than not, the government offers challenging, meaningful work. As Lois put it, "You don't get jobs just because you're friends with someone and then never show up. You are expected to work. You will be held accountable." As with other options, if you get comfortable with your role in government, so will those around you.

Politics and bureaucracies. Face it. This is government—politics and bureaucracy exist. On the other hand, most companies also have their share of politics and bureaucracy. Patricia describes her experience: "You have to be pretty determined to get something done. You have to learn how to manage it. But it is possible. The bottom line is that you are still working with other people. You can appeal to their senses. You have to get past letting the process get under your skin. If I need to get something done, I will get it done."

You're not going to get rich working for the government. You will make a reasonable wage, but you will not accumulate wealth. Most women we spoke to felt that government salaries were not significantly under market, but there are no stock options and no annual bonuses. On the other hand, there usually is a favorable pension program. As Roberta put it, "I'm making a living wage, and I actually have the free time to enjoy it." In her former life in the private sector, Roberta earned more but felt that the money was wasted because she never had time to enjoy it.

Your work environment—slower and not on the cutting edge. While not true in all agencies, some women mentioned that the pace of work in their divisions was slower than what they were used to in the private sector. This slower pace is exactly what makes many work/life programs work. However, if you like a frenetic pace, many government jobs may not be for you. Similarly, limited government budgets make it unlikely that you will work in lavish surroundings with the latest in technology on your desk. More likely, you will work in basic surroundings with functionally sufficient equipment.

Is Moving into the Public Sector Right for You?

Ask yourself these questions:

- Will the opportunity for more responsibility and advancement excite you? Will it help make the trade-off in compensation worthwhile?
- Is money a key driver in your life? Are you willing to trade some income for more free time?
- How important are private-sector perks—prestige, cutting-edge technology, more-luxurious travel budgets, and well-appointed offices—to you?
- Are you tenacious? Are you willing to persevere to get things done? Can you be diplomatic yet persuasive in sharing your ideas? Or will bureaucracy frustrate you?
- Will you be proud of your contributions to your community through your work? Or, will you feel like you took a "step down" in your career if you leave the private sector for the public?

"I WANT TO MAKE A DIFFERENCE":
MOVING INTO NONPROFIT WORK

Catherine says of her nonprofit life, "I'm totally fulfilled here. For the first time in my life, I like what I do every day." With an idealist's dream to make a difference, Catherine spent much of her career in the mental-health field. She was largely disillusioned. "I had doctors hitting on me. . . . I saw my company recommending hospitalization for women who clearly didn't need it in order to make more money. . . . I found I had better diagnostic skills than most of the doctors." She went back to school so that she could assume more responsibility and have greater control over how the patient care was delivered. Catherine moved into administration so she could be a voice for the patients. As the insurance industry began to take over health care, Cahterine explains, "I was doing less and less of what I wanted to do. I felt caught between the patients, the insurance companies, and the CEO of my company. The patients were missing out."

Catherine thought that moving to a more senior position at an alternate health-care facility would make her work/life better. It only became worse. Catherine found herself in the middle of a political battle. She was instructed to just keep quiet. "I hit a low point in my career. I was so mentally stressed that I would shut and lock my office door and lie down on the carpet to take a break. I'd wake up with drool on my face, the carpet imprinted on my cheek." Catherine knew it was time to move on.

Catherine began looking for a new job. She was evaluating numerous intriguing, well-paying offers when a tiny ad for a nonprofit organization caught her eye. "I knew I was tired of the dog-eat-dog life." Catherine went through six interviews, competing against 180 highly credentialed individuals. She was offered the executive directorship at a local nonprofit that serves disadvantaged women. "The job appealed to me because, for the first time in my career, I would really have the full say of how things would go."

*Catherine walked into a bankrupt organization that was oper-
ating in chaos. "I virtually had to re-create the organization from
scratch." Catherine went from a highly structured company to an
organization that completely lacked structure. "I was overwhelmed. I still had offers on the back burner and considered giving up. What kept me here were the women who were being helped
by the organization."*

*Catherine became a vocal advocate, speaking nationally on
the program she ran, teaching other municipalities how to create a
similar program in their communities. She was able to make an
impact on an individual level as well as work to change the system
on a broader scale. "My life wasn't fragmented anymore. All of my
former skills and even skills I developed from my hobbies are now
being used." Catherine is passionate about her work. She feels
personally complete. "When I'm here, I'm at peace."*

*Catherine asks, "How many people go into work and start
their day with a hug from one of the women they have helped?"*

"What Is This Option Really Like?"

The opportunity to make a real difference. Like Catherine, women
who move from the private sector to a nonprofit are primarily
driven by two interwoven motivators. First, these women have
a strong desire to give back to their communities. Second, they
want their profession to have greater meaning. For Catherine,
the move to nonprofit met both of these criteria.

Other women who move to nonprofit work express this dual
sentiment in a variety of ways. Working for a children's nonprofit,
Mona is developing a pilot program, creating a for-profit enterprise under a nonprofit umbrella. If successful, it will sustain the
nonprofit in the future and can be replicated by other charitable
organizations. "There is a great sense of accomplishment in pio-
neering a way for nonprofits to sustain themselves." One woman

who moved to nonprofit says, "It's not the position in a company or how much money you make that matters. It is how you feel at the end of the day." Adds another, "I like the fact that the work I am doing is for a good cause, not just to make a corporation more money." Still another woman pipes in, "The best part is the way I feel about myself." Hope, an associate dean at a top university, sums up the feelings of most nonprofit women: "The best thing is that I truly feel I am the luckiest person I know when it comes to career. I love what I do. . . . I am doing what I want to do, and it is having a positive effect on others too."

The two for one: making a living and a difference—simultaneously.
Many women want to include numerous things in their life collage. By earning a living at the same time that they are making a difference in their communities, there is more time for other collage elements. Sandy, chief financial officer for a national charity that fights hunger, put it succinctly: "I'd always wanted to do some volunteering, but with small children at home, I lacked the time. Now I have a job that is good for my career and helps people. It kills two birds with one stone." Like women who move to the public sector, women who move to a nonprofit do not have to carve out separate, personal time to volunteer. They contribute to their community every time they step into their office. As one woman put it, "I feel like I have been given an opportunity to serve others effectively *and* earn a good living."

Movers and shakers and other passionate people. Women who have made the move to nonprofit often mention the fascinating people they meet in their new world. "I have a much broader exposure to very interesting people," says one woman. The people who sit on nonprofit boards are some of the most accomplished in any community. Working in the nonprofit sector enables women to meet and get to know leading businesspeople as well as others at the top of their professions whom they might not otherwise encounter.

These contacts can provide a future career boost in both the for-profit and nonprofit sectors.

Another benefit is the opportunity to work with people who really care about what they are doing and whom they are helping. One woman shared, "[Nonprofit] is filled with people who surpass those I had worked with previously. People who commit not only their time, but their life and heart, were the people I wanted to find as my coworkers and supervisors." Another convert to nonprofit adds that the people in nonprofit "work that hard because they are passionately driven to do what they do. It is a burning desire within them." Many times the people who are drawn to nonprofit are well-rounded, successful people who feel a calling to their work. That makes for some fascinating coworkers and clients.

A kinder, gentler workplace. While your nonprofit colleagues are likely to be passionate about their work, they are also just as likely to be passionate about their lives. Consequently, the pace of work tends to be slower, the atmosphere calmer, and interpersonal relations more respectful and appreciative. As Mona recounted, "It's a different pace here, compared to my former investment-banking position. A 37½-hour week is normal, and people here really stick to it." This more relaxed workweek has added immeasurably to Mona's personal time. Sandy compares the antihunger charity where she currently works to her former life as a private-sector accountant. "It's a calmer, gentler place."

In a nonprofit setting, you may feel more respected and appreciated than is often the case in corporate America. Stephanie, who works for an arts-related nonprofit, says, "I have a skill here that no one else has. It's a skill that is greatly needed and sorely lacking. . . . So many things I say are treated like gold." She went on to talk about interacting with her arts clients: "The first time that a client said, 'thank you' to me, I was shocked. I'd never had a client say, 'thank you' to me, ever [in the corporate world]. . . . When was the last time you had the head of a major philanthropic foundation call to tell you you're a genius?" At the same time, nonprofits' budgets are tight. You may find yourself under increasing pressure to be more and more productive.

Not surprisingly, and like their public-sector counterparts, women who move to nonprofit work generally find themselves working in basic, utilitarian office space with functional, but not state-of-the-art, equipment.

Hints to Help You Move into Nonprofit Work

Finding a job in a nonprofit is much like finding a job in the private and public sectors. Networking is often the key. As you leverage your personal network, ask your contacts about the organizations where they volunteer their time. A personal reference from a valued volunteer is a sure way to be considered for a position in a nonprofit. There are a few additional steps you can take to find the job you want in the nonprofit of your choice.

Volunteer. Volunteering is a great way to sample the nonprofit world and determine if it is truly right for you. If you have identified a specific nonprofit where you would like to work, become a volunteer for that organization. Establish the value you bring to the organization as a volunteer. When a position on the professional staff opens up, you will likely be given serious consideration. As one woman put it, "I began volunteer work at a nonprofit organization, which led to a part-time job, which led to a full-time position there." Proving yourself as a volunteer is an especially useful tool for women who are looking for positions that are significantly different from the jobs they have held in the private sector. Catherine says, "I would consider hiring someone who was looking to change fields, but they must have a compelling reason why. They must have thought through why they want to make the change." In considering job candidates from corporate America, most nonprofits will want to see volunteer experience. Catherine says, "If someone has volunteered before, then I know they have at least some idea of what they are getting into. I want to know they have a real taste of what nonprofit work is like versus what's in their head."

Consider a freelance project. Nonprofits often have projects that need to be done, but lack the staff to do them. Taking on a defined project is a good way to see what it would be like to work for a particular nonprofit. It is also a good way for the nonprofit to get to know you. Mona was in the midst of trying to decide what was next for her when a former colleague asked if she would be interested in taking on a consulting project for a nonprofit. She jumped at the chance. When the project ended, the nonprofit hired Mona in a permanent position.

Recruiters can be helpful. There are headhunters that specialize in nonprofit jobs. In addition, make recruiters you have worked with before aware that you are interested in a nonprofit position. Most recruiters assume that people in corporate America want to stay in corporate America and will not suggest nonprofit opportunities. As Libby, a former corporate marketer recounted, "A recruiter called me about another marketing position. I mentioned that I wasn't interested, that I was wondering if there was something else out there that might offer a new challenge. The recruiter all of a sudden became so excited! She said, 'We present only marketing jobs to marketing people because usually that's all they want. But now that I know you'll think about other opportunities, that opens up a whole new realm of possibilities I can offer you.' I was aghast. I didn't know there was this secret world that I had just been made privy to. I was really excited about the new possibilities."

"I've Found the Job I Want in a Nonprofit I Care About. Now What?"

Once you have found the nonprofit job you want, you can still expect to confront some issues unique to the nonprofit sector. In her autobiography, *What Women Want: A Journey to Personal and Political Power,* Patricia Ireland, president of the National Organization for Women, describes her move from partner at a prestigious Miami law firm to national officer of this nonprofit:

The practicalities seemed obvious enough ... my salary would be cut in half ... I had to accustom myself to working in surroundings that were far from luxurious, too. Without realizing it, I'd been spoiled in Miami; over the years, I'd gotten used to all the perks of working at a posh downtown Miami law firm. NOW's national action center in D.C. was a different story. The workers there were still using manual typewriters. And there were no assistants or secretaries to take dictation or run off copies for me. ... While looking for someone to type up and file a reply [to a lawsuit] in court, I was struck for the first time by how dramatically my circumstances had changed and by how limiting that change from for-profit to not-for-profit work could be. The carpet stains and the peeling paint were constant reminders: In many ways the party was over. *But in other very important ways, the fun had just begun* [italics added].[1]

Financial trade-offs. There is no getting around the fact that nonprofit jobs pay less than private-sector jobs. If you move to nonprofit from a prestigious corporate position, you are likely to face a financial trade-off. Mona said her position provided a "normal salary," a livable wage, but one that is far less than what she was making in investment banking, which tends to pay at the high end of the corporate pay scale. "It was hard to give up the money. It's still hard. There are things I can't do or buy now that I used to be able to."

At the same time, women acknowledge that they receive compensation in nonfinancial terms. They cite a sense of satisfaction

---

[1]Patricia Ireland, *What Women Want: A Journey to Personal and Political Power* (New York: Penguin Books, 1996), 194, 197–8.

in helping others, greater self-esteem, and richer relationships in their lives due to an increased focus on humanity. To prepare for this trade-off, several women advise, "Reduce expenses as much as possible and beef up savings to prepare for the salary drop when going from corporate to nonprofit."

Failure is more painful. Women who cite the nonprofit benefit of making a real difference in others' lives also cite the downside. Making a mistake can be costly. Making a mistake can make a real difference in others' lives—a negative one. As one woman said, "It is very, very difficult. . . . People never expected anything [meaningful] from me before. Now, if I make a mistake, I'm really letting people down."

Getting over the nonprofit stigma. "A nonprofit job can be seen as a waste of time by those around me who work in for-profit organizations. I seemed to lose a lot of my credentials due to the change," says one woman. Stephanie shared that her biggest challenge in making the shift from corporate America to nonprofit is debunking the myth of nonprofit incompetence. "I do get frustrated dealing with the attitude that everything has to be compared against the standard of for-profit."

But, women say, the myth of incompetency is easily debunked. As Catherine said, "I saw the resumes of the people applying for my position as executive director of this nonprofit. There were 180 applications—highly credentialed individuals. I'm talking real high flyers."

Corporate big shot to nonprofit pariah: In taking their business skills to the nonprofit world, some women found that they met with resistance by some hard-line nonprofit career professionals. While their skills were needed and valued by many, some women encountered people who viewed their contribution as a threat to the customary way of doing things. As Mona put it, "It was really lonely sometimes. I was viewed as a pariah by many of my co-officers. . . . I was used to being the center of things, people liking me, being the fun one in the group." Most women say that this resistance tends to dissipate as you perform. But you will have to work to persuade some of your new peers.

Jack-of-all-trades. Working in a nonprofit, you will have fewer resources at your disposal. Consequently, you will have to be more resourceful. You will be called upon to perform a wide variety of tasks, some of which may seem far afield from your core job description. For Catherine, this was a big adjustment. "It's very similar to running your own business. It took me a week after I started to realize no one was going to empty my garbage can." Catherine also recounted how, when her computer crashed, there was no technical-support person to call. Instead, with the help of a staff member, Catherine got her system back up and running herself. On the positive side, "you don't get pigeonholed like you do in corporate America," says Stephanie. "Everyone does everything, so you get a much broader experience."

Is Moving to Nonprofit Work Right for You?

Ask yourself the following questions:

- Do you have a burning desire to make a difference? To make your living in a way that makes a difference? Is having a passion for your work important to you?
- Are you resourceful? You will have to make resources stretch further in the nonprofit world. For some, this is a creative challenge. Will it frustrate or excite you?
- Are you willing to pitch in and do the scut work as well as the fun stuff? Remember, you are unlikely to have the kind of support and technological staff you are accustomed to.
- Are you willing to make the financial trade-offs?

Part III

"Whew! Work Is Contained":

Creating and Maintaining

Your Collage and Making the

Collage Possible for Everyone

Preparing for a Rough Patch

*"I had always wanted to own my own business,"
Kathy recounts. "I was not prepared for the major
bout of anxiety that gripped me when I left my corporate job to go out on my own. I thought making
the break would be the hard part. I had no idea how
terrified I'd feel after making that first big leap.
Once I started my business, I thought, 'I'm finally
living my life's dream. What if I mess this up? How
will I recover?' All of a sudden, there was no goofy
boss to blame if something went wrong. There [was]
just me."*

Now that you have decided to make a change, you can look forward to an exciting new life. Possibilities are everywhere around
you. Yet, at different times, anxiety is everywhere inside you. For
some women, the multitude of possibilities creates feelings of

uncertainty about which is the right path to choose. Other women, like Kathy, make a move to pursue their life's dream only to be gripped with anxiety. Freelancers wrestle with anxiety every time they have to pursue new business. While these feelings are normal responses to taking positive steps forward, they are unpleasant. As career coach Miriam Krasno counsels, "Expect that it's not going to go smoothly. Plan. What are likely to be the hardest spots? What steps can you take to minimize those difficult times?"

"OH, MY GOD! WHAT HAVE I DONE?": HOW TO HANDLE BOUTS OF ANXIETY

The following may help reduce the level of anxiety you may feel by putting things into perspective. Reread the next several paragraphs as often as you need to when those bouts of anxiety grip you.

Regrets are rare. Rarely do women regret leaving their former work/life habits behind. As Chris, now cofounder of a women's alternative-health products company, recounts, "I thought that two to three months after selling my electronics firm I would think, 'What did I do?' [I left this really successful business behind]. But I never did." Out of nearly one thousand women who contributed to this book, only a handful expressed significant regrets.

This too shall pass. No matter how anxious you are at any one moment, that anxiety will not last. Women across the country, from all walks of life, have made it past this uncomfortable transition phase to a more satisfying life. As Jillian, an entrepreneur, said, "I know myself. Fears feel very pronounced at the time, but a week later, they go away. . . . I remind myself, 'Remember last time . . . you got through it . . . it was okay.'"

The first major step is the scariest. If you can steel yourself to get past this first major hurdle, the rest will come more easily. Just keep Mindy's story in mind: "That first month really scared me," she recalls. "For one month, I was catatonic. I wasn't sleeping at night. My face was breaking out. I was eating a lot, watching TV. I was hiding all of this from my husband because I didn't want him to see me falling apart." She took small steps like working out and engaging in some creative activities to get herself going again. She met freelance writers and photographers at her health club, which led to her first freelance writing assignment. She went on to forge a successful writing career, one step at a time.

For many women, once they take that first big step, all future "risky" steps become considerably easier. These women realize that they can take a risk and survive. They gain an increased sense of courage and self-esteem, which creates more possibilities in their life—and not just for their career. Some women take on new hobbies, volunteer opportunities, or travel adventures. Taking the first big step breaks the shackles that the security of their former life created.

When putting things into perspective is not enough to reduce your anxiety, try these strategies that have worked for other women.

This is not an endurance test. Some women who shared their stories said, very stoically, that they did not receive, ask for, or need any help. Americans seem to think it is a sign of weakness to ask for support. Think about times when someone has asked you for help. Remember how good you felt to help another person? Imagine how great the people around you will feel when you call on them and they are able to be there for you. Imagine how much better you will feel to get some of your anxiety out in the open. Holding anxiety in is what makes it worse. Felicia, a freelance marketing consultant, relies heavily on other freelancers. "I have a fair number of alliances—other people who work on their own. We provide each other support—people I can call and say, 'Jesus, I haven't worked for a month.'"

Surround yourself with cheerleaders, not critics. If the people around you think you are nuts, it is time to broaden your network to find some supportive new friends. Look for other people on a similar journey so you do not feel alone. Ask one of them to be a phone buddy, someone to call when you are hitting bumps along the way. Felicia says, "When I have a case of the 'shoulds,' I obsess about it. My friends and close advisors challenge me: 'Why do you feel that way?' I stop and ask myself, 'Do I like what I do? Yes. Is it financially rewarding? Yes. What is the problem? You never really wanted to do (whatever the should was).' The reinforcement from others helps me to give it to myself. . . ."

Imagine. Think of someone who has always been supportive of you. Imagine her sitting across from you as you tell her all the things that make you anxious. Imagine her supportive words reaching out to you, giving you the encouragement you need. Pretend that you are one of those supportive people. Write a letter to yourself, as if from them. What would the letter say? Now is also a good time to pull out the exercises you did in Chapter 4 to reinforce why you made the move you did. Look at the disconnect you had in your Desire Gap Analysis. Remind yourself of how little your old life looks like the one you envisioned and how the moves you have made are putting you on the track to making your dream a reality. Think about all the trade-offs you used to make that you no longer do.

A formal group. Some women take advantage of groups or organizations that help people in career transition. Early in her journey, Bridget, who is currently exploring her options, found a group that provides weekly speakers covering a variety of subjects of particular interest to people looking to make a move. Roberta shared her story of moving from private law to government law. Finding a group that helps lawyers in transition was, as she puts it, "the best thing that ever happened to me." Ruth joined NAWBO to give her the formal support she needed. Lia learned from her group: "Sometimes people are afraid to admit that they're in trouble—their pride gets in the way. You get the most support when you are open and honest about what's troubling you."

Write it down. It is amazing what a relief it is to get all of your fears out on a page. Shining the light of day on your concerns goes a long way to dispelling their power. Frequently, you can see them for what they are—irrational fears that are standing in the way of your ability to move forward. When she gets really nervous, Beth writes down why she is nervous and what is the worst thing that could happen. Then she writes down—honestly—how likely it is that that worst thing will happen. Invariably, the worst thing that could happen is not that bad and the likelihood that it will happen is small.

Do not be afraid to ask for professional help. For many women, redesigning work is a major life transition. It is about more than a job change; it is about a lifestyle change. This is no time to keep a stiff upper lip. Just as someone asks for help from an accountant or a lawyer or a doctor as special needs arise, professional counselors are available to help you with the more significant bumps in life. These professionals can be helpful even if you are doing a good job of managing your own anxiety. If you are experiencing persistent stomach upsets, backaches, the inability to go to or stay asleep at night, or shortness of breath due to chronic feelings of anxiety, it is probably a good idea to seek professional help.

■ **Career coaches.** Career coaches can help you discover what is next. A good career coach will help you look at the big picture and determine how you want your career to fit into a more well rounded lifestyle. She will highlight your interests and talents and direct them toward a career that is in sync with your desired lifestyle. Barbara saw a career coach when she was considering a move from marketing management for a Fortune 50 company to freelance. "I worried—will there be work? Won't I be lonely? [My coach] helped me realize I could separate from moving up in a big company and emerge as something new."

■ **Life planners.** Life planners are similar to career coaches in that they help you look at your whole life. They differ from career coaches in that they work with you to make changes in many areas of your life rather than just your work/life.

■ **Psychiatrists, psychologists, and psychotherapists.** These mental-health professionals focus their attention on helping you get to the root of the roadblocks that are stopping you. They may focus less on specific career direction and more on patterns of behavior that need to be modified so you can move on successfully.

Engage in relaxation activities. Deep breathing, going on restorative walks, doing yoga, taking a bath, or getting a massage are all tried-and-true strategies. Catherine, executive director of a nonprofit agency, regularly engages in activities that help her feel "centered" so that she can focus on the task at hand.

Engage in physical activities. Just as physical activity makes women feel better about their bodies and improves their mood, it is also a good way to burn off the energy created by anxiety. If you feel anxious, hop on that treadmill and get going! Or better yet, go to a beautiful place, be it a park, the lakefront, or a shopping district where you can do some brisk walking while enjoying the scenery. Lia recalls, "I work out consistently. It clears my head. If I have a wimpy workout, it's okay—as long as it clears my head."

HANDLING A FUNK—TAKING CARE OF YOURSELF

Anxiety tends to hit hardest when you make your first move. Once you are on your journey, an occasional blue day may set you back and make you feel like you are not making progress. Some days, the uncertainty will get to you. Know that this is a temporary state. But have some strategies in place that will ease your blue mood.

Relaxation activities are always a good place to start. As described previously, baths, massages, deep breathing, and restorative walks are all great self-nurturing activities.

Exercise your mind. Go to your local library or bookstore and dive into an engaging novel or thought-provoking nonfiction. Get your mind off your funk by stimulating your brain. Mindy used this strategy while she was still at the ad agency to get her mind off her unhappiness with her position. It can work equally well when a funk derails your journey.

Distraction. Movies, live music, a visit to your local museum or gallery, or an interesting lecture are great distractions from what is making you feel blue. Reveling in the creative talent of others works well, not only as a distraction, but can also act as inspiration. Jane, a commercial–real estate developer, would occasionally head to her city's art museum during lunch to get inspired and needle her out of a mood.

Take action. To ward off worry, take one step—even a small one—forward. SARK, the creative author of numerous inspirational books, suggests "micro-steps." If you cannot face updating your resume and getting on the phone with a number of people in your network, break the action step down into tiny steps. The first day, make a list of people you would like to call. The second day, make notes on your resume of things you would like to change. The next day, turn on your computer and pull up your word-processing software. The next day, type the changes into your resume and print copies. The next day, make one phone call. You get the point. You will feel empowered taking some action, any action, and it will make you feel better. It might just get you going enough to tackle a big step!

Throw a pity party for yourself. Sometimes, the best strategy is to thoroughly indulge your self-pity to get it out of your system. So, set aside the day or evening (or both) to really go for it. Rent a movie that will make you cry. *Terms of Endearment* and *Steel Magnolias* are good tearjerkers. Remember to have a box of tissues handy when the tears come. Make a big bowl of popcorn or dig into a pint of ice cream. Light a fire in your fireplace, put on your pajamas, and climb under a blanket. If you do not have a dog, borrow one, or grab the teddy bear you saved from your youth and stroke her fur. Then, go for it. Just remember that when the party is over, it is over. Return the movie and get on with your life.

Volunteer. One of the best ways to put your troubles into perspective is to help the less fortunate. Many volunteers often talk about the volunteer "high," that feel-good feeling that comes from helping others. Many collagers regularly volunteer some of their time to a favorite charity. By doing so, they help keep a funk at bay permanently.

Engage in a hobby. In the next chapter you will explore how to redevelop your interests. If you are already participating in a hobby, take some time and lose yourself in the familiar rhythm of an activity you enjoy. Many people talk about the meditative quality of a hobby. Kathy finds tremendous benefit from gardening; she really misses it when faced with a week that does not allow her to get her hands dirty. "It's physical and mental. It's a great way to get my mind off things and get back in touch with nature—the beautiful colors, the great scents. Seeing how much progress my garden has made over the years is very restorative. Watching the butterflies and birds play in my garden, knowing that the work I did now attracts them, is very nurturing."

Meet a friend for lunch. Interacting with others is a great way to get out of a mood, particularly if you can submerge yourself in something a friend is doing. This is particularly valuable for telecommuters and freelancers who are prone to feelings of isolation. Kathy relies on calls to former colleagues or a midweek lunch to cheer her up: "When I'm feeling down, I call a friend [from my former company] and hear how terrible her life is, working all the time. It always reminds me of how good I truly have it now, and it makes me feel so much better."

Experiencing moments of anxiety or the occasional blue mood is normal when blazing a bold, new direction for yourself. Accept that these moments will come and you will handle them when they do.

Why Collage? Let Me

Count the Ways . . .

You may know you want and need to make a change, but still feel tenuous. What if it does not work out? You might be thinking, "Sure, it worked for other women, but who is to say it will work for me?" The overwhelming majority of women who contributed to this book were thrilled they made the changes they did. When they were asked, "If you had it to do all over again, what would you do differently?" the most common answer was, "I would have done it sooner." Many other women answered that they would not change a thing—including those women who gave up some income, moved to a less prestigious position, or had a minor bout with anxiety.

Becky, an advertising executive, recalls the benefits she received from switching companies and setting boundaries around her work:

"Life is so much easier and more fulfilling. I feel as if I can accomplish anything. The hardest part is forgiving myself for sacrificing so much for so long. I have gained self-esteem, health, prestige, increased salary, and benefits. I have gained better relationships, both inside and outside the office. I have gained clarity about who I am and what I have to give to others. I have lost nothing worth having."

THE BENEFITS OF COLLAGING

Women share the benefits they received as a result of building their life collage. Generally, the benefits cited fall into six categories:

Richer relationships. Most often women identify richer relationships with family, friends, and community as a benefit received from living a conscious collage. Sally beams and says, "This lifestyle breeds good relationships, good partnerships. It's conducive to [nurturing] kids." Women say they now have the time and energy to devote to these relationships—and they are enjoying the results of their efforts. Says Felicia, a marketing consultant, "I find that I have many more acquaintances than before . . . and deeper, closer relationships." One woman noted a "marked [positive] change in [my] children. They're now more self-assured."

Career coach Miriam Krasno describes a relationship benefit to collaging: "Many women in their thirties and forties expected to be married and have kids. For one reason or another, it didn't happen. Yet I find, when they get their conscious collage all worked out—they determine what they need, they identify ways to meet their needs, and they structure their life in a more meaningful way; frequently, within a year it happens—they meet that special partner they so desired."

Time for self. Women indicate that they now have time for themselves. This self-care time keeps their creativity fresh, their energy and psyche "up," which in turn further fuels their self-esteem and self-confidence. As one woman puts it, "The best part about making this change has been the amount of self-confidence I have gained. . . . I feel like I am in control of my world and that is the best way to gain self-worth. . . ."

Barbara, owner of a marketing-consulting business explains, "I'm more myself. I get to grow and be who I'm supposed to be. I have flexibility. I can pursue achievement and my mothering side. I'm very blessed. I need to give back, and now I have the time to do that." One East Coast lawyer shares what the best part was for her: "Raising my self-esteem and feeling that no matter what else happens, I can handle it. I might fail, but it won't be the end of the world."

Greater satisfaction with work. Once established in their new career structure, women experience a high level of satisfaction with their work. One woman said, "I no longer dread getting up in the morning. When it's time to go to work, I really look forward to it. . . ." Some women indicate a greater degree of pride in their work than they ever knew in their previous, more traditionally structured job. Jillian, an entrepreneur, notes the impact her work satisfaction has had on her daughter: "She's already said, 'Mom, I want to be like you. I want to work out of my house. . . . I want to work and I want to be home with my kid.'" An entrepreneur shares the power she now feels over her destiny: "The best part . . . is that I rely on myself, create my own schedule, and answer to myself. My successes are mine, as are my failures."

Bobbie, an independent consultant, likes the freedom she has to structure her work around her needs: "I've learned my rhythms. Writing kicks in late in the day, around four P.M. I can manage around that. I work a Saturday or Sunday, then on Tuesday I go play golf." Still other women had these things to say: "There are so many benefits. The most important is that I do work that flows from my heart, and is in alignment with my deepest spiritual beliefs. . . ."; "I *love* what I do now. I don't dread going to work. . . . I feel like a more well-rounded and complete person."; "I feel happy about going to work. I feel no stress. I have energy when I get home from work. . . ."

Time for other activities. Women say that they have time for hobbies and/or community activities that allow them to use their creativity. One woman shares, "I have more time for hobbies—needlepoint, painting, ceramics. I am also a happier and more relaxed person." Nicole, a marketing manager, recounts, "My life feels a lot less frantic now. The difference is conscious choice. I am still overcommitted, but I choose to be overcommitted. Because I don't do any last-minute travel anymore, I'm able to plan ahead. I always have something to look forward to. I've chosen my commitments."

These activities provide a release from the stress of work and family and give women a sense of satisfaction from doing things they enjoy. One grandmother smiles, saying, "I have more time for myself and my grandchildren. I love going to the library and enjoying books that I have always wanted to read. I've taken a few courses at college; I'm developing more culture and knowledge, going to the movies, etc."

Bobbie reflects, "I see how restricted I was. I used to work from 8 A.M. to 6 P.M., five days a week. I had no time to do anything, except after dinner and on Saturday and Sunday. I see how busy people are on weekends. Stores are crowded [and as a result, waits are longer]. Everyone looks to the weekend as the be-all and end-all of life. For me, Tuesday is the same as Saturday. I do what I want. . . . Every day can be a good day—not just Saturday and Sunday."

Another woman enjoys the time she now has for her community activities: "I used to think that success meant money, but now I think it means peace of mind and well-being. You can't enjoy your money if you are constantly stressed and don't have any time. . . . Now I work fewer hours. I have time to work with a youth program twelve hours a week, and I have time and energy to participate in social activities with my friends and family. . . ."

Sense of fulfillment. Collagers enjoy an overall sense of fulfillment, a sense that they are living an authentic life that enables them to creatively express their true selves. "The *best* part?" says one woman. "The best part has been my sense of self is back. I feel 'like me.' I feel alive again!" Mindy says, "I used to always feel as though I was going against the grain. Not anymore. I realize I'm doing what I'm supposed to be doing. I'm happier. I'm not sick as often. I'm more laid back." One woman sums it up: "I feel more like a whole person. . . ." Chelsea, a telecommuting journalist, explains, "My collage? I have blobs here and there of my making. The colors are appropriately balanced and all of my design. I'm living my life—not someone else's." A Midwest manager says, "I feel more creative, have more energy, and my self-image has vastly improved."

Sense of peace. Even though a collager's pace of life may remain the same, rounding out the work/family picture with personal and community activities offers many women a sense of peace. "I am a much calmer and more relaxed person. My relationships have grown stronger now that I no longer feel the need to compete so much," explains one West Coast marketer. By adding other activities to their lives, these women relieve the stress of combining professional positions with an active family life. One woman enjoys "coming home relaxed and happy instead of clenched and stressed."

A finance manager takes a broader view: "I'm setting longer-term goals versus feeling like everything has to get done today." Sally, a nonprofit consultant, explains, "It's the little things. Being able to do lunch with friends without worrying about when I have to get back to the office. I can leave in the middle of the day to do yoga. I have energy. I'm refreshed enough to brainstorm about new ideas. I can play golf with my husband in the middle of the day." One manager said, "I discovered that THIS is my life. I no longer live for days off or vacation. I don't know what I was waiting for, but when I worked in full-time management, I felt as if I was 'waiting' to start being happy. . . ."

Sarah's sense of peace translates to freedom. "Freedom is fun. Freedom means I get to make my own schedule. . . . Now I can have REAL conversations with people." She has learned that her creativity comes in spurts. She doesn't force it. "I take a lot of naps. I work when it strikes me [which may be off hours]." Finally, another woman explained, "I'm more relaxed, less tense, and have a lot more patience."

REDISCOVERING YOUR INTERESTS

Once you have successfully wrestled some of your free time from that all-consuming job, you get to decide how to spend that newfound time, rather than having it decided for you. You choose what interests you and then pursue those interests. A word of caution though: If you are not careful to fill that free time with interests you enjoy, work is likely to suck you back into its fold.

Some women are at a loss with what to do with their reclaimed personal time. They are so used to saying no to personal endeavors that it is difficult to rekindle their interests. Family and friends are so used to hearing no to every invitation that they have stopped asking. It is time to say yes to things you would like to do. You will need to extend yourself to those around you to let them know you are ready and willing to go see a play, go out to dinner, or go to the latest art exhibit.

Felicia experimented with many things. "The first couple of years, I explored—art classes, painting, refinishing, antiques, flea markets, stained glass. I got involved in nonprofit volunteering. I made sure there is more to me than just work. Now, the answer to the question 'Who am I?' has many parts." Felicia's strategy is one that you can use—sample many things to see what you like best. If you are not sure what you would like to add to your life collage, pull out the envisioning exercise you did in Chapter 4 to see if glimpses of your interests came through. If you do not see any specific things you would like to try in the work you have already done, take a minute and add to your envisioning project. In addition to your career and family, what other interests come to mind? Is there a hobby you long to try? A musical instrument that is woefully out of tune due to lack of use? Do you have some cracked and rusty tubes of paint at the bottom of your junk drawer?

Maybe there is a favorite charity that has always intrigued you. Think through how these activities can work in tandem with the rest of the life you envisioned. To help you flush out your passions, some suggestions for rediscovering your interests follow. Look at what calls to you. Do what kids do—if it interests you, just try it! Do not worry about whether you are good at it. Just concern yourself with adding more fun and joy to your life.

Look to your childhood. When you were a child there must have been some activities that you loved. What were they? Did you like to play tennis? Grab a friend and head out to the tennis court. Is an instrument gathering dust in the corner of your home? Dust off that guitar and take some lessons. Did you love to write or draw? Were you good at making homemade gifts for others? Did you enjoy cooking or baking? Buy a bunch of magazines and comb them for inspiration.

Long-time longings. Are there things you have always wanted to try but did not have the time or courage? Have you always wanted to bungee-jump, to take singing lessons, or learn to build houses by volunteering through Habitat for Humanity? Perhaps in-line skating looks appealing to you. Or you have envied that neighbor's garden and long to turn that barren clump of earth you call a yard into a beautiful retreat for you and the butterflies. Or you flip through decorating magazines and long to add some color to your walls. Try a new activity this weekend. Fulfill a long-time longing and see if it is right for you.

Look at what your friends are up to. Is there an activity your friends are doing that looks like fun? Perhaps some of your friends are interested in a wine-tasting class or some other activity. Libby, a marketing manager, had several friends who formed a book club and invited her to join. Or perhaps you admired a vase at a friend's house only to find out she made it in her pottery class. Or maybe another friend has started a play group for her little ones and has asked you and your children to join in the fun. If a writing class your sister has been taking at the local community college has been a source of inspiration and creative expression, call and find out more about it. See if it is something you would like to try. You get the idea.

Educational opportunities. Many colleges offer adult education or extension courses that are noncredit, thought-provoking curricula. There are also many nonprofit art organizations that hold a wide variety of art-related classes. Junior colleges offer a broad range of inexpensive classes to either develop new skills or strengthen old ones. Call the school and request their catalogue. See what you are drawn to. Make a list and prioritize what you would like to try first. Then give them a call and register. Kathy always makes time to take some classes—be it gardening, writing, or personal growth.

Health clubs have come a long way. In addition to the weight machines and the traditional aerobics classes, health clubs now offer nutrition and wellness classes, yoga, Pilates, meditation, and behavior modification. Cindy, Sally, and Becky all make time for their weekly yoga classes. Mindy is experimenting with Pilates.

Try something new to freshen up your weekly workout. Make a commitment to try one new fitness activity a month.

Wander around a bookstore. What sections draw you into their aisles? Self-help? Cooking? Redecorating? Home repair? Go with your instincts and pick up a book for inspiration. Becky has devoured home-remodeling books as she refashions her condominium. Join a book club. Get to know some new, fascinating women while reading books you may not have considered reading. The monthly stimulation has become a must for many collagers.

Look for volunteer opportunities. Your local church or synagogue, school, homeless or battered women's shelter, are always looking for people who are willing to donate some time. Many times volunteering inspires whole new interests and introduces you to new friends. Look to your community paper for ideas. Judi is involved in a literacy program for children. Beth is an active board member of a domestic-violence agency. Becky provides fund-raising support for her favorite charity.

Often you can turn a hobby into a volunteer opportunity. Successful collagers look to local botanical gardens to combine a hobby with a community-service project. Many cities, due to a shortage of funds, are privatizing such public facilities as zoos and museums. These newly privatized organizations are looking for volunteers. What a great way to learn and contribute to your community!

eleven

Maintaining the Collage

There will be times after you redefine work and create your collage when adjustments will be needed. Life demands may create a week where you are barely treading water. As you move into and out of various life stages, your collage will continue to evolve. Collaging allows you to make those adjustments when they occur.

COLLAGES CHANGE IN SHAPE, COLOR, AND COMPOSITION

Your life is made up of many dimensions, dimensions that evolve over time to meet your life stages. Collagers' lives are full of activities; their lives may be equally, if not more, complex than they used to be. Demands on collagers' time come from many sources rather than a few, sometimes necessitating more coordination.

As Lindsay, the director of advertising for a communications company, advises, "You have to ask yourself what propels you day in and day out. Decide what is unbending for you and what can flex in your life. You have to have a filter by which you can make certain decisions to reduce the conflict you are experiencing. And that filter evolves over time based on your life stage—you will make different decisions based on your position in the company, your ambitions, if you have children, the age of those children, the number of children, where you live, etc. You have to ask yourself, does my filter still work? Do I need to change my criteria? Are these the right criteria to be using?" As Lindsay suggests, not only will the roles you play evolve over time, but so, too, will the filter by which you decide what roles to play and to what degree. Understanding your filters and refining them over time allows you to catch yourself when you get off track and make the necessary adjustments.

There are three levels of collage maintenance—short, intermediate, and long term.

SHORT TERM—COLLAGES OCCASIONALLY COLLIDE

There are short-term accommodations your collage must make for a tight client deadline, a special class for your child, or caring for a sick parent. A collage can ebb and flow to accommodate the short-term changes in your weekly schedule. Few people experience a day where all aspects of their collage are represented. A realistic goal is one where your collage reflects the life you want over the course of a week or month. With the freedom gained from getting work under control comes the responsibility of meeting your various, and sometimes conflicting, commitments.

When things get out of control for Lindsay, she says, "I go back to the basics. There are some things in life that are non-negotiable. You have to have some constants to live by, which help you determine what goes or gets adjusted in crunch times. For example, I have a best friend that I keep in touch with regularly. We used to go out to dinner, just the two of us, with some regularity. Lately, with our work and kids' schedules, it's been tough. So now I've been keeping in touch with her via phone calls during my commute. It is not ideal, but I have a commitment to stay connected with her, and that was the time and place we found to keep the connection going. I had to look for spaces between my commitments to get some things done."

Lindsay had a project that required a short-term work crunch. She was trying to figure out how to get the work done and still respect the evening time she had with her daughters, helping them with their homework. Her solution? "I pulled out my laptop on the same table they were doing their homework. I was doing 'Mommy's homework.' I was there for them if they needed assistance—I was able to stay involved in what they were doing and get the work done. They had the opportunity to learn more about what I do and ask me questions about it. It worked so well, now they ask me, 'Does Mommy have homework tonight too?' They look forward to it. I created an esprit de corps with my children."

You can recognize when your collage is colliding when you feel that momentary sense of panic, and think, "How will I ever get this all done?" Take a deep breath and calm yourself a bit. There are several strategies to use when your collage collides.

 EXERCISE 9
Trimming or Rearranging the Collage

Step 1: "Take the emotion out of it," counsels Lindsay. "Speak up for what you need. During a crunch week, I may say to my husband, 'I know we need time as a couple. I just need ten minutes to get my head together.' Don't be afraid to let your kids know you need time. One of my kids wanted to play volleyball. I said, 'I can't do that right now. I need about an hour to get this task done, and then I'll play with you.' They understand. Rely on your support community at work. My mother died a month ago, and my work community was incredibly supportive to me, both emotionally and pitching in to see that the work got done while I was out."

Step 2: Identify all the roles you are currently engaging in— professional, mother, gardener, board member, etc. Identify the pressing demands under each role.

Step 3: Prioritize each of these demands. For instance, for mothers, their children are frequently a top priority. But if a mom is in a situation where a tight client deadline is pressing, perhaps help can be deployed from family or a neighbor to make sure the kids are taken care of temporarily while she attends to the client's needs.

Role	Demand	Priority	Delegate/delete/ move due date
Professional	1.		
	2.		
	3.		
Mother	1.		
	2.		
	3.		
Volunteer	1.		
	2.		
Hobbyist	1.		

Step 4: Determine whether some of the tasks can be temporarily or permanently delegated. Can they be scaled back? For example:

■ Can you have your groceries delivered? Ruth used this tip when she was put on bed rest during her second pregnancy while her business was in a growth phase.

- Can your baby-sitter drop off the dry cleaning? Kelsey's baby-sitter agreed to do this to save Kelsey some time.

- Can the parent of a child in your daughter's ballet class give her a ride to class? Caitlin relied on other moms from her children's school to keep her on top of her children's school commitments.

- Can your client's deadline be moved?

- Can your significant other alter his schedule? Barbara often negotiates her schedule with her husband's so they can meet each other's needs.

- Can the location of the activity change? Lindsay moved her workout routine to her home from the health club, saving her travel time and allowing her time with her children.

- Can some activities be combined? Kathy uses a cordless phone with headset to stay in touch with her folks while she is straightening up the house.

- Plan ahead—Barbara has a family meeting when she is anticipating a client crunch period. She not only looks to her husband for help, but her children also volunteer to pitch in where they can. "My kids have a great sense of satisfaction that I can count on them and trust them to help out."

Lindsay offered this tip: "Remember that quality moments can happen at any time—while you're grocery-shopping or making dinner. If you have to make a presentation, bring the kids along so they can learn. You don't have to create separate, special time. Make any time with kids, [friends, and loved ones] special. I had to learn that it is okay to do 'nothing' with my kids. You don't always have to plan activities. Some of my best family moments are when we're all together around the house, doing nothing. You don't have to choose between work and family. Find ways to connect that don't necessarily require you to be there at two P.M."

INTERMEDIATE EVOLUTIONS—THE DOMINANT
COLLAGE-THEME CHANGES

Rather than stopgap measures, occasionally the collage evolves permanently to reflect changes in your needs. As you move in and out of various life stages—e.g., single careerist, dual-income marriage, parenthood, empty-nester—the needs at each stage instigate greater evolutions to your collage. For instance, activities that were once important to you as a young careerist may become less so when you become a parent. Learning to consciously increase or lessen the importance of roles or activities as your needs change is a healthy way to evolve the collage.

Keep in mind, most collages have one color or theme that dominates. Many times the other components do not go away; they just play less importance. For instance, when women become mothers the demands of a baby and a career are such that many other activities get scaled way back, but they do not go away. As the child enters her school years, mothers typically have more time for participating in their communities and seeing more of their friends. Then when children go off to college or start their own careers, moms can move more of their focus from developing their children to developing themselves—creatively, professionally, intellectually, and spiritually. At each of these phases, different parts of the collage take center stage. For non-moms, sometimes life moves from a major focus on building a thriving career in their twenties and thirties to refining the direction in their forties so that community service, hobbies, and spirituality can play a larger role. Perhaps in their fifties and sixties the career levels off so that there is more time to travel. The other parts of the collage are still alive; they are just not as active.

In knowing when it is time to make an intermediate move and deciding which roles to change, one woman put it as "listening to the [internal] discourse in your life." Where is your discomfort coming from? Perhaps you have outgrown a particular friendship.

Olivia, a speech pathologist, said, "I loved to play soccer with other women. But I got to the point where I would be in so much pain for days afterward. I had to face that I was getting older and it was just too hard on me. I had to let it go."

Maybe you have found that after-hours, work-related entertaining is not as much fun as it used to be, but that local art class is now sounding interesting. Or perhaps you want to get more involved in your children's school. That board you have been invited to sit on will introduce you to some fascinating new people. The garden that used to be a chore is now a wonderful source of reward for your efforts and offers great time for contemplation. Or perhaps you are tiring of being a committee chair but do not want to give up volunteering altogether so you scale back your commitment to committee-member participation.

When you sense it is time to rearrange the collage, ask yourself these questions to identify what needs to change:

■ Are there activities that you participate in that have begun to feel stale? Are there other activities that you find yourself drawn to lately that you would like to try?

■ In reviewing the roles you listed in Exercise 9, are there roles that make you cringe? Is there a way to redefine the scope of this role so that it takes less precedence in your collage, thereby reducing its impact?

■ Rather than being thrilled by an opportunity, does it make you feel exhausted, exasperated, or frustrated just thinking about it? Are there other opportunities that inspire, motivate, and excite you?

Beverly, general manager of a communications company and single mother of two, talks about her participation in the PTA. "I was miserable. I wanted to participate for my kids' sake, but I felt shunned. Women would whisper, 'She works,' as if to somehow discount everything I had to contribute. I was recounting all of this to my girls, who finally said, 'Mom, if it makes you miserable, don't do it!' What a relief! I resigned and now contribute my volunteer time where my talents are appreciated."

If there is a role that is not the type you can resign from, perhaps it can be redefined in some way to make it less draining. As you did in Exercise 9, consider:

■ Can pieces of this role be delegated or deleted?
■ Can your deadlines be moved?

Now is the time to consider what you want to permanently cross off your list and what new activities, if any, you would like to try.

Sometimes, in order to take on a new hobby or activity you will need to scale back something else. For example, one woman loved horseback riding and used to horseback-ride every week. She was finding it increasingly difficult to keep this commitment. She was looking at it as an all-or-nothing proposition—either she kept riding once a week or not at all. Colleagues encouraged her to consider riding once a month rather than once a week. That way, she could still enjoy a passion of hers while at the same time relieving some of the pressure on her time.

Another example of an intermediate recomposition is the decision many women face when having children: The question many ask is, should I take time off from my career to care for my children full-time? This is a very personal decision that each woman needs to make within the context of her own family, based on her own values and goals. If you are facing this dilemma, one of the things to consider is: What are your long-term goals? What will it take over the course of your career to achieve them? If you are a woman who sees herself shooting for the CEO spot some day, taking time off to care for children full-time, in today's workplace, may limit your ability to reach this goal unless you start your own business. However, if your goal is to be a director in your company, then time off with the children may not preclude you from reaching this goal. It just may defer it a bit.

A word for all of you workaholics: once a workaholic, always a workaholic. It is important to remember that while getting work under control is intended to allow more time for other activities in your life, the goal is not to continue "working" relentlessly, even if it means some work time has been replaced with fun things in your life. If you are continuing to feel stressed out by your life, you probably still have too much on your plate. For example, Kathy was so excited with the time she reclaimed that she signed up for numerous volunteer responsibilities and fun classes. A few months into her new schedule she looked ahead over the following several weeks and realized she had something scheduled every weekday evening for three weeks straight. "Ugh! How did this happen?"

It is easy to get a little carried away when you finally have the opportunity to engage in things you have been putting off. To ensure you do not self-destruct, some behavior modification needs to occur. Once you get work under control, you may want to ease into fun activities initially to see at what level your life feels fulfilled without feeling out of control. After all, the idea of collaging is not to take your formerly stressed-out, overbooked life and re-create it by overbooking it with other, albeit fun, things. It is okay to take on new activities; just be realistic about how much you can take on and when.

LONG TERM—BEGINNING THE EXPLORATION STARTS ANEW

People are living longer these days, and as such, they are working longer. They have a greater period of time to achieve their goals than was possible in the prior generation. Arlene Rossen Cardozo, author of *Sequencing,*[1] encourages looking over the course of your lifetime to accomplish your goals, rather than assuming that all goals need to be accomplished now. Taking the long view enables you to consider multiple careers. Who wants to have the same career over fifty years anyway? For instance, your first career probably was the career your parents encouraged you to go into so that you "always have something to fall back on." Your second or third career could be a dream realized. Saying no to an activity now does not necessarily mean saying no forever. Work/family consultant Dawn Gray describes this as "dreams deferred." Gray encourages women to expand the time line over which they plan to realize a particular dream. For example, Gray is writing a play. But rather than planning its completion in two to three years, she knows, given the other priorities in her life, it is more likely to be completed in ten years. The dream does not go away, it is just deferred.

Evolving your collage will become natural as you make moves to meet your needs. Becoming aware of this process gives you the freedom to evaluate and modify your life as needed. Rather than living with discomfort, you can spot the problem and address it.

[1]Arlene Rossen Cardozo, *Sequencing: A New Solution for Women Who Want Marriage, Career, and Family* (Brownstone Books, 1996).

twelve

Conclusion:

Where Do We, as a Society,

Go from Here?

Thus far, this book has looked almost exclusively at what you can do to further your own career while at the same time developing "a conscious life collage" —a multifaceted life made up of the activities and roles you love. And yet, families and communities also benefit as people take on these multiple roles.

Ask yourself, what example should be set for the next generation? One where life is two-dimensional, composed of work and family, with little creative expression and commitment to others, and fraught with stress? Or one where career is important and rewarding, but textured with many other aspects of life, including consideration for others in the community?

Communities need to encourage individual-citizen involvement. For so many individuals, work has grown to consume an overwhelming part of life, making meaningful community

involvement nearly impossible. If society wants citizens to participate in arts councils and science associations, mentor children,
coach Little League, help at the Special Olympics, or volunteer in
schools, it needs to help provide the time for people to live up to
these commitments. Communities—and the government, media,
businesses, and individuals that comprise those communities—
need to support and encourage people to redesign work to permit
time for these other activities—activities that benefit all.

WHAT CAN YOU, AS AN INDIVIDUAL, DO?

No matter what position or title you hold, there are several things
that you, as an individual, can do to help make it possible for
everyone to create a conscious life collage.

Do not be part of the problem. If, in the past, you have made heroes
of your peers who regularly pull all-nighters to meet deadlines,
STOP. Do not perpetuate the "face time" culture. Instead, applaud
those people who develop and stick to achievable work plans,
enabling them to manage their time effectively and leave the office
at a "normal" hour most days. Recognize people like Becky, profiled in Chapter 5, who maintain "grace under pressure."

Do not judge others. Just as you designed your life collage to meet
your specific needs and desires, others craft their collages to meet
their needs. Spend less time judging working moms versus stay-at-
home moms. Stop comparing women who have children to those
who do not or those who are married to those who are single.
Instead, support everyone's right to a life of their own design.

Join the "community labor force." As you redesign your work and
create your life collage, include a community commitment as an
element of your collage. Lead a Girl Scout troop, join the board of

a charity, or serve meals to the homeless. Take an active role in a cause that matters to you. You will make a difference by example. Every woman who realigns her life to pursue a financially and emotionally satisfying career while simultaneously nurturing family and contributing to her community, furthers the efforts of all women who want to forge their own collage.

Celebrate success. If you have successfully redesigned work to make it work in your life—whether you have negotiated a part-time arrangement, established a job share, or initiated telecommuting—share your success with others. The public relations will be good for you and good for your peers. Make sure managers and senior staff see what you have accomplished and how it has benefited the organization. By spreading the word, you increase the likelihood that others in your organization will be able to do as you have done. And, you will become less of an anomaly. Be generous as others seek your advice on crafting their own solution.

Alternative work arrangements are not favors. Lynn Martin, former U.S. Secretary of Labor, advises, "Stop viewing your company's accommodations as favors. Helping employees manage work/life issues is good for business. You have ensured that. If you view being able to take advantage of alternative work options as a favor, guess what will get cut when the economy heads south?" Your managers should know that, at a minimum, they saved the cost of replacing you by meeting your needs in a way that is good for business.

Form alliances with others in your company. Kay, the editor at a communications company, counsels, "Women need to look to one another, support and encourage one another. See if you can craft a unique solution. Don't be a victim. You can create a solution that works." Do not look only to other women at your level or in your department. Women in all areas—professionals and support staff—and with all lifestyles—married, unmarried, with children and childless—are facing these issues. So are many men.

Increasingly, men look to women to lead workplace transformation. Many men want to have their own conscious life collage but feel that it is more difficult for a man to advocate for work/life issues. Rather than hide your work/life needs and pretend to be "one of the guys"—a strategy that will almost certainly leave you exhausted, emotionally drained, and isolated—enroll other like-minded men and women to work toward change, both inside and outside your organization. Many voices have more impact than one. Get together, brainstorm solutions, and present one proposal for all.

Adapt the "quilting bee" concept to your company and/or your neighborhood. Martin explains that "the 'quilting bee' concept invites people to get together to help one another out." Together, the group can complete the quilt more quickly than an individual quilter. For example, if you are part of a work team, look around at the total skill set on the team. Propose the cross-training of skills so you and your colleagues can substitute for one another. Be willing to substitute for one of your colleagues so she can attend her art class. In exchange, ask her to sub for you so you can coach Little League. In addition to facilitating your life collages, this cross-training will benefit your career as well, providing you with new skills to offer the workplace.

The quilting bee is useful in your neighborhood as well. Martin continues, "Form a baby-sitting club where parents can swap baby-sitting as needed. Or create 'errand central' where one member of the club takes care of everyone's drugstore errands each week, while another handles the dry cleaner, so everyone does not have to spend time running every errand individually." The concept can be adapted to include leaf-raking, snow-blowing, and other chores. Imagine the time you could save—and add to other elements of your collage—if you did not have to do every errand or chore yourself.

Get out and vote. Finally, as an individual, no matter what job you hold, you can pay attention to public-policy issues that impact people's ability to create a conscious life collage. You can bring these issues to the forefront. Ask candidates for their positions on work/life issues. Has the candidate given any thought to how to encourage businesses to support alternative work arrangements? How does the candidate propose to ensure that affordable child care is available to all families? Would the candidate support a tax incentive for employers who have a certain percentage of employees who telecommute or job-share? Or a company that has a formal policy that supports employees in undertaking a regular volunteer commitment? Or a company that provides health care to part-time employees as a matter of policy? Get the answers to these questions and vote for candidates who are cognizant of work/life issues and who will advocate for solutions.

WHAT CAN YOU, AS A MANAGER, DO?

Perhaps one of the most discouraging aspects of interviewing women for this book was that most of the management women interviewed had thought long and hard about their own collages but had given little or no thought to supporting work/life balance for their subordinates. The few who had any response to their subordinates' needs offered inadequate examples. One manager said, "Once a year we have a company party where spouses are invited, and we thank them for their support and understanding when their employee spouse had to work late." It may be human nature to blame the person who is enthroned above you in the hierarchy and to forget the people perched on the rungs below. But it is unacceptable. You can do more. Here are some steps you can take to help your subordinates manage work/life issues:

Be open-minded to proposals for alternative work arrangements. Kay, editor at a communications company, offered this challenge: "As a manager, it's important to be flexible, for both single and married employees. . . . Employers need to be creative. Give people leaves of absence. [People need a break]. Allow them to come back. Be open to job-share arrangements."

Provide proposal guidelines. If your organization has not developed a policy, Lindsay, director of advertising for a communications company, advises, "Give subordinates the guidelines for how to present a proposal to you and define what you expect to see. For instance, managers are worried about how the work will get done. They also want to know that making the accommodation will not cost them anything—better yet, it will save them some expense. Instruct employees to anticipate a trial period." As Lindsay suggests, creating a well-crafted proposal should not be a mystery. Clearly identify the issues you need addressed so that employees spend their time addressing your concerns rather than wasting time on a proposal that does not resolve the departmental issues.

Stop being a roadblock. Are you helping your employees create their life collage or are you a roadblock for them to get around? In 1997, Lia, who owns her own accounting firm, found that her primary assistant, Angela, was due to give birth on April 1—right in the heart of tax season. Lia felt strongly that the company and the employee could make it work. "I had been an active voice on women's issues. If I couldn't make it work in my company, then I had been full of hot air all these years."

The company communicated with clients about Angela's pregnancy. Deadlines for submitting tax materials were communicated far in advance. Clients were warned that, while in past years the company had been lax in enforcing these deadlines, this year deadlines would be enforced. At the same time, to demonstrate her commitment to making it work, Lia let her existing clients know that for this year only, she would take in no new clients. She would dedicate herself to taking care of her existing customers. In summary, Lia asked for some assistance from her clients, but she also gave some herself. It turned out to be a win-win-win. Clients were impressed with Lia's commitment. The company retained a valuable employee. And Angela is an even more loyal employee than she was before.

Try new things. Be willing to try new ways to work on a trial basis—and then evaluate the results fairly, based on productivity. Gwen, the telecommuter profiled in Chapter 5, initiated her firm's telecommuting policy on a trial basis to determine whether her organization could make it work. The pilot period enabled Gwen and the firm to work out the kinks before rolling out the program company-wide. The firm made sure it had the proper systems in place to ensure the work would get done.

Encourage cross-training. Cross-training allows one employee to pinch-hit for another when the need arises. Allow your employees to stand in for each other so that the group's work is done while each individual's life is respected. This cross-training will have other benefits. If one of the members of your team becomes ill or resigns, you will have ready backup.

Be an exemplary role model. One woman described her former manager as a role model. "He was an outstanding manager, first of all, just in terms of knowing his stuff. He was smart. He was organized. He made some clear priorities for himself. He was on the 6 P.M. train to go home to his kids. So if you wanted him to see something you had to be in his office by 4 P.M. or 5 P.M. so that he could get on the train. He had a very good sense that the work he was asking you to do could reasonably be accomplished between Monday and Friday, during reasonable work hours. If you ended up working more, it was your own fault. He was very good at isolating what was important, doing what was important and cutting out the fluff."

Lindsay puts her pediatrician appointments on her calendar for all to see. "Some managers believe in 'don't ask, don't tell.' I'm less concerned about someone being out on a personal appointment, as long as the work is getting done. My philosophy is, work smart. Don't sit on the expressway in the middle of a snowstorm, when it will take you two hours to get to work. That's not working smart." Lindsay has also been known to bring her kids into the office occasionally when there is a snow day. She lets employees know, by example, what is okay and what is not.

WHAT CAN ORGANIZATIONS DO?

First and foremost, organizations can support alternative work arrangements. Create, disseminate, and support policies that encourage employees and their managers to innovate how and where they work.

Flexibility is key. Many women are not looking for fewer hours. They simply want to respond to their life needs as appropriate. For example, school plays sometimes occur during the day. Also, plumbers do not make house calls at night. Women wish to fulfill their work responsibilities while at the same time attending to their personal needs. Organizations can provide this flexibility by measuring output, using business metrics, not face time.

Provide the toolbox. Organizations should structure policies that include a format for how employees should propose to alter their work/life, a method for trial and measurement and a threshold for success. Such policies encourage managers to support pilot programs and to evaluate results based on business metrics. Lindsay says, "Most managers are not philosophically opposed to giving people flexibility. They just don't have the toolbox to make it all happen. Companies put work/life policies on the books, but managers get stuck trying to figure out how to make it work. Companies need to provide the toolbox so that managers are equipped to meet the needs of their employees and the company. Make policies simple for managers to implement. The company standards need to be clear: What are okay flextime parameters? If someone is telecommuting, what is the company's standard response time? How quickly is someone expected to return a phone call or e-mail? How quickly do they need to get in the office in the case of an emergency? If the company allows telecommuting, give me the tools to manage results, not face time."

For example, when Gwen's company introduced telecommuting, they began using a project-management software that facilitated communication of work progress between employees and their managers. This software gave managers a standard structure to review their subordinates' work. Using this software helped Gwen's firm move from a face-time measurement system to measuring productivity based on business results.

Companies also need to be flexible when setting alternative work arrangements by giving managers discretion to meet their department needs. Lindsay continues, "Understand that some adjustments will need to be made to company-wide policies to address differing division needs. For instance, my company has casual dress on Fridays, and yet my division vice president will not permit it in our division. We are a sales organization. At any time, a large client could walk in the door for a meeting. The VP wants to ensure we present a professional look to our clients."

Organizations should be clear on the career impact, if any, of participating in alternative work arrangements. For instance, if going part-time will delay an employee's consideration for promotion, organizations need to spell out the time implication so that people can make meaningful decisions based on fact rather than fear.

Get over the lemming myth. Many organizations are reticent to support alternative work arrangements based on the "lemming theory"—the idea that if they accommodate one person's needs, others will want to follow. First, not everyone is going to want to alter their work/life. Examples abound at peer companies where alternative work arrangements have been in place for some time and only a small percentage of workers took advantage of the programs.

Second, companies can set parameters around their alternative work arrangements. Supporting part-time work, boundary-setting, job sharing, telecommuting, or some other work option, is not an anything-goes free-for-all. Lindsay says, "For those managers who worry about employees slacking off through alternative work arrangements—I have news for you. They're going to slack off anyway. There are some people who will work hard, regardless, and some people who will slack off, regardless. Having alternative work policies has no impact on that front. If you have an employee problem, deal with that. Don't base the decision to put a policy in place or not, due to concerns over a few slackers. Fire the slackers." One suggestion is to set a minimum work-quality threshold before an employee can be considered for alternative work arrangements. The minimum threshold could be that an employee must receive at least a "meets expectations" on their annual performance review to be considered. That way, companies do not feel that they have to make accommodations for underperforming employees and it provides incentive to the employee to ensure her performance meets company standards.

Organizations can, and should, set policies to standardize and measure alternative work option–productivity. Lindsay continues, "It's easy to measure output rather than face time. All of my people have quarterly business goals and annual development goals. It is easy to see who is performing and who isn't." Weekly project-status reports, discussed in "Setting Boundaries" in Chapter 5, are another method for measuring output. Companies that successfully deploy these arrangements have specific measurement systems in place to ensure the work is getting done in line with company goals. These measurement systems also provide the tool by which an employer can terminate an arrangement in the event the arrangement is not working or the employee is not performing.

And third, so what if everyone wants to take advantage of an alternative work option? Play "spot the assumption"—the company may be assuming that if everyone wanted to take advantage of the policies the end result would be negative. Rather, it might be the case that the organization will be full of satisfied, loyal employees. Productivity might go up. Expenses might go down.

Many organizations that support alternative work arrangements find that employee retention rates go up—while recruiting, hiring, training, and absenteeism costs go down. As Gwen said, "I don't know if I could ever leave this job." Many organizations also see productivity gains in some alternative work arrangements. With standardized policies and the appropriate use of technology, employees working in different places on different schedules can be managed.

Reward the behavior they say they value. Just as individuals should acknowledge their peers who are productivity leaders but work normal hours, so should organizations. Organizations must accept—even applaud—work/life balance. Employees should not feel that they have to lie about their life obligations in order to keep their jobs. Many women described situations where they told employers that they had a "dentist's appointment" in order to go catch their child's school play. These situations hurt the employee as well as the employer.

REALLY value diversity. "Diversity," for many, is just a code word for race and gender. There is also diversity in views and in ways to get the job done. "Corporate America needs to understand that there is no one career path," advises Stephanie, a former advertising supervisor turned nonprofit arts consultant. "Know that there are many ways to get the job done. And this difference is very viable—it provides a vital, fresh perspective."

Collaboration among differing perspectives yields exponentially greater results. Corporations can use this to their advantage rather than seeing different points of view as a problem to be overcome. Creativity is often drummed out of employees by years of demands for conformity. Many a corporation in trouble has found that it did such a "good" job of inculcating employees into its corporate culture that the employees were no longer able to respond to competitive threats. Rather, employees continued to do things the standard way, the only way they knew—which was often inadequate to meet the current needs of the business.

WHAT CAN GOVERNMENT DO?

Government has the ability to induce behavior by using the carrot (i.e., tax incentives such as empowerment zones) or the stick (i.e., legislative mandates such as the Family and Medical Leave Act). Many people may argue that it is not the government's place to regulate business. They argue that the power of the free market will eventually persuade companies to allow alternative work arrangements. In some cases, market forces do work to alter business's behavior. But, often, market forces work slowly or not at all. As Lindsay says, "Without the Family and Medical Leave Act, many companies still would not offer maternity leave. Sometimes it takes outside forces to encourage organizations to act responsibly." The government need not regulate—but it can advocate and encourage. And you can use your right to vote— indeed your responsibility to vote—to influence government to do just that.

Create incentives to encourage businesses to support alternative work options. Some of these options not only help women and men and their children, they also improve other aspects of American life. Telecommuting, for example, is good for the environment, minimizing the pollution that results from Americans' daily drive. It may also help decrease violence by reducing road rage. In another example, encouraging women to start businesses is good for the economy, creating jobs and spurring growth. By utilizing alternative work arrangements, private citizens are more likely to have time to contribute to their communities, benefiting all.

Eliminate the marriage tax penalty. For the vast majority of people, marriage is an important element of their collage. Much of government rhetoric touts "family values." Making policy consistent with this rhetoric requires that the marriage tax penalty be repealed. Saddling married couples with an added tax burden is contrary to public interest.

Make quality day care available to all. Government can also ensure that quality day care is available across the economic spectrum so that workers at all levels and of both genders can perform their jobs without constant worry and distraction. The public school system is, in effect, day care (albeit with an all-important educational component) for children beginning at age five. Since when does a child's life or education begin at age five? Since this society is no longer agrarian, why does a child's need for education cease to exist in the summer? Public education should begin at an earlier age and continue throughout the calendar year. Research indicates long summer breaks contribute to developmental lags as students must ramp back up each fall, relearning what was lost over the summer.[1]

---

[1]Doris R. Entwisle and Karl L. Alexander, "Summer Setback: Race, Poverty, School Composition and Mathematics Achievement in the First Two Years of School," *American Sociological Review* 57 (Feb 1992): 72–84.

If government is unwilling to extend public learning to early-development years, then it must offer tax incentives to working parents to increase their ability to contribute personally to quality child care. The government can also offer tax incentives to day-care organizations that surpass national quality standards, thereby creating an incentive for day-care operators to improve their quality.

Affordable, quality day care will save money in the long run, benefiting all community members, parents and nonparents alike. Research is increasingly demonstrating the importance of intellectual and emotional development during infant and toddler years. In *Meaningful Differences,* Betty Hart and Todd Risley draw an important connection between early language development in the first three years and later accomplishment. Cognitive experience is sequential. Early intervention in disadvantaged communities is critical to addressing the language deficits that exist between disadvantaged and advantaged children. According to Hart and Risley, "the longer the effort is put off, the less possible the change becomes."[2] By investing in early childhood education, society will have better-adjusted, contributing adults in the future. Over the long haul, less money will have to be spent on prisons, drug-treatment programs, and the like. Remember: *It is easier to build a child than to repair an adult.*

Given the seemingly daunting task of creating quality child care for all, it is easy for some people to argue that women should simply stop working and return home to care for children full-time. This argument says that making day care and early childhood education available simply makes it "easier" for women to shirk their parenting responsibilities. Today's economic reality contradicts this argument. Today, most families need two incomes to pay their mortgage, cover other living expenses, and save for college and

---

[2]Betty Hart and Todd R. Risley, *Meaningful Differences* (Maryland: Paul H. Brookes Publishing Co., Inc., 1995), 203.

retirement. In 1998, 62 percent of mothers with children under age three worked outside of the home.[3] While some of these women (or their husbands) may not "have to work," most are working to help pay their family's basic expenses, not frivolous luxuries.

At the same time, whether women are working because they "have to" or because they "want to" is irrelevant. The sad truth is that roughly half of all marriages end in divorce. And divorce is one of the leading forces pushing women and their children into poverty. Domestic violence and the sudden, tragic death of a spouse also often plunge women into poverty. A woman's ability to support herself and her children is her own invaluable insurance policy. Simply put, women who have been out of the workforce for many years will find it difficult to earn a living wage for their family. Alternative work options make it possible for women to contribute to their families' livelihood while still having time to nurture their families. And, alternative work options make it possible for women to maintain their skills and marketability in case they need to become their families' sole support.

HOW CAN THE MEDIA HELP?

Stop featuring the cat fight. "The media is responsible for perpetuating the conflict between stay-at-home moms and working mothers," complains Kay. "While there are complainers on both sides, for the most part I find this a nonissue between my working friends and my full-time mom friends." Through both entertainment and news vehicles, the media can showcase how women are supporting one another in designing their own unique life collages, rather than focusing on working women and stay-at-home moms who point guilty fingers at one another.

[3]Stacy Kravetz, the *Wall Street Journal,* 18 Jan. 1999: 1.

Change the definition of success. Most important, the media can help change the prevailing definition of a successful American life—for both men and women—from one that is focused on traditional career success to one that encourages a multifaceted life full of the interests and values of the person living it. *Working Mother* magazine has done a terrific job of celebrating the success of work/life programs and the women thriving in them.

Stop focusing on the problem and start focusing on the solution. Most of the media glorified the stay-at-home mom of the '50s and elevated the superwoman to new heights in the '80s. The '90s found the media reporting such items as *Fortune* magazine's cover story "Is Your Family Wrecking Your Career? (and Vice Versa)"[4] The gloom-and-doom message is that work/life balance does not work, so do not even try. Not only is this message pervasive and destructive, it is also inaccurate. Collaging is possible; there is proof if you look for it. Nearly one thousand women contributed their success stories to this book. Each issue of *Working Mother* magazine features successful women enjoying a life collage. Other media outlets, particularly business publications, should follow suit.

The media needs to remove its blinders and shift focus from the "problem" of work/life balance to solutions—many of which are captured in this book. The media has the opportunity—and responsibility—to extol the virtues of the collage at the start of the new century.

As you create your conscious life collage, it is incumbent upon you to use your individual skills as well as your position in organizations, government, and the media to extend a hand to help others join you in redesigning work to reclaim their life.

[4]Betsy Morris, "Is Your Family Wrecking Your Career? (and Vice Versa)," *Fortune,* 17 Mar. 1997: 71.

Note from the Authors

Thanks for reading. We hope you found this book inspiring and useful in building your own life collage. With creativity, ingenuity, and effort, you can redesign your work and reclaim your life. In an effort to perpetuate more collage success stories and tips, we would like to hear about your experiences in creating your own conscious life collage. Please e-mail: thecollage@aol.com. *Note that these stories may be used in a future publication. Individual stories may or may not be acknowledged. However, as in this book, names and other details will be camouflaged.*

We wish you the best of luck in redesigning your work and creating your conscious life collage!

—Kathy McDonald and Beth Sirull

Resource Guide

Suggested Reading

MORE INFORMATION ON TELECOMMUTING:

Kugelmass, Joel. *Telecommuting: A Manager's Guide to Flexible Work Arrangements*. Lexington, KY: Lexington Books, 1995.

Langhoff, June. *The Telecommuter's Advisor*. Newport, RI: Aegis, 1996. Also see www.langhoff.com.

Niles, Jack. *Making Telecommuting Happen: A Guide for Telemanagers and Telecommuters*. New York: John Wiley & Sons, 1997.

Piskurich, George M. *An Organizational Guide to Telecommuting: Setting Up and Running a Successful Telecommuting Program*. Alexandria, VA: American Society for Training & Development, 1998.

MORE INFORMATION ON JOB SHARING:

Olmsted, Barney, and Suzanne Smith. *The Job Sharing Handbook*. Berkeley, CA: Ten Speed Press, 1996.

MORE INFORMATION ON ENTREPRENEURSHIP:

Gerber, Michael E. *The E-Myth Revisited: Why Most Small Businesses Don't Work and What to Do About It*. New York: Harperbusiness, 1995.

MORE INFORMATION ON FREELANCING:

Fast Company Magazine (See www.fastcompany.com.) Those interested in freelancing should see the November/December 1997 issue in particular.

MORE INFORMATION ON YOUR RELATIONSHIP TO MONEY:

Dominguez, Joe, and Vicki Robin. *Your Money or Your Life: Transforming Your Relationship with Money and Achieving Financial Independence*. New York: Penguin Books, 1992.

MORE INFORMATION ON UNCOVERING YOUR DREAM CAREER:

Boldt, Laurence G. *Zen and the Art of Making a Living: A Practical Guide to Creative Career Design*. New York: Penguin USA, 1993.

Cameron, Julia. *The Artist's Way.* New York: Putnam Books, 1992.

Sher, Barbara, with Barbara Smith. *I Could Do Anything if Only I Knew What It Was: How to Discover What You Really Want and How to Get It.* New York: Dell Publishing, 1995.

Sinetar, Marsha. *Do What You Love and the Money Will Follow: Discovering Your Right Livelihood.* New York: Dell Publishing, 1989.

MISCELLANEOUS:

Levine, James A., and Todd L. Pittinsky. *Working Fathers: New Strategies for Balancing Work and Family.* Harvest Books, 1997.

Morgan, Hal, and Kerry Tucker. *Companies That Care: The Most Family-Friendly Companies in America—What They Offer and How They Got That Way.* New York: Simon & Schuster, 1991.

Organizations

FAMILIES AND WORK INSTITUTE

330 Seventh Avenue, 14th Floor
New York, NY 10001
212-465-2044; www.familiesandwork.org

INTERNATIONAL TELEWORK ASSOCIATION AND COUNCIL

204 E Street, N.E.
Washington, D.C. 20002
202-547-6157; TAC4DC@aol.com; www.telecommute.org

NATIONAL ASSOCIATION FOR FEMALE EXECUTIVES

P.O. Box 469034
Escondido, CA 92046
800-634-6233; www.NAFE.com

NATIONAL ASSOCIATION OF WOMEN BUSINESS OWNERS

1100 Wayne Ave. Suite 830
Silver Springs, MD 20910
301-608-2590; 800-55-NAWBO; national@nawbo.org

THE NATIONAL PARTNERSHIP FOR WOMEN & FAMILIES

1875 Connecticut Avenue NW, Suite 710
Washington, D.C. 20009
www.nationalpartnership.org
(See publication #55—"Ask Your Candidate About Work/Family Issues")

NEW WAYS TO WORK

785 Market Street, Suite 950
San Francisco, CA 94103
415-995-9860; www.nww.org
Also offers *The Job Sharing Handbook,* $15 plus tax

U.S. SMALL BUSINESS ADMINISTRATION

800-8-ASK-SBA; www.sbaonline.sba.gov for information on offices
    around the country; www.onlinewbc.org—Women's Business
    Center Web site

WOMEN'S CONSUMER NETWORK

P.O. Box 660
Holmes, PA 19043-0660
www.womensconsumernet.com

Recruiting Companies for Professional Temporary and Part-time Work

EXECUTIVE OPTIONS

8707 Skokie Blvd, Suite 300
Skokie, IL 60077
847-933-8760

IMCOR

(See Web site for offices around the United States.)
www.imcor.com

M2

235 Montgomery Street, Suite 760
San Francisco, CA 94104-2910
415-391-1038; www.m2net.com

MACTEMPS

(Specializes in computer professionals; see Web site for offices around
    the world.)
www.mactemps.com

Other Resources

BRIGHT HORIZONS
One Kendall Square, Bldg 200
Cambridge, MA 02139
617-577-8020; www.brighthorizons.com
(Consults to companies on how to become more family-friendly)

DAWN GRAY MOMENTS
312-850-3597

JOB SHARE ADVANTAGE
Rita Brown and Sheryl Goodman, founders
510-443-7427
(Consulting service offered to potential job shares on how to set up job
    sharing)

MENTTIUM CORP.
8009 34th Avenue South
Suite 1350
Minneapolis, MN 55425
612-814-2600; www.menttium.com
(Provides assistance in developing and using mentor relationships)

MIRIAM KRASNO, CAREER DEVELOPMENT AND LIFE PLANNING CONSULTANT
847-679-5960
MiriamKrasno@sprintmail.com

WOMEN'S WIRE
1820 Gateway Drive, Suite 100
San Mateo, CA 94404-2471
650-378-6500; www.women.com
(Information on career issues facing women)

WORKING MOTHER
www.workingmother.com
(Information on family-friendly companies as ranked by the
    magazine)

Index

About the Authors

KATHY MCDONALD AND BETH SIRULL are dedicated to researching, developing, writing and speaking about, and advocating solutions to the work/life dilemma. They conduct workshops and speak regularly on redesigning work, work/life balance, workplace flexibility, and related topics.

KATHY MCDONALD leveraged her eight years' experience in corporate finance and marketing at Fortune 50 companies to successfully launch and grow two businesses. She received her M.B.A. from Northwestern University's Kellogg Graduate School of Management. Kathy holds a leadership position with the National Association of Women Business Owners. In addition to these professional endeavors, Kathy's collage includes roles as wife, parent, avid gardener, pet owner, painter, good friend, active family member, and lover of books and the arts. Kathy and her husband, John, live in Chicago with their two children.

BETH SIRULL successfully established a market research and consulting company following a ten-year corporate career. She has held adjunct professorships at both DePaul University and Dominican University. Other elements of her life collage include serving on the board of directors of a domestic-violence agency, taking an active role in her synagogue, and being a wife, mother, friend, regular aerobics attendee, and cooking enthusiast. Beth and her husband, Jon, live in the Chicago area and recently welcomed their first child.